Creative Advances in Groupwork

of related interest

Dramatherapy for People with Learning Disabilities
A World of Difference
Anna Chesner
ISBN 1 85302 208 X

Group Action
The Dynamics of Groups in Therapeutic, Educational and
Corporate Settings
T. Martin Ringer
ISBN 1 84310 028 2

Foundations and Applications of Group Psychotherapy
A Sphere of Influence
Mark F. Ettin
ISBN 1 85302 795 2
International Library of Group Analysis 10

The Group as Therapist
Rachael Chazan
ISBN 1 85302 906 8
International Library of Group Analysis 14

Creative Advances in Groupwork

Edited by Anna Chesner and Herb Hahn

Jessica Kingsley Publishers
London and Philadelphia

First published in the United Kingdom in 2002
by Jessica Kingsley Publishers Ltd
116 Pentonville Road
London N1 9JB, England
and
325 Chestnut Street
Philadelphia, PA 19106, USA

www.jkp.com

Copyright © Jessica Kingsley Publishers 2002

Library of Congress Cataloging in Publication Data
A CIP catalog record for this book is available from the Library of Congress

British Library Cataloguing in Publication Data
A CIP catalogue record for this book is available from the British Library

ISBN 1 85302 953 X

Printed and Bound in Great Britain by
Athenaeum Press, Gateshead, Tyne and Wear

Contents

Introduction

Herb Hahn and Anna Chesner

The idea for this book germinated in the dying months of the last millennium in the context of the British Association of Group Psychotherapists Executive Committee, of which Anna Chesner and Antonio Fazio were members. Encouraged by David Glynn, the chairperson at the time, Anna initially took on the role of editor, and they established a link with Jessica Kingsley as potential publisher. Shortly after this, Anna withdrew from the task of editor due to an aversion to this role as she had perceived it from the point of view of chapter contributor in the context of another book. David approached Herb Hahn, who took on the task with a burning sense of motivation. He telephoned Anna as a courtesy. During the course of that conversation between colleagues who did not know each other, in which we both shared our experience and fantasies of editing, the idea emerged that we would work together in a spirit of dialogue as co-editors and that the book itself should have something of the spirit of going 'beyond orthodoxy'. Anna suggested a joint meeting with the publisher, which was then arranged.

Herb came to London to meet Anna and Jessica Kingsley. It was his first ever meeting with a publisher and he had only a vague idea of what the book might contain. He arrived to meet Anna at the publisher's door and they were ushered in through a busy book-bursting ground floor to a tiny upstairs room in which Jessica Kingsley was waiting. There were two stools for us to perch on and her editorial assistant, Della Gray, was then invited to join us with her own chair which she parked in the doorway.

'Tell us about your book,' said Jessica.

There was a silence of at least ten seconds.

A voice emerged from Herb. He found himself saying that in recently preparing a chapter for another book, he had been disappointed about the lack of dialogue between the contributors about their subject matter. This had led him to reflect on other edited books he had read in which it had also been apparent that the contributors had no knowledge of each other's chapters. He felt that this book, as it was to be about work with groups, should itself develop in the context of an interactive group of contributors who were doing innovative groupwork. The authors would meet to outline their chapters, engage with each other's ideas, develop their chapters on their own, meet again, explore further, work on their own again, and so on, until an organic book was produced. Herb's enthusiasm grew as he spoke. When Della Gray wrote in due course to enquire about the delivery date, Anna and Herb initially suggested nine months (!) hence, but then opted for twelve 'to be on the safe side'.

In gathering our contributors we sought kindred spirits whom one or both of us knew and whose work excited us. Geographically we ranged from Devon to the north of England and operationally from internal consultancy in an international business, to a dedicated, largely dyadic, private practice. Our first all day meeting was at Anna's house in London. There we embraced the possibility of encompassing our overlapping applications of spiritual values, and action and reflection methodologies in our clinical, organisational, and other developmental contexts. We envisaged adding an interactive dialogue by all of us as an addendum to each chapter and excitedly went on to explore the idea of our book being published on the internet in a way which also encouraged interactive dialogue among readers. Then we settled down to focusing on a hard copy book 'just to begin with'. We ended the day with a lively experience of playback theatre, which Anna describes in her own chapter later in this book.

After that first day, one of the contributors, who is an established author, wrote to Anna and Herb as follows:

Thanks so much for asking me to contribute to the book.

Thanks also for yesterday, which was, for me, momentous.

The afternoon served to convince me that I very much want to be involved in the process, whatever it takes. And I know that this venture will be very different from anything I have ever been part of – in the sphere of putting thoughts and ideas down on paper. Perhaps it has never been done quite like this before and we are establishing a new (novel) book form. (A sense of inflation there!) Some of our fantasies about shuffling the pages about, cutting them, having a space for each chapter to be commented on by others and CD-ROMs etc. seemed to imply something of this nature for this book (or the next effort!).

If I were to try and describe what the meeting was like for me I would say that it resembled the process of creation: but in the company of others, so as to feel acknowledged, encouraged, supported, but without being told what I should or should not be doing/saying, by 'parent' editors who *know* in advance what the outcome is going to be. The nearest I can get to describing the experience, perhaps, would be to say that it felt like an experience of mirroring and being mirrored. This was aptly concretised by the final and individual experience of playback.

The nearest I can get to the experience is remembering the days when for 15 years I headed a team who put on an annual arts and therapy conference. Both the planning of it, as well as the week of the conference itself, invoked this 'shared yet alone' feeling. And the whole week was devoted to personal creativeness, on the premise that 'Art is Wholemaking' (healing).

Another way of describing my experience of the day (and perhaps what the book may turn out to be like) is the painting of a mural by a group of people who don't have a finished product, or a pre-fixed design in mind when they begin, only an intimation, and a commitment to the work and the pushing out of boundaries as barriers.

All that I have written here is, of course, also in the nature of an 'aide-mémoire' to remind me of yesterday's experience, as well as its effects and my affects, which will help me when I tackle the next stage.

The next stage involved each of us working alone. We came together for two more whole days over the next few months, and also exchanged and commented on chapters in progress in various permutations. Herb and Anna met for six days over three weekends to read the emerging chapters and engage with the authors.

With regard to our contributors, we lost three of them, two because of time factors, and the third because personal circumstances stood in the way of participation in the group meetings. We also had our difficult moments not only of group conflict and confrontation, but also of anxiety about survival when one of our group experienced acute palpitations during one of our meetings.

As Anna and Herb spent their final weekend together working on their editorial task they felt intimately engaged with all of the contributors and with the book as a whole and they both had dreams which, in the spirit of social dreaming, they feel belong to the matrix of the book.

Anna dreamt:

Dream One: 'Bath Spa, I am with a man in the context of a group, and he is or we are composing a piece of music. I am not sure if it is for me. The number nine figures strongly. There is also the image of arthritis, something growing in the joints, calcifying.'

Dream Two: 'At a playback type gathering of workshops I am in a room and notice a GIANT yellow beak of a blackbird or crow penetrating the upper right corner of the ceiling. A sense also of fire breaking through there. Somebody on the workshop, perhaps a Greek, maybe a fraud, not having done the full training. Walking outside in Findhorn type landscape myself and one other, we see a stable, where the gigantic blackbird is looking after the cattle, they are being winched up off the ground.'

Our associations were as follows. *Dream One*: Bath Spa is a Roman city built on a previous, earlier city. The bath spa is still there, and the new spa is currently being built on the ancient roots. This could be an analogy to our endeavour – a book entitled 'Creative Advances', involving new applications and approaches built on the foundations of tradition. Archaeology has the task of connecting with ancient roots. We can relate to the challenge of connecting with the original and yet building anew. These reflections take us back to our first dialogue, over the telephone, about going beyond orthodoxy.

The implicit question in the first part of the dream, whether this composition is for Anna, relates to the tension between the individual and the group. We all have our selfish motives for participating in this project.

The number nine. We both registered that this introductory chapter would be the ninth chapter to be written. In retrospect, we miscalculated. It should have been the tenth chapter, but turned out to be the ninth when a colleague had to withdraw at a late stage!

Herb resonates with the theme of pairing in terms of Bion's concept of a group avoiding its task by shifting the burden of the work onto a pair (Bion 1961). We had hoped that, by working through face to face dialogue amongst all the contributors, we would avoid some of the authority issues we were familiar with from other co-authored writing projects. In these the editor/s took on authoritarian parental roles in relation to which the other contributors were infantilised as siblings. We hoped for a greater sense of shared ownership of the project as a whole. In this sense there would be stronger sib-links. Towards the end of the project our experience differed from this hopeful vision, in that we did take on the task of editors in a more traditional sense of the role, meeting together as a pair to work through the various contributions.

Arthritis in the joints. Anna fears that this is something negative, calcifying. Herb associates it punningly with 'us writers' and feels it positively.

Dream Two: The square hole in the ceiling is the size and shape of a book or A4 sheet of paper. The creative task involves a breakthrough from above, perhaps from the transpersonal or spiritual realm, a dimension beyond ego and narcissistic preoccupations.

The idea of the fraud resonated with earlier discussions in group. Antonio Fazio had said at one meeting that none of us is a 'group analyst proper', which Herb had framed as an advantage in terms of not having too narrow an allegiance. The shadow side of the group, as the converse of our conscious identity as self-reflective co-operators, is competitive, and projective in the sense of looking 'out there', rather than within, for someone who may be a 'fraud'. We could say that all the writers are writing from the perspective of the alien/observer/outsider in its glamorised or professionalised form, the consultant!

The giant blackbird with the golden beak. Perhaps this relates to Bion's theory that the group seeks a saviour when it experiences its task as impossible (Bion 1961). The golden beak has echoes of divine presence (see the Golden Fleece, Golden Calf, and golden rain in the myth of Zeus and Danae). In the socio-cultural matrix it is like the British Prime Minister being burdened with the responsibility of saving the animals during the foot and mouth crisis current at the time of writing.

In the final scene of this dream the cows have their feet off the ground, despite being earth-based animals. Is this bird trying to teach these cows to fly, by mechanical means? Is this what we are doing as contributors – writing about our differing group technologies, the methods and means by which we make the impossible possible? As group workers we are trying to make the herds of cows fly with our particular winches and methods of magic.

We discuss the setting of this final scene. It is viewed from the outside, an open-sided stable, like a theatre lacking the fourth wall. Within the Christian tradition the stable is a birthplace and a place of transformation. The setting of this final scene ensures that the process and frame are visible. As in the ritual of playback theatre the invitation is there to 'Watch!' The dreamer, like the reader of this book, is an active participant.

The following night Herb had a dream. An image remained constant as the setting in which other events were happening. Herb could not remember the events when he woke up, but the setting was clear. 'It is a house built on sloping ground so that part is on solid foundations and part raised on stilts. The part on stilts also supports a balcony with a balustrade, which gives a view of the surrounding area. A sense of mountain and valley.' It was not a place Herb knew on waking, but it seemed natural, familiar and like home in the dream.

Our associations were as follows. We saw the book as the house, partly built on solid foundations, partly needing propping up. Our experience as editors has certainly been that we have needed to support, cajole, and prop up different contributors to a different degree. The book, like the house, is built, created and constructed to give a view and a perspective. It is both seen and a place to see from.

We think of Europe, perhaps Switzerland or southern Germany. At Lake Constance there is a settlement of primitive stilt houses at the edge of the water. Antonio Fazio's chapter explores our identity as Europeans. Perspective is an important feature of the contributions in the book. The role of the consultant, the one who stands back to gain perspective, is in all the chapters. Sometimes this role is called the dream matrix leader, sometimes conductor, consultant, supervisor or facilitator.

The chapters begin with Amélie Noack's chapter which focuses on the special task of group facilitation for trainees in clinical analytic dyadic work, and end with Chris Johnstone's chapter which explores the way in which he enables those he works with to relate to our whole world. Anna Chesner's and Peter Tatham's chapters elaborate and contextualise their understanding of playback theatre and social dreaming respectively. Anna Chesner embeds her work in her experience of dramatherapy, psychodrama, and group analysis, and Peter Tatham draws on his profession as a Jungian analyst. Herb Hahn shows how his approach to facilitating groups among the helping professions developed from his personal and professional experiences, and Angela Eden keenly examines the trials and treasured moments of the matching process between a consultant and client. Ron Wiener's chapter has the immediacy of a personal journal and introduces us to the person behind the mask of the sociodramatist and organisational consultant. Antonio Fazio draws on his British and Italian roots to explore the dynamics of inter-European relationships, and links this to an illuminating glimpse of the cultural dimension in clinical work.

The book we offer you ranges over commercial, training, environmental, and community contexts. The methodologies referred to include therapy, and broader applications beyond. Our foci include the intrapsychic, intragroup, intergroup, organisational and international. The mediums are language, ritual and action. The theoretical underpinnings are mainly analytic and include systemic, cognitive, narrative and role theory. The title of the book relates both to our experience of producing it and to our ongoing aspirations in our work. In our joint endeavour, we have shared moments of containing, exploring and building bridges across troubled interprofessional and interpersonal borders and boundaries. On the margins of our engagement there have been glimpses of the unconscious and even precious moments when we could engage with it playfully. This book is a celebration of the work we are privileged to engage with individually, and of our relationship with each other, our publisher Jessica Kingsley, and most recently her new editor Graham Sleight. Some of our journey has been in the shadows. We have encountered the constraints of our limitations as we strove for the realisation of our hope and aspirations. We hope that you enjoy this book, find it stimulating and useful, and experience it as a whole.

Anna Chesner and Herb Hahn, 30 June 2001

Reference

Bion, W. (1961) *Experiences in Groups*. London: Tavistock Publications.

CHAPTER I

Working with Trainees in Experiential Groups

Amélie Noack

Introduction

This chapter aims to explore the processes and dynamics in experiential groups with trainees of individual counselling and psychotherapy courses. While group training programmes obviously expect their trainees to undergo group therapy, individual counselling or psychotherapy training programmes usually require of their trainees individual therapy only. However, there are quite a few individual training courses which offer in addition an experiential group experience as part of their training. I will argue that participation in an experiential group as part of an individual therapy training course is of great advantage for the individual trainees, personally and professionally, and for the training organisation itself.

The lack of relevant literature in this respect could be explained by the fact that experiential groups are usually conducted along general analytic or group analytic lines and therefore do not seem to warrant separate theoretical consideration. I believe there are identifiable issues pertaining specifically to experiential groups which are worth discussing.

It is important to realise that different training organisations produce different groups and therefore different group experiences. Depending on the particular training course and context, different developments will be triggered in an experiential group. The groups I will be describing reflect the context of their particular training course based on Object Relations and Jungian theory, and these approaches are reiterated together with the group analytic model in my choice of theories to describe the groups' process. Ten years prior to this I ran several experiential groups for a more broadly psychoanalytical organisation, and here the Jungian element remained more in the background. My insights and thoughts about experiential groups therefore do not describe a generally valid model, but are reflections on my way of working with a particular sample.

Theoretical background

Group analytic thinking is underpinned by psychoanalytic thinking and in fact evolved historically as a combination of psychoanalysis, sociology and biology. In addition to some major group analytic principles based on Foulkes I have selected ideas from Winnicott and Jung to explain the dynamics and processes in experiential groups. D.W. Winnicott's ideas in regard to the facilitating environment and his concept of holding illustrate the basic qualities and preconditions for any successful psychological work, and this naturally also applies to groups. I will refer to Winnicott's writing about group processes and also use his idea of the transitional space as a space for transformative processes occurring within the group.

C.G. Jung's contribution to the understanding of transformative processes based on his writings about alchemy will be another theoretical orientation utilised for the exploration of group experience. Jung's psychological interpretation of the alchemical processes in a sealed-off container, the alchemical vessel, will be described as a model for the integration of psychotic processes during the course of analytical work. As far as I can see, this aspect of Jung's work has not been appreciated fully or understood on even a basic level up till now outside of the Jungian community. An interesting aspect of the application of alchemy to groups, I believe, is the fact that the transformative processes of alchemy are much more palpable in groups, at least they can become so at certain times. In individual work the therapeutic space is still often thought of as the containing mental space of the therapist or in more recent interactive models it is defined by the processes occurring in the container provided by the consulting room space or within the therapeutic relationship. However, the therapeutic space in individual work presents itself visually to both participants always as that of a dyad. In contrast, the group setting of the circle offers a therapeutic space which is actually visible to all participants including the conductor as the space within the group's circle. The centre of the space provided by the circular setting of the group can be seen to represent the inside of the alchemical vessel of the alchemist. Analytic groups are described as slow open groups, because people leave and join the group at times, and experiential groups as part of a training programme have, unlike analytic groups, to deal with all kinds of links and overlaps with the training organisation, so neither provide a sealed container in the strict sense. However, I believe it is valid to use the alchemical metaphor and describe the group space as a securely or hermetically sealed-off container at least for the time of any given session after the group's matrix has become established. I am hoping to show that this central space within the group can serve as a projective screen for the symbolic condensation of phenomena occurring in the matrix of the group, where transformative processes can become visible.

For the third theoretical perspective I will make use of concepts deriving from the group analytical model based on S.H. Foulkes' contribution, which incorporates social, collective and environmental aspects into the psychological processes occurring within the group as well as within the individual. His theory of group analysis is the attempt to develop an integrated viewpoint of the individual as a social being. Like Winnicott and Jung in their theories, Foulkes had to resort to a paradoxical stance, which still gives rise to misunderstandings in the group analytical community, because his theory tries to encompass the individual together with the group as a whole. I am hoping to clarify some of these misunderstandings in the course of my argument.

Outline of argument

I am going to describe the processes and the dynamics in experiential groups which I have conducted over the years. The observations mainly derive from several years of running the experiential group for the first year trainees of an analytic psychotherapy training course. In addition to the first year group, I also conducted each year a single one-off session with the trainees who had progressed to the third year of the training.

I am hoping to show that participation in an experiential group offers an advantage to students on individual training courses in that they are encouraged to reflect together on the training process which they are undergoing. The experience of membership in such a group can enable the trainees to develop mutually respectful and understanding relationships with their peers and future colleagues. This provides support for the development of the trainees' new professional identity and promotes a healthy sense of professional community. The developing awareness of group-related interactions in relation to the authority figure of the group conductor and to the training organisation as a whole, I will argue, provides a much needed balance to the dyadic and therefore limited view of traditional psychoanalytic understanding. I will also attempt to clarify in which way an experiential group, which is in fact not a therapy group, can nevertheless develop a therapeutic function. This may have an effect on the trainee's individual therapy, but also promotes the trainees' understanding of processes of change and transformation in the more general context of the group. Trainees can observe in the group the broad spectrum of circumstances which encourage and support change and reflect on these conditions which will enrich their professional competency at the end of their training.

Differentiation from therapeutic groups

I have run experiential groups for trainees for a long time and I find this a particularly interesting and rewarding type of groupwork, because in experiential groups the conductor is faced with a variety of issues beyond the usual group therapeutic task.

Experience of change

The group consists of individuals who are not coming for help with their personal problems, but are hoping to become professionals in their own right. The trainees are working towards one day becoming colleagues of their trainers, including the group's conductor. The transferences and countertransferences in experiential groups reflect this particular dynamic, which surfaces especially around conflicts regarding envy and competitiveness and colours various psychological mechanisms and defences, such as projection and idealisation. It can be argued that the primary focus of an experiential group is not the process of personal change in the individual as such, as in a therapy group, but that its main task is an educational one with emphasis on the observation of group dynamics and process in addition to the individual expression and integration of affect (see Yalom 1995, p.523). However, individuals in professional training programmes are expected to change as well. They are expected to change into competent and confident professionals who are able to initiate and facilitate change in their clientele. They themselves also expect to change and develop a solid and reliable professional identity.

The experiential group as part of the training programme can provide the space to experience this process of professional maturation consciously from various angles. The regular group sessions allow time to reflect on the process in exchanges with peers in the same position; this also includes a mutual monitoring of everybody's progress. Experiential groups as part of a professional training programme also demonstrate that personal and professional change cannot be separated from each other in any simple way. Any change in the individual will affect the whole of the personality, and a professional training that is effective will without question turn out to be a life-altering experience. This highlights the additional interaction between the group process and the ongoing individual analytical process of each trainee which can be supported and enriched by the group experience, but also come into conflict with it.

Responsibility and control

The setting of an experiential group is qualitatively different from that of a therapeutic group. While the time frame is usually the same, of one and a half hours duration, I have also conducted experiential groups for slightly shorter sessions, for instance of one hour and twenty minutes duration, due to restraints in the training set-up, which does not seem to restrict the effectiveness of the group experience. However, the experiential group does not take place in a private consulting room, but usually in the premises of the training organisation, often in the same room as the seminars. This means the group conductor has not the same control in regard to the physical environment as in privately run therapy groups. I once ended up with a trainee group for the last session of the term in a private consulting room where we had never met before, because the usual premises were inaccessible due to the caretaker's illness.

The lack of control might also become a feature with regard to the seating arrangements in that for instance only a variety of chairs might be available and not the same type of chair for everyone in the group. However, this can become grist for the mill for instance in the discussion of status and power differences. I have run several groups where only a limited number of armchairs was available and several people had to sit on normal, rather uncomfortable chairs. These ordinary chairs, which were out of the ordinary in the group setting, assumed the power to assign roles to those seated on them alternating between the scapegoat position on the 'hot seat' and the position of the leader on the 'throne' presiding over the group. In a therapy group where individual patients usually identify themselves, at least to begin with, as inferior in the role of the sufferer and as feeling too vulnerable to address issues with regard to power differences or authority, this added inequality would be avoided. However, for an experiential group of trainees the relation to authority figures and the negotiation of power relationships are part and parcel of the training and need to be acknowledged as inherent in any training set-up. The experiential group can therefore benefit greatly from an opportunity like this to verbalise these issues and negotiate power differentials in an open way.

Power relationships

I believe that the experiential group on counselling and psychotherapy courses has a political function. In my role as conductor of experiential groups on professional training courses I make the attempt to foster an atmosphere of openness and flexibility and apart from maintaining the boundaries of the setting I refuse to establish any rules myself. My aim is not first and foremost a therapeutic one, like reducing anxiety, promoting warmth and the development of trust; instead my aim is to create a group climate and initiate interpersonal processes between the trainees as peers and future colleagues which are based on co-operation and collaboration. While every analytic therapy group aims to develop co-operative interaction between peers, this aspect is often neglected as a part of the teaching on individual counselling and psychotherapy training programmes. Here the teaching is directed at and often limited to the dyadic setting of the interaction in the patient–therapist relationship. The experiential group offers the opportunity to develop a sense of mutual understanding and consideration between trainees, which can serve as a foundation for the forthcoming interaction in the professional community. This, I believe, is badly needed in the psychotherapeutic profession where people are often mainly working on their own and may become isolated. Training courses which do not expect their trainees to participate in an experiential group forego this opportunity.

The role of the conductor in experiential groups

The conductor of experiential groups holds considerable power as a role model and as an authority figure. This is even more pronounced when the conductor also takes part in the assessment procedure of the trainees. To counterbalance possible inhibiting effects of this, Yalom suggests that the leader should model openness and the universality of human problems, even be more self-disclosing (1995, p.522). I would disagree with this option, because I regard the crossover between the functions of conductor and assessor as extremely complicated and ultimately undesirable. It seems incompatible with the need for confidentiality which is indispensable for the experiential group to work in a satisfactory way. This does not mean, however, that the conductor cannot give general feedback on the group process to the training organisation, if the confidentiality of individual members is safeguarded. This is important, because on the one hand the conductor models the behaviour of a senior and well-experienced therapist to the trainees, who will unconsciously adopt this model for identification which will later inform their own practice. By preserving confidentiality for the individuals, the conductor is on the other hand setting and maintaining the boundaries for the group as a whole. While an experiential group is indeed not a therapy group, it nevertheless is undergoing a therapeutic process when it works well. This process may prove not to accomplish its expected therapeutic potential due for instance to resistances or defences in individual trainees or owing to the composition of the group. However, for the group to feel safely contained in the first place a facilitating environment needs to be established, which enables trust, openness and learning from experience, and this requires the guarantee of confidentiality.

The training context of the groups

I have been running the experiential group for first year trainees for the same therapy training organisation for several years. The group meets for thirty sessions during the first year, ten sessions each term, with two long breaks of up to six weeks between the terms. It takes place in the same room as the seminars, following them after a twenty minute break. Each of the groups I have run was distinctly different in its own way. For instance one group was able to start interaction and exploration very soon, while another group was much more cautious and people needed until the second term to learn to communicate more freely. A third group in contrast struggled for the whole year and never quite came together to be able to use the group for the exploration of the relationships amongst themselves, with me or with the training organisation. It turned out to be an extremely painful group experience for everybody in the group including me, and I will describe it later on in more detail.

Over the years I have found, however, that all the groups were showing comparable dynamics and were going through a similar process, even if the timing was different in each case. I will be using my insights to describe the developmental patterns of these experiential groups as I have observed them over the years. It should be understood that I am not reporting any personal information regarding any individual trainees, but that I will give a general idea of the group process and its dynamic, conflating information where individuals are concerned. The groups I was running were confidential and the group experience did not count as part of the official assessment or evaluation process of the training. In addition, the trainees had the right to discuss their own experience of the group with the trainers if they felt the need to do so. Also all the trainees were asked to give anonymous feedback about my performance as the conductor at the end of the year.

I am aware that some training organisations even provide experiential group experience throughout the whole of the training course, for instance for three or four years running. While I have not done this work yet myself, I gather from colleagues who run experiential groups for three years with the same trainees that the processes can be of a similar nature. In a one year group the processes are obviously condensed and the dynamics become intensified. In a longer lasting group the same stages of group life may and can be repeated and reworked in a new way as the group matures. Nevertheless, I believe that the processes I will be describing are able to serve as one valid description of the processes and dynamics in experiential groups with trainees.

The composition of the groups

People who start the training course have obviously freely chosen to embark on the training. They will have been informed that the training entails participation in an experiential group and some people will even have had experience of this kind of group through former training or attendance of an introductory course somewhere else. Nevertheless, the group is not optional but is an integrated part of the training, which may be welcomed or not. Indeed the experiential group may be dreaded, if there has been a negative group experience before or if there is a fear of exposure to the powerful dynamics in groups due to earlier damaging experiences in the family or at school.

Each individual who has passed the selection procedure of the organisation will become a member of the group. The selection procedure does not necessarily pay attention to the suitability of a candidate to group exposure or to the question of whether the selected individuals will in fact be able to form and come together as a group. The task of the conductor is to facilitate this initial process of group formation, which is not an easy one nor always successful. However, the trainees' usual enthusiasm can be employed as the original bonding agent to initiate the first processes of communication in the group.

The group process in action
The beginning of the groups

The individual trainees usually do not know each other at the start of the training and this allows space for projections and powerful transferences onto each other. If the trainees want to go on with their training, the group will have to learn to deal and cope with these mechanisms. The students will have to recognise their transferences and own their projections. This particular training organisation has also a policy that none of the trainees should know the group conductor beforehand and because of this even discouraged somebody applying for the course. The conductor's role serves as a unique projection screen for authority issues in general and the trainees will see her (the conductor) as a critical and judgemental agency intricately linked with the training organisation. As the projection carrier of parental authority the conductor may be unconsciously perceived by the group as functioning like a severe super-ego, which creates reservations or even unconscious resistances. This holds true even if the group conductor has no part in the assessment procedure of the course and the students know this. As the designated facilitator of the group the conductor holds in the beginning all the power, at least in the eyes of the trainees. Trainees are mature adults, usually already working in some or other professional capacity and they experience the loss of adult power and control at the beginning of the training as extremely threatening. However, in order to pursue their intended professional aim they will have to develop ways to utilise the group and the conductor, whether they like it or not.

However, sometimes it becomes apparent in the first session or soon after that a particular group will have enormous difficulties in developing a common matrix. Without this shared foundation the group will not be able to do any satisfactory work. It will be the task of the group conductor in such a case to make every effort to help the group communicate openly in order to resolve the difficulties.

The first term

THE ESTABLISHMENT OF THE MATRIX

Regular group attendance is one of the basic prerequisites for the group to establish a sense of security. While attendance can be erratic in therapy groups, experiential groups usually benefit in this respect from the fact that trainees are professionally motivated, are eager to get on with their training and do not want to miss sessions. However, this is a new beginning and exultation is coupled with hesitation or even reluctance to get involved. People are concerned with safety and trust, boundaries need to be clarified, and anxieties and fear of rejection are voiced. How does one become a group member? How much can be said? How to engage with each other? How to use the group? What are the rules?

At the start all these questions are directed towards the conductor and Winnicott describes this attitude as a request for 'covering'. He introduced this term for group processes in his paper 'Group influences and the maladjusted child' (1994) in parallel with his concept of 'holding' provided for the baby by the mother. The immature group, he says, is developmentally only a collection of bits, which to begin with needs to be held together or 'covered' by a containing and supportive agency. Before integration, he says, there exists '…only a primitive pre-group formation, in which unintegrated elements are held together by an environment from which they are not yet differentiated. The environment is the holding mother' (1994, p.193). Winnicott's concept of the interdependent existence of mother and baby and his parallel formulation for the individual and the group allows him to transfer the parameters of the parent–infant relationship (1987b) to groups by analogy. For a group to be functional in a real sense, the group must be understood theoretically and conducted practically as a facilitating environment for the individuals in it. If a group is able to fulfil the function of a facilitating environment, the individuals in the group can develop at their own pace and according to their individually inherited potential. In the group it is the conductor who performs the function of holding or 'covering' and guarantees that the group provides a facilitating environment.

It certainly is a good sign if everybody in the group contributes and talks freely, is able to air fears and anxieties or to express scepticism about the group and the training as well as hopes. However, equal contribution is not automatically a sign that the group matrix has become established. The group matrix is the necessary foundation of any group and is based on as Foulkes says '…the common pool of meaning, the network of communication…' (1986, p.122).

Example

Students are describing how they made their original commitment to the training. They are reassuring each other that this training is a good choice and – since everybody seems curious in a genuine way – they urge the next person to tell their story. However, I notice that this is happening in a kind of going-around-the-circle exercise initiated and maintained by group pressure. The temperature rises and individual information is exchanged in a somewhat frantic way. 'A lot of "to-ing and fro-ing" is going on,' I wrote in my notes. Suddenly, a direct communication from one member of the group to another is made: a comment about how he presents himself to the group. Startled, people open up to listen and everybody takes note of the honest and upfront response.

A real connection has been made, the group is at the threshold of change. A few minutes later I notice that the pattern of exchange in the group has changed and that there is interaction through the centre of the group space.

This transition from the circular movement of contributions around the circle of the group to a criss-crossing pattern of direct interactions going through the centre of the group space constitutes the first transformative group event and symbolises the establishment of the matrix.[1] This event has become visible as an alteration in the pattern of exchange in the group and is an example of my idea that the central space within the group can serve as a projective screen for condenser phenomena occurring in the group. The establishment of the matrix, I believe, represents a condenser phenomenon (Foulkes and Anthony 1957, p.199) and signifies a transformative process. The emotional charge generated by this shared group event led to a deepening of communication in the group and allowed further group development. The alteration of the pattern of exchange in the group from a circular movement to interaction through the centre of the group space occurred in the group I described above unusually early in the third session. From now on the matrix can serve as a secure container; the group has become a group.

From this moment onwards the conductor will be watching and able to monitor group analysis 'in action'. The matrix of the group, 'the web of intra-psychic, interpersonal and transpersonal inter-relationships, in which the individual is conceived as a nodal point' (Behr and Hearst 1983, p.5), has been successfully launched and from now on it will develop and mature in its own way for the remainder of the time.

The individuals in the group, described by Winnicott as a collection of bits, which up till now needed to be held together or 'covered' by the conductor, have become nodal points within the network of a greater unit, the group as a whole. The conductor will now be able to relinquish her containing function to a certain degree and join the newly established network as another nodal point. However, each individual in the group remains an individually recognisable unit or separately identifiable cell with a particular function even as part of this greater organism. Like each cell in an organism, each individual entity has a specific function in the network of the group. It remains the conductor's task to monitor the processes of the group organism in order to maintain a healthy state of affairs and if necessary to intervene for the sake of it.

BELONGING AND BEING PART OF A WHOLE

Now that the group has started to function on its own, questions are no longer directed exclusively at the conductor, as they were at the beginning. What is allowed in the group and what has to be avoided, what belongs to individual therapy and what to the group, can from now on be discussed and negotiated amongst the group members and at times settled by mutual agreement. Moreover, people are becoming aware of the group's containing function and are starting to use the group. The need to belong and to be part of the newly integrated unit of the group brings anxiety-provoking concerns with regard to experiences of isolation, rejection and abandonment to the fore. In conjunction with the first integration as a group the individual defences are lowered and the recent and still unstable integration of the group precipitates a paranoid emotional state in the group as a whole.[2]

Anxieties are expressed either in direct relation to the group or the training, such as for instance, 'I don't know how to be really a part of the group' or 'Others understand the theory much better than I do' or in relation to events in the individual's life. People have talked at this time about being separated from parents or siblings, about feeling unwanted for instance when sent away to boarding school and about the frightening isolation of childhood loneliness. People with greatly different backgrounds and experiences poles apart, are working together to weave the pattern of the group's matrix. Some of the individuals now feel safe enough to step symbolically into the transitional space in the centre of the group to allow themselves to be seen. 'How can I get into the middle?' asked one trainee, who wanted the group's attention and to be in the centre, like a baby in the maternal container of the matrix or womb.[3] The image of the baby in the womb could be understood as a second condenser phenomenon appearing in the matrix. Again, as I described above, the central space within the group serves as a projective screen for an emotionally charged event occurring in the group signifying transformation. The awareness of 'being at the centre of the group's attention', symbolising the baby in the womb, is more or less consciously shared by all group members and leads to a deepening of communication, which allows further group development. It is not surprising that at this point people might squabble for space and attention. Will there be space and enough to go around for each of them? There are so many siblings – will they all be able to survive and complete the training? Will they all get their needs met or will they have to kill each other off to have enough space for themselves? Competitiveness and envy emerge in the group.

LOSS AND DEATH

In several of the experiential groups I have been running actual deaths have occurred in the lives of the trainees during the first term, that is, some friend or relative died. This is obviously due to the fact that psychotherapy trainees are mainly middle-aged adults with relatives in advanced years. However, the emotionally loaded themes of loss and death have been themes during the whole year for all the experiential groups in one way or another, paralleling the preoccupation with loss and separation in small groups in general. In addition, I relate the feelings of loss and particularly death, mourning and grief to the fact that all the trainees are in fact contemplating the possible end of an old way of life and are preparing for a new career. During the initial period of training these feelings are especially acute, and pain and grief about what has to be left behind are unavoidable. The group has to debate whether these feelings can be expressed and tolerated or whether they need to be denied. When people feel safe enough and the environment is facilitating the expression of feelings and thoughts, they can usually address these issues.

The second term

FEAR OF DISINTEGRATION

After the first break the second term continues the themes of pain, loss and death. People have missed each other, had time to contemplate things and are often more aware of the great changes they will have to make. The experience of separation during the break is often described as the 'gap'. For me the notion of the 'gap' is an indicator of psychotic anxieties, signifying the fear of the abyss of disintegration.[4] Since the conductor's understanding is part of the matrix, it is not surprising that my viewpoint makes room in the group for the experience of psychotic processes, such as splitting, denial, disavowal and so on. If the group's container is sound, the 'gap' of the break serves as a vehicle to explore unbearable or intolerable feeling states. Verbalising and sharing these intense emotional states with others strengthens the ego and facilitates the possibility of developing alternative ways for dealing with them.

Example

One trainee has not returned after the break; he has decided to leave the course. There is helplessness and fury that there is no chance to discuss it or at least say goodbye. 'How do you make contact with somebody who is not there anymore?', 'How do you connect with a person who has died?' people ask. Somebody talks about the anniversary of a death: 'It's not getting better, the loss!' Anxiety is rising. 'Will all the men leave?' How can they connect with each other again, if they are not sure that everybody will stay? Will they be able to reach out and link up after such a big gap? To think about all this seems unbearable. 'It's too painful.' One woman says that she is not feeling anything. People are talking about the need to cut off. 'Sometimes it's healthy to cut off' and, 'Sometimes it's healthy to leave, because you can't stand the pain' are some of the comments. Two sessions later one woman says that she feels she revealed too much, she feels raw, mauled and destroyed. Somebody supports her: 'Yes, the group behaved "awful", people were not human.' A sense of anger rises in the group and a rather sharp and argumentative tone develops. 'Like scorpions!' somebody comments. In the next session the group talks about the anxiety, shame and guilt that aggression creates: 'I felt mad! Like a mad woman!' one participant verbalises. 'But you need aggression to do what you want!' another person says.

GETTING WORSE

The example illustrates that feelings can now be expressed more easily, but are often experienced as unbearable and acting out can occur. People may feel exposed and either manage to express their feelings or withdraw, and individuals have run out of the group room at this stage of the process when feelings became intolerable. They did return in each case, I must say thankfully, either in the same or in the next session and things could be discussed.

After the initial experience of unity through coming together as a group, this second stage provides a chance to work through anxieties about separation. Fears of disintegration alternate with fears of confrontation. The associated emotions of aggression, fury and rage seem often unacceptable in the groups and it is a challenge for the conductor to create an opening in this respect. Some groups are more able to use this opportunity than others. If these anxieties can be faced, they ultimately lead to a sense of individual identity and the discovery of differences for the group members. If the group feels safe enough to do so, aggressive feelings of fury and rage also make space for the unfreezing of grief, and an awareness of the successively repeated 'layering' of the emotional experiences of grief and anger in the psyche can develop. In this course of events people also have a chance to experience and to express shame and guilt. The group is often profoundly moved by these difficult experiences with each other.

In groups which work really well anxieties concerning madness, badness, destructiveness and in some more mature groups even sexuality can be conscious themes. The fear of getting lost in all this 'primitive stuff', as trainees have called it, evokes doubt, even panic at times and the desire to disengage. The decision to train can begin to be questioned anew. Towards the end of the second term the forthcoming second break seems to become a life and death issue: 'Will we survive the break?' is the anxious question. The break looms like an enormous and unbridgeable abyss during which the group may disintegrate after all. However, these feelings concerning the break can this time become a conscious theme for discussion before the break – not after it, as in the first term – and most groups are able to do so. The conscious preparation for the break has a containing function preventing further drop-outs from the training at this stage.

In 'Group influences and the maladjusted child' (1994) Winnicott describes the second stage of a group's process, following the first stage of establishing safety, as people 'exploiting' the situation, since they seem to get worse, start acting out and allow themselves to be dependent and regress. Another well-known theory of group development divides the process into four stages of forming, storming, norming and performing (Tuckmann 1965), and the second stage of 'storming' also captures this quality. In short, useful work which has a therapeutic function is done in the second stage and my experience of experiential groups in the second term as described above seems to support this view. When the group works well, the group members usually develop in the second term of the course the capacity to 'use the group as an object' for their own developmental processes and needs.[5]

BAPTISM BY FIRE – THE ALCHEMICAL METAPHOR

I see this second stage of the group process with its turbulence and upheaval as an important training experience and opportunity. The trainees are immersed in processes which seem at times unbearable and overwhelming. However, if these feelings can be contained in the group and talked about, they turn out to be invaluable for the trainees' understanding of paranoid-schizoid experience and psychotic processes. This phase can then be appreciated as a baptism by fire for the therapists coming into being. My vantage point for this particular view is provided by alchemy, using alchemical metaphors for specific psychological states of mind and transformational experiences leading to further development.

Jung's interpretation of alchemy[6] is based on the notion that the alchemists resorted to mechanisms of projection of psychological contents onto the chemical processes for the purpose of reflection on the qualities of the materials and procedures they were working on. He showed that their description of qualities of chemical elements and the transformation these elements were undergoing when mixed with each other were more often than not in fact projections of psychic contents activated in the experimenter and his attendant or between the two of them. In parallel to this Jung described the therapeutic relationship as an alchemical process between therapist and patient, following a pattern of certain stages and leading to psychological development in both participants. I am here extending his approach to the application in groups.

When two or more substances mix a new combination with new qualities is created. I demonstrated before that the establishment of the matrix of the group constitutes a mixing of a complex kind, because here several substances are involved, that is, five, seven or more people come together to form a group. When the individuals in the group have been successful in forming and becoming part of the new combination of the group network or matrix, the alchemical vessel of the group as a whole is symbolically sealed and the turbulent processes of transformation can start. From now on the centre of the space provided by the circular setting of the group can be seen to represent the inside of the alchemical vessel of the alchemist, ready to receive the projections of psychic contents activated in the group.

The first stage of the alchemical process is called nigredo, the black stage of lead, which is laden with darkness and despair. The alchemist experimented in fact especially with heavy metals, such as lead, copper, mercury and so on, which are toxic and induce, as we know today, a psychotic-like state with depressive features. From the start of their work, the alchemists were therefore subjected to this toxic state, which they called nigredo, the blackness, and which they described as a preoccupation with dark and heavy matters, such as loss, abandonment, death and despair. The alchemists saw this as the original stage of primal chaos symbolised by lead, and their goal and expectation was to transform it through hard work and devotion into gold, a more ordered stage suffused by light. From a psychological point of view we could say the alchemists were trying to transform a confused, poisoned and depressed state of mind into a more healthy one.

The psychological processes of change and transformation in a group following the establishment of the therapeutic container of the matrix can be understood in analogy to this. After the mixing together of people in a group, experiences akin to the alchemical nigredo are activated, because individual differences are becoming mixed up and this creates feelings of possible chaos and confusion. As I have described above, after the establishment of the matrix the group finds itself time and time again in a state of black depression preoccupied with loss and despair. If the temperature of the emotional turmoil and intensity, the parallel to the alchemical fire heating the alchemical vessel, can be endured and consciously observed, there gradually emerges an awareness that during this process of emotional smouldering the old state of affairs is crumbling, disintegrating and dying. The former psychological structure and organisation in the individuals and in the group as a whole are falling apart. The expected new structures, which would give new solidity and security, are not formed sufficiently yet to be noticed or seen.

When the initial combination of substances had crumbled to dust the alchemist would add water and other solutions to initiate the second alchemical stage of the albedo. The alchemists described their experience of the albedo as a white, milky and watery stage and related it to silver, the soft light of the moon and the longing of love. Psychologically speaking, a liquid binding agent is added in the form of sweat and the tears of sorrow and grief to the broken-down pieces in the alchemical vessel. If the group feels safely contained throughout the upheaval of break-up and the shifting of personal boundaries, the heat of the emotional turmoil initiates a melting of the defences against pain, sorrow and grief and this unfreezing ushers in the next stage of the albedo. Here the dregs of the old psychic state are washed away by the watery flow of emotion to make room for something new. The milk of human kindness, empathy and compassion is being added to the mixture and starts to create a new cohesion. The old structure is no more and the remains now cohere to form a new shape. A new structure is emerging and things are coming together in a new way. The heat of envy, competition and murderous rage and the liquidity of compassion and sadness alternate in the group at this time in the effort to produce the new psychic structure, gradually forged in the group by rhythmic alternation between confrontation and empathy. Emotional responses of shame and guilt are often evoked at this point and some trainees have the courage to talk about them. Frequently group members express during this stage of the process how deeply moved they feel by listening to each other's difficult experiences. 'It's like being a witness' and 'You don't feel so alone' are comments from the different sides of the experience. Being genuinely stirred or moved deeply by witnessing and accompanying another person through profound changes is another aspect of the liquid experience of the albedo. Clinically speaking, the trainees at this time have a chance to observe and possibly practise projective identification in action.[7] Slowly an awareness of mutuality and reciprocity develops in the group and trainees often remark on their growing awareness of interdependence.

The last term

The original excitement of starting the training and entering a new phase of life has by now mostly faded into the background. It has been replaced by sober contemplation of the losses that will have to be faced and by the consideration of the price the trainees have to pay, for the actual training course as well as in personal terms. The monetary price of the training always becomes an issue in the third term, because the trainees are preparing to take on their first patients at the beginning of the second year of training. This means sometimes giving up existing work to make the space, and in any case a supervisor will have to be paid and the financial sacrifice can breed resentment.

GROWING UP AND COMING OF AGE

I usually interpret the preoccupation with a time some months ahead as a resistance to facing the coming end of the experiential group. The group is trying to avoid the psychological task of separation and ending by splitting and projecting the shadow side onto the seemingly cruel and demanding training organisation.[8] Separation or individuation within the context of the group, which was the assignment of the second term, has now to be replaced by the realisation of the actual impending ending and separation of the group. Will the group be able to function in the future as a mature workgroup independent from the conductor or will it break down? These themes are usually raised in the last term around the time when I tell them that I will leave them to meet on their own for a session. The discussion usually moves from 'We finally have to grow up' through 'Let's meet in the pub instead' to 'This will be interesting, let's see how it goes'.

Example

The session (first session of the last term) has started, but two people remain standing chatting to each other outside the circle of the group. I comment lightly: 'There obviously is a resistance to start the ending.' A woman feels cold and wants the fire lit and somebody else turns it on. 'It makes a sound like a faltering heartbeat,' somebody remarks. One trainee starts talking about aged parents, they will not live that much longer. Another trainee, who has lost his parents, expresses envy that others still have parents. One mother does not want to know about her daughter's private life, a father cannot remember his child's early years – he was not there. The responsibility for oneself and having to grow up seem a burden; people do not feel ready. In the next session I tell them that I will not be there in four weeks time and the talk turns to the theme of 'murdering mother.' They play with the idea of going to the pub when I am not there, but then decide to meet in the group without me.

The theme of growing up is often discussed in the groups in relation to growing old and ageing. Again, I believe, this happens to a certain extent because the trainees are mostly mature adults. However, the impending ending of the experiential group is also a coming of age for the group and the individuals in it. The group will need to develop the capacity to function in a new way without me. I believe that my absence gives the group a chance to achieve a sense of maturity, individually and in relation to the group. Winnicott says that a mature group formation is created and maintained by the organisation which well-integrated individuals bring to the group, and that the mature group benefits from the personal experience of the individuals in it, each of whom has been seen through the integration moment and has been 'covered' until able to provide self-cover (1994, p.193). My absence provides an opportunity for the trainees to explore their independence and to experience themselves as a workgroup able to perform a task and achieve objectives, in this case, to conduct a session without me.

THE NEED FOR FATHER

The example of the session given above already illustrates that at this stage the figure of the father and the parental couple as a unit can become conscious preoccupations. I became fully aware of this focus while running the third group for this organisation. In addition to the aspects mentioned in the above example there were repeated allusions to couples, and I recognised after a while the virtual image of a couple in loving embrace in the middle of the group space – another condenser phenomenon on the projection screen of the central group space, generated by the emotional charge of the group's preoccupation with the oedipal couple.[9] While theoretically aware of the importance of the negotiation of the oedipal situation for the individual's maturational process, I had not considered this consciously in application to separation processes in groups. After becoming aware of the image of the couple, I went back to my notes and found that in both groups I had run before, the parental couple had also been a theme in the second or third session of the last term. I believe this image is partially evoked by my announcement of non-attendance, which goes with the idea that I have a separate life from which the group is excluded and reiterates the oedipal trials and tribulations on the way to growing up. The group often interprets my absence as a paternal act forcing them to start to take responsibility for themselves. However, even in the first group I facilitated for this organisation, where

I did not miss any sessions in the third term because a third year of trainees did not exist as yet, 'parents' and 'father' were topics of the group conversation at this point in time.

Generational differences can now be addressed and thought about together, often again in the disguise of disagreements with the training organisation. The envy of those who have gone before and who have made it already is present in the form of negative transferences, but if acknowledged may turn into respect and the recognition that one's elders also provide a mirror or models to identify with. The need for a constructive and positive authority figure called 'father' can be verbalised. The importance of healthy dependence as well as independence is assessed and evaluated: 'When do you ask for help?' is contrasted with 'When do you trust yourself?'

ENDING AS CHANGE AND CHANCE

There is often a major crisis half-way through the third term for the group, usually after I return. 'We are running out of time!' 'The group is almost over and we have just started!' This usually gives rise to a discussion of missed opportunities, in the group and in life. Some groups are at this point in time able to weigh up the place and function of psychotherapy as a whole. As a rule, at this time, limitations, disappointment and disillusionment are highlighted themes. I make a point of emphasising these concerns as important stepping stones for healthy development and for a realistic and mature attitude to life. If the group is able to grapple with the emotional impact of these subjects, the experience of the experiential group and its process throughout the year can be appreciated as enriching. In the group which has weathered the storms of crisis and conflict and has understood that the group was a chance for change, a sense of achievement and satisfaction arises. Often people are also aware of development and growth in their fellow trainees and these observations can be exchanged, sometimes like gifts in the last few sessions. An awareness of the ending of the experiential group as another change, but also as a further chance, may develop.

In the alchemical process the image of the sexual couple is one of the symbolical representations of the dawning of the third stage, the reddish golden state of the rubedo. It stands for the possibility of birth and new life and the rising of the sun on a new day. The third stage is solid, symbolised by the stone of the philosophers; it is luminous and sparkly, symbolised by the alchemists' gold. It reflects an attitude of achievement, accomplishment and success.

Something bad and smelly – a group is stuck

Sadly, groups do not always work well and the conductor's efforts are not
always successful. One of the groups I have run, for instance, was not able to
work constructively and develop the common ground for the transformational
processes of change I have been describing. The group was very small to begin
with, which created great anxiety, because there was enormous fear from the
start that the group might not survive. In addition, all my efforts to transform
the anti-group factor (Nitsun 1996) into a workable matrix failed. The group
never seemed able to create any valid space for thought or reflection, despite
long silences. The group never quite gelled to become a group as a whole, but
remained a collection of individual bits which were never able to develop into
one shared unit able to work together.

Personal resistances and transferences towards other group members and
the conductor were strongly negatively coloured. I was experienced as cold and
tough. During sessions I regularly experienced extremely intense emotional
states due to projective identification. I felt controlled, suffered attacks of fury
and murderous rage, and experienced isolating icy contempt, utter despair and
helplessness in cyclical repetition, to name only a few of the feelings I experienced. I often developed a headache or other physical symptoms just before or
during the sessions and repeatedly struggled in vain to connect with a sense of
compassion, for the group members as well as myself. I felt that I had been designated as a bad object and I had to remain one; letting go of it or changing it
seemed impossible. Despite all my attempts to tackle this desperate situation I
found no way to change it. As became apparent, all members of the group had
had somewhat negative therapeutic experiences in the past, but this revelation
made no great difference to the group's process as a whole. In the third session
before the end of the year people in the group commented: 'The group is
coming to an end – has it even started?' 'The group is a pot with a firmly closed
lid.' 'There is shit inside it.' 'Something bad and smelly.'

This short portrayal indicates that in fact even this group got off to a start
after all, because there was an alchemical vessel, a pot, and it was sealed, the lid
was on – a matrix existed. However, the comments also depict that the group
was stuck in the first stage of the alchemical nigredo, the first station of this
process of psychological change, where things are rotting and decaying. The
alchemists called this stage of decomposition and corrosion 'putrefactio'. It
seems that after all some kind of work was in progress, the heat was on, but it
was work of a particularly stinking and shitty variety, only able to produce

unpleasant stenches and disgusting odours, and any step forward out of this foul-smelling hell-hole was blocked, because people were too afraid to move, which could only be acknowledged at the end of the group. The result was that nothing was shifting, projections could not be withdrawn, and the group as a whole could not progress. In the last session one group member said: 'We did not work as a group, there was too much fear.'

Discussion
The paradox of the individual and the group

Winnicott, Jung and Foulkes, whose theories I have used to describe the development of experiential groups, are all struggling to make sense of a phenomenon which is one of the basic dilemmas in understanding human experience. Psychological processes in the individual are enormously complex and even more so are psychological processes in groups – how do you reconcile or even combine the two? Different schools of thought have tried to make sense of one or the other side of the phenomenon; for instance, psychology has over the last two hundred years attempted to explain mental processes in the individual, and sociology has made an effort to define interaction in the social sphere or with the environment.

The complex situation of understanding human experience in relation to individuals and groups has been made even more confusing through the fact that the dilemma has been transferred onto the individual itself by splitting the bio-psychological unit into mind and body. We conceive of ourselves as separate three-dimensional creatures, while we in fact know that the actual world around us is a multi-dimensional one. During the last century the natural sciences have demonstrated that it is not in accordance with reality to think of even inorganic matter in that way, that is, to consider an event in the physical world as separate from any other. A theory which views human beings as being individuals only, that is, separate entities unrelated to each other, has become more and more questionable. Chaos theory (Gleick 1988), for instance, and quantum mechanics (Mansfield 1995) have shown that we live in a universe that is through and through interactional and that all events are in some way interrelated to one another (Bohm 1995).

To think about human experience in a way which does not prioritise either the individual or the social group is extremely difficult, because it requires a viewpoint which is paradoxical and difficult to maintain. It requires an awareness able to keep the balance between the two extremes or 'to hold the tension of opposites', which are Jung's words to describe the goal of individuation (1981, p.200) and which incidentally is also the aim of the alchemical opus (Jung 1980). I hope to be able to make a clarifying contribution to a better understanding of this dilemma.

To demonstrate the needed new viewpoint I want to paraphrase Winnicott's statement, 'There is no such thing as a baby' (1987a, p.99) by changing it provocatively into: there is no such thing as an individual! This is the standpoint promoted by Dalal in *Taking the Group Seriously* (Dalal 1998). Dalal tries to do away with the individual in his attempt to illuminate Foulkes' viewpoint of the group by formulating an understanding of the individual as formed and defined purely by the social. In my opinion his viewpoint turns out to be lopsided and seems to leave one side of the equation out altogether.

However, Winnicott explains his statement that, 'There is no such thing as a baby' with the further declaration '...that if you show me a baby you certainly show me also someone caring for the baby...', concluding with '...the unit is not the individual, the unit is an environment–individual set-up' (1987a, p.99). Following his train of thought, my statement that there is no such thing as an individual also needs to be completed by pointing out that in relation to the individual we are also always dealing with an environment–individual set-up: there is no such thing as an individual, there is always only an environment–individual set-up. Individual and environment are always intricately connected, they constantly interact and define each other in relation to each other.

To make sense of the individual–group dilemma I want to apply Winnicott's famous dictum also in reverse and this would read: 'There is also no such thing as a social world whatsoever. There is always only a social–individual set-up. The social world also does not exist on its own, because the social world itself is composed of and composed by individuals.' In this way Winnicott allows me to define a new understanding of the individual–group paradox, which is, that the group constitutes an environmental factor with regard to the individual in the group, and while the individual is part of the group, it is also contributing to and defining the group through participation in it.

Psychoanalysis has provided a foundation for the understanding of the human psyche during the last century, but I believe it is reaching its limitations when practised with the focus on the individual only in the traditional way. Foulkes, who was one of the founders of group analytic theory and practice, was trying to expand those limitations. He was hampered in his attempt,

however, by the disdain and criticism from his former psychoanalytical colleagues, who could not stomach the implied devaluation of the individual as
they saw it. I believe the research into and the development of an understanding of human group processes is of such immense importance at this point in
time, because the group paradigm is needed to complement our understanding
of the individual. Human life is defined by our capacity to communicate and
co-operate with each other.

I believe Winnicott's formulation of the mutually interdependent environment–individual set-up describes the practically lived experience of various
social units, such as families, groups and communities and also of humanity as a
whole. I have described before how the individuals in the group become nodal
points within the network of a greater unit, the group as a whole. This can also
be applied to the notion of humanity as a whole. We as individuals are all nodal
points in the newly established network of humanity as is becoming increasingly apparent. One of the obvious examples to demonstrate this today would
be the worldwide web. However, each individual in the network as a whole
remains an individually recognisable unit or separately identifiable cell with a
particular function even as part of this greater organism. Like each cell in an
organism, each individual entity has a specific function in the network of the
whole. The individual and the group are both real interdependent aspects of
one reality.

I hope this shows that the paradox of the group and the individual cannot
be resolved, but needs to be perceived as the possible basis for a new understanding of human experience: 'Paradox…is…fundamental to human
life…the individual and the group are paradoxically formed by and forming
each other at the same time' (Stacey 2000, p.402). As I have pointed out above,
this new paradigm is already widely used and applied for instance in the natural
sciences. The recent application to human sciences, as suggested for instance by
Stacey (2000) in his theory of complex responsive processes, demands the
effort to develop the flexibility and the freedom of at least a bi-focal, if not a
multi-focal, point of view, and a realisation that these different points of view
are all equally valid. This new viewpoint comprises also, I believe, the capacity
to move between a variety of levels of reality. These different levels are not necessarily directly accessible to ordinary physical perception, as for instance the
symbolic level of alchemy as described above, but can be approached for
instance through analogy or metaphor. However, it seems to me that what we
call psyche or psychic reality is in itself an example of symbolic reality. Working
as psychotherapists we may enter into and inhabit the reality of the psyche in

every session. The concepts of transference and countertransference and other psychological mechanisms could be seen as ways to monitor and record this specific level of reality. They help us to design functional maps enabling us to exchange our growing understanding in communication with others. By using the alchemical model, I believe, we are able to add colour to these charts to make them even clearer and easier to read.

Conclusion

I hope I have been able to show that the experiential groups I have conducted moved during the year of their duration through profound processes of change, in successive phases of loss, recovery, separation and reparation. In the therapeutic profession, which struggles with problems related to competitiveness, status and power, the experiential group experience offers a way of exchange complementary to the isolating work situation in the consulting room through enriching and mutually validating relationships between equals. As I have described, however, it is not always possible to facilitate this process of open communication between equals due to the composition or the context of the group. I have also made the attempt to show that the psychological interpretation of the alchemical process can be used as a tool to locate a group's developmental process in relation to certain transformational stages. In addition I hope I have been able to make a contribution to a new way of understanding and conceptualising a dilemma, which is still perceived as a serious problem leading to misunderstandings in the therapeutic community, by describing the paradox of the individual and the group.

Notes

1. For a detailed elaboration of the establishment of Foulkes' concept of the group matrix in reference to Winnicott's understanding of the development of the individual, see James (1982).

2. For the elaboration of the paranoid psychological state following integration to unit status see 'Anxiety associated with insecurity' in Winnicott (1987a) pp.97–100.

3. The term 'matrix' is derived from the Greek and means 'womb'; for more information see Roberts (1982).

4. For further elucidation of this understanding see 'Fear of breakdown' in Winnicott (1989) pp.87–95.

5. For further elucidation of the term, see 'The use of an object' in Winnicott (1989) pp.217–247.

6. For further elaboration of the alchemical opus see Jung (1980).

7. For an excellent description of projective identification see Rogers (1987).

8. For a description of the shadow see Jung (1979), pp.168–176.

9. For the clinical importance of the oedipal situation for psychological development, see Britton *et al.* (1995).

References

Behr, H. and Hearst, L. (1983) 'Group analysis: A model of group psychotherapy developed by S.H. Foulkes.' *Midland Journal of Psychotherapy 1.*

Bohm, D. (1995) *Wholeness and Implicate Order.* London: Routledge.

Britton *et al.* (1995) *The Oedipus Complex Today.* London: Karnac Books.

Dalal, F. (1998) *Taking the Group Seriously.* London: Jessica Kingsley Publishers.

Foulkes, S.H. and Anthony, E.J. (1957) *Group Psychotherapy.* London: Penguin.

Foulkes, S.H. (1986) *Group-Analytic Psychotherapy.* London: Karnac.

Gleick, J. (1988) *Chaos: The Making of a New Science.* London: Heinemann.

Hearst, L.E. (1990) 'Transference, countertransference and projective processes in training course block sessions.' *Group Analysis 23*, 341–346.

Hutten, J.M. (1996) 'The use of experiential groups in the training of counsellors and psychotherapists.' *Psychodynamic Counselling 2.2*, 247–256.

James, D. C. (1982) 'Transitional phenomena and the matrix in group psychotherapy.' In M. Pines and L. Rafaelsen (eds) *The Individual and the Group.* New York: Plenum Press, 645–661.

Jung, C.G. (1979) *Man and His Symbols.* London: Aldus Books.

Jung, C.G. (1980) *Psychology and Alchemy.* Collected Works, Volume 12. London: Routledge and Kegan Paul.

Jung, C.G. (1981) 'The psychology of the transference.' In *The Practice of Psychotherapy.* Collected Works, Volume 7. London: Routledge and Kegan Paul, 163–323.

Mansfield, V. (1995) 'A participatory quantum universe.' In *Synchronicity, Science and Soul-Making.* Chicago: Open Court, 97–107.

Nitsun, M. (1996) *The Anti-Group: Destructive Forces in the Group and Their Creative Potential.* London: Routledge.

Roberts, J.P. (1982) 'Foulkes concept of the matrix.' *Group Analysis XV*, 2, 111–126.

Rogers, C. (1987) 'On putting it into words: The balance between projective identification and dialogue in the group.' *Group Analysis XX*, 99–107.

Stacey, R.D. (2000) *Strategic Management and Organisational Dynamics: The Challenge of Complexity.* Harlow, England: Financial Times Prentice Hall.

Tuckmann, B. (1965) 'Developmental sequences in small groups.' *Psychological Bulletin 63*, 384–99.

Winnicott, D.W. (1987a) *Through Paediatrics to Psychoanalysis.* London: Hogarth Press.

Winnicott, D.W. (1987b) *The Maturational Processes and the Facilitating Environment.* London: Hogarth Press.

Winnicott, D.W. (1989) *Psychoanalytic Explorations.* London: Karnac Books.

Winnicott, D.W.(1994) 'Group influences and the maladjusted child.' In *Deprivation and Delinquency.* London: Routledge, 189–199.

Yalom, Irvin D. (1995) *The Theory and Practice of Grouptherapy.* New York: Basic Books.

CHAPTER 2

Playback Theatre and Group Communication

Anna Chesner

My aim in this chapter is to explore the fundamentals of playback theatre as a way of communicating in groups. To experience playback theatre for the first time is often to be struck by its immediacy and simplicity. At the same time it can be both subtle and profound in its impact, for reasons which I hope to explore. I shall begin with a brief description of the method. I shall then consider its impact for a group from a variety of perspectives: playback as a ritual form serving an aesthetic and social function; its relationship with therapy; its foundations in creativity and spontaneity; its function as a medium for narrative and dialogue. My interest is in its value as a means of aiding communication in groups and I shall give some examples of its application.

Personal prelude

My engagement with playback theatre is part of a process, which began at Bristol University where I studied drama. This was during the mid-1970s when the theatrical work of Grotowski (1975) was seen as the cutting edge. I joined a group inspired by his Theatre Lab, in which we investigated improvisation, ensemble and devised approaches to theatre as well as powerful 'paratheatrical' activities, often in the open air. This work intrigued and impressed me as a vehicle of self-discovery, interpersonal exploration and encounter with the external landscape. After a year as a postgraduate at Sussex University studying Intellectual History I took a job as a drama lecturer in York, where my approach to production was heavily influenced by the exploratory work from Bristol. I struggled with the identity of theatre director, one of the expected sub-roles of drama lecturer, but facilitated work that was transformative for the students, and we produced provocative performances based on their personal process.

It was a logical step from there to train as a dramatherapist, particularly since my time in York corresponded with the foundation of the first dramatherapy course in the north of England, located at the college where I taught. The emphasis of my work was changing. It was clear to me that theatre work could be therapeutic, and as a dramatherapist I could legitimately give the therapeutic priority over the theatrical as I saw it then. The 1980s and 1990s were a period of increased professionalisation in the field of therapy and personal development work, and as a dramatherapist I felt inadequately trained for the depth of work I was interested in. I had been involved with psychodrama psychotherapy for some years, and finally decided to complete my training by undertaking a double course in psychodrama and group analytic psychotherapy, approaches which have since formed the basis of my clinical work.

When I came across playback theatre in the early 1990s it represented a refreshing return for me to emphasising theatre and performance. The direction I had taken professionally had meant that 'creativity' and 'artistry' had a place in my work, but were seldom the explicit focus. Through playback theatre I am currently exploring a new balance between the elements of theatre and therapy, an exploration which I am finding personally revitalising and expansive in terms of focusing on a wider social field.

A brief description of the method

Playback theatre was developed as a form of non-scripted theatre by Jonathan Fox and his company in New York State in the 1970s. Since then it has developed across the globe, where it is used to aid communication and understanding in groups, organisations and communities in a variety of contexts.

Playback theatre is a ritual form of improvised theatre created in the moment by a unique collaboration of audience and players (see Figure 2.1). The *conductor* (a role including aspects of a master of ceremonies and a shaman) introduces the performance and acts as a conduit between audience and players. He or she elicits a personal sharing from the audience. This can be a brief description of a here-and-now feeling, or as the performance progresses, a more detailed story, an account of a current situation, a memory or dream. The *teller* always figures in the story. With the conductor's words 'Let's watch!' the story is passed over to the performers (actors and musician), who give the story dramatic form, spontaneously and without discussion. They work without props, except for the boxes or stools they sit on, a variety of coloured cloths, and

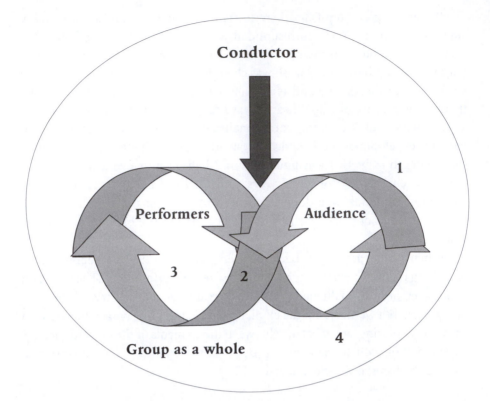

1.   A story is held by an individual

2.   The story is told – in dialogue between the individual and the conductor

3.   The story is performed to the group as a whole

4.   A new story is elicited and the cycle continues

Figure 2.1 The flow of communication in playback theatre

the instruments at the disposal of the musician. So they rely on physical and vocal expressiveness to capture the essence of the story. At the moment the enactment concludes the players come to a point of stillness and with a look of *acknowledgement* symbolically return the story to the teller. The conductor checks with the teller that there was some congruency between the story told and the performance, and gives them the opportunity to say how the enactment impacted on them.

A vignette

It is the end of our first all-day meeting of contributors for this book. Contributors have introduced their areas of interest and there has been some dialogue. In order to convey more directly something of the quality of playback theatre I take on the role of conductor and invite four group members (actors) to stand in a line facing the rest of the group (audience). I ask someone from the audience group to describe in a few words their experience of the day. 'I'm tired, intrigued and stimulated by what we have discussed, but feeling pretty full.' As conductor I invite the actors to let the words resonate with them and in a moment to express directly with movement and sound something of the essence of what they have heard. With the words 'Let's watch!' the attention is on them, and one by one during the following moments they produce physical movements, facial expressions, sounds and the odd word as a response to what they have heard. Each person does something different and a composite picture develops. One looks ready to drop, another ready to burst, another appears to be grabbing at exciting ideas (or are they fruits?) from the air. Few have come across playback before, so I indicate to them to hold the image and cast their gaze towards our colleague whose words inspired the enactment. This moment is the acknowledgement.

I ask our colleague whether he recognised what he saw (i.e. the conductor checks back with the teller). He laughs affirmatively. The process is repeated for other group members.

As a performance progresses, and the level of warm-up of audience and players increases, there is often a move from short forms of enactment, such as *fluid sculptures* (the form described above) and *pairs* (in which ambivalent and conflicting feelings are expressed), to the longer form, *story*. There are usually several of these in a performance. This constitutes a change of gear, a greater degree of risk-taking for teller and audience. The shift is reflected also in the spatial positioning of the teller and conductor. Initial contributions from the audience take place from the teller's own space amongst fellow audience members. This convention takes into account that any contribution will have some feeling of risk. So a number of audience members are given the opportunity to explore that risk, to share something personal but brief; to tolerate the spotlight of the audience's attention, but not for too long.

As the culture of give and take between stage and audience is established and the level of trust in the process increases, the conductor may invite a fuller story. At this point a teller is invited to sit with the conductor in two chairs positioned on stage, but to the side of the acting area, and constituting a third zone, both physically and psychologically. From this position the conductor elicits the story, bearing in mind the needs of the teller, the audience, and players. The teller is usually requested to choose one of the players to represent him or herself in the story, that is, to become the *teller's actor*. Other roles may or may not be explicitly allocated. The words 'Let's watch!' again introduce the spontaneous enactment, which is performed for the teller and the audience. Once the enactment begins, the teller and conductor remain as onstage witnesses, and the players have complete autonomy until the *acknowledgement* as described above. The conductor checks with the teller how the enactment touched them. There is the opportunity here for the teller to have the final word, also for the players to redress gross inaccuracies if necessary. The conductor may also on occasion consider the playing of a *transformation scene* in the event of a teller being left with a desire to see an alternative outcome to their story. This convention is analogous to the psychodramatic use of *surplus reality*. More usually, the moment is used to share the teller's immediate response to their experience of witnessing the enactment. The teller and actors are then thanked, perhaps with applause, and the teller returns to their seat.

Vignette: encounter with Kali

It is the afternoon of a one-day introduction to playback theatre hosted by Middlesex University. There is an explicit focus of exploring questions of culture and difference. The group is varied, comprising students and professionals from the worlds of theatre, social care, law and computers. Group members come from England, Mauritius and Hong Kong. During the morning we have explored short forms and now we move on to full story.

The space is arranged with chairs in a line on stage, cloths draped over a flipchart board to one side and musical instruments to the other. To one side and between audience and performance space there are two chairs, one for myself as conductor, the other ready for a teller.

As conductor I introduce the teller's chair and ask if there is a personal story waiting to be told. A young woman from Mauritius comes to the teller's chair and volunteers from the group take the actors' chairs. My colleague and co-facilitator of the day takes the role of musician. The teller recounts a memory of her visit to India with a female friend. They visit the Kali temple in Calcutta, queue expectantly for several hours to enter the temple, but are moved through within moments, having completed a short ritual, which seems to be over before it has begun. As they leave they witness the sacrifice of a goat and then continue on their way. Close by they come across Mother Theresa's mission, which they also enter. They are struck by the relative quiet, the contrast of atmosphere and colour, a place of coolness and blue after the black and red of the temple scene.

As she tells the story I ask the teller to choose someone to play herself in the story, and someone for her friend. The challenge for the other actors is to play all the other relevant parts of the story (Calcutta, priest, goat, nuns etc.). When she has finished telling the story I summarise briefly and with the words 'Let's watch!' hand over to musician and actors.

The musician starts to play an overture, evoking the busy atmosphere of Calcutta and singing of excitement and expectation. During these moments the actors have the opportunity to use the cloths and chairs to set the stage and to prepare for the enactment. The music pauses and the action begins, with the friends standing in the queue, observing the scene around them. Someone takes the role of the priest who quickly moves them on and out of the inner temple space. The scene changes to Mother Theresa's mission and the ensemble try to convey something of the sense of contrast. The enactment ends, with some closing phrases of music and a coming to stillness of the actors, who turn to look in acknowledgement at the teller, returning the story to her.

This is the first attempt at enacting a full story for this group. I sense that the challenge of conveying such a colourful and multi-layered story has been at best partially met. As conductor I turn to the teller and ask her how the enactment of the story impacted on her and what we had managed to capture. She confirms that it did not really capture what was important in the story but that watching it enabled her to identify what the significant elements were for her, something she had not been aware of during the initial telling. 'What it's really about is the questions that came up for me about religion, about my feeling of expectations that were disappointed, which led me in the end to wondering: where is the spirit?' Rather than trying to replay the whole story as a correction, I invite the actors to offer the teller a fluid sculpture on these elements. She expresses her satisfaction and returns to the audience.

So far I have been describing the visible, external form of the method. The content of each story has an impact not only on the teller, but also, at many levels, on the audience. In contrast to psychodrama, where a piece of protagonist-centred work is always followed by a *sharing* (a process in which group members talk about the impact on themselves of the work, and their own points of identification with it), in playback theatre the response to the story usually comes in the form of another story. The dialogue between stories over the course of a playback event is subtle. It emerges through the individual's spontaneous impulse to tell and yet also belongs to the particular group of people present at that particular time. The content and mood of the stories can be very varied, and the connecting or 'red thread' (Hoesch 1999) may emerge during the performance, for example, as a subtextual dialogue about worldviews, the nature of suffering, power, spirit. In the above example the group came up with two subsequent stories. Connecting themes were friendship and the challenge of being confronted with difference.

The interplay between individual and group is described in Figure 2.1. As the figure-of-eight shape of the diagram suggests, the process is characterised by both continuous flow and containment. From the point of view of the playback event those present constitute one group. Within that group there are two sub-groups, who *between* them co-create the event: the playback company and the audience. The conductor is the conduit and central point between the two. He or she facilitates the process by which the voice of the individual is heard, amplified and dramatised by the players. Each sharing or story is returned to the teller, but is also tangibly present in the shared space, inspiring or provoking another contribution from the audience, which in turn becomes part of the collective dialogue. While playback actors train themselves to *serve* the teller's story, that is, to do justice to its meanings as fully as possible, they also respond to it with their own interpretations and resonances. This is inevitable. Indeed the whole event is predicated on the notion of such resonances between people. By not discussing the story before the enactment, the dramatic interpretation emerges spontaneously *between* the players, and tends to be multi-dimensional, thus revealing familiar and new perspectives of the story as told, both to teller and audience. Perhaps this can be compared with the 'multiverse of meanings' within social dreaming (see Chapter 3).

The language of playback

Playback theatre uses verbal, non-verbal, physical and spatial language. In terms of its emphasis on embodiment and gesture it sits comfortably with the feminist tradition of expanding the notion of language beyond the 'phallogocentric' sense of disembodied, decontextualised words (Laderman and Roseman 1996, p.4). In playback enactments spoken language is often condensed; there may be repetition of single words or phrases, or the use of nonsense language and non-verbal sound to convey a feeling or dynamic in a new way. This use of language is an attempt to communicate more directly, to ground expression in the realm of the physical. Moreno, too, had an interest in the early development of language. He writes of the 'sound matrix' preceding the 'language matrix' and how the infant imitates the sound of the mother, its body being a sound-producing instrument: 'The physical spontaneity of soundmaking is an inherent skill of his body' (Moreno 1978, p.717). Playback theatre, by approaching sound and language in this playful way, has the capacity to cut through or comment on the veneer of over-verbalisation, which can have as much to do with disguising as conveying meaning. At best it can help to reveal essential dimensions to personal and shared experience, although the reality does not always live up to the aspiration, as demonstrated in the playing of the Kali story above. It is possible to miss the point or fail to do justice to the story as told, which is why companies spend time and energy developing their listening and performing skills through training and practice sessions.

Playback performance style varies from company to company, but there is a common tendency in the direction of condensation in both movement and verbal language. Particularly in its short forms playback aims to have something in common with the haiku, which is 'meant to carry a truthful moment into heads and hearts with the speed of an arrow in flight' (Matsuo Busho, quoted in Usher 2000). Significant here is its economy and the direct-ness of its impact at emotional and cognitive levels.

The language of playback is dynamic, a continual process. Part of the enjoyment is in watching it emerge between performers on stage and between performers and audience. The fluid sculpture offers a form for the emergence of a short multi-meaning image or statement. The task of each actor is to convey in gesture and sound one aspect of the teller's experience. Each actor steps forward with their unique contribution, and makes a physical connection to one or more of the preceding actors, so that the final image or statement is ambiguous, a plurality of co-existent perspectives in dialogue with each other, and creating a whole.

Connections to the therapies: psychodrama, dramatherapy, and group analysis

Moreno's vision of therapy and of 'the theatre of spontaneity' (Moreno 1983) can be seen as one of a number of sources of playback theatre. Like psychodrama playback theatre is based on a relational view of human beings and the practice of creativity and spontaneity. Fox himself augmented his theatre background with a training in psychodrama, and acknowledges the connection between these forms (Fox 1999b, p.134). Playback theatre is not itself a therapy, although it can be deeply therapeutic at individual, social and community levels. Some practitioners use it within a therapy frame, for example as part of a psychodrama or dramatherapy group, or in closed groups as a method in its own right.

Moreno's philosophy of psychotherapy is itself radically different from that of the psychoanalytic mainstream of his day. His focus is on *creativity* and *spontaneity* rather than psychoanalytical psychopathology. His concern is with the existential encounter between people. He develops the notion of the 'co-unconscious' which he describes as 'joined *inter*association' (Moreno 1975, p.52). Foulkes suggests a similar perspective: 'What is mind…the mind that is usually called intrapsychic is a property of the group, and the processes that take place are due to the dynamic interactions in this communicational matrix' (Foulkes 1974, pp.227–8).

From a Jungian and group analytic perspective Zinkin writes of a 'mental entity, which is shared by the group', an image which is 'a kind of we-production rather than an I-possession' (Zinkin 1998, p.152). He refers to Henderson's concept of the 'cultural unconscious' (Henderson 1967).

Playback theatre may be a way to access the 'cultural unconscious'. It is certainly a dynamic way of giving form to the 'communicational matrix', and facilitating an 'existential encounter' through personal story.

On the basis of his interpersonal and relational view of humankind Moreno points to a need for therapy to deal with 'social or cultural pathology' (Moreno 1975, p.57). His vision goes beyond the dyad and the closed group: 'A truly therapeutic procedure cannot have less [of] an objective than the whole of mankind' (Moreno 1978, p.698).

Playback theatre operates within the spirit of this vision, honouring the individual and their story, but importantly in the context of the group, where the story needs to be heard. Zinkin, on the relationship between the individual and the collective, invites us to consider that 'collectivity, far from being a

danger to the individual, actually creates the possibility of individuality'
(Zinkin 1998, p.153). He proposes that: 'Meaning is derived from the collective, of which each of us is a part' (p.155).

A playback company trains to be able to achieve what Moreno describes as
a 'spontaneity state' (Moreno 1983, p.44) in performance, a degree of vitality,
openness and intuitive expressiveness, which informs the performance, and in
turn has a transformative impact on the level of spontaneity experienced by the
audience. Moreno, too, recognises the impact the spontaneity state has on
others in its presence. He describes it as motivating 'not only an internal
process, but also a social, external relationship, that is, a correlation with the
[spontaneity] "state" of another creating person' (Moreno 1983, p.44).
Playback theatre promotes this creative interplay initially within the ensemble,
and later, in performance, also with the audience. 'The first character of the
creative act is its spontaneity, the second character is a feeling of surprise, of the
unexpected' (Moreno 1983, pp.42–3). Such moments of surprise in a playback
event act as a call to further spontaneity. In this sense playback theatre can be
said to be an 'Invitation to an Encounter' (Moreno 1914).

A central difference between psychodrama and playback theatre is that in
psychodrama the protagonist (the equivalent to the teller in playback, the one
whose perceptions, roles and relationships are staged) participates as actor in
his or her own drama. Indeed the deepest therapeusis within psychodrama is
often perceived as being brought about by the act of role reversal, the protagonist's participation in the action from the role and perspective of the other/s,
through which projections and internalisations can be explored and new
insights achieved. In playback theatre by contrast the teller remains in the
position of witness throughout the enactment, albeit an onstage witness, sitting
with the conductor to the side of the action. Even here, however, there is a
parallel technique within psychodrama, that of *the mirror*. The psychodramatic
mirror is a device by which the protagonist takes a step back within the psychodrama, viewing a scene through the eyes of an observer, that is, as witness. The
greater degree of distance afforded by this technique can serve a variety of therapeutic functions. It can protect the protagonist from being overwhelmed by
the emotional intensity of a particular role; it can increase their ability to reflect
on the dynamics of a scene; it can move them to a new level of spontaneity, a
new vision and a new impulse towards action.

Within playback theatre, from the witnessing position of the teller's chair,
there is an experience of both containment and intensity. The intensity comes
from a number of factors. Amongst these are the narrating and disclosure of a

personal story, the sense of having been heard and understood, as evidenced in the 'truthful' playing back of the story. The teller's identification with the teller's actor in action induces a trance-like experience where the teller feels paradoxically both inside and outside the action. Intensity arises also from the aesthetic transformation of a personal story in a way that suggests a dimension beyond the personal. The sense of containment is provided by the clarity and discipline of the ritual form, an important element of which is the teller's position as witness throughout the enactment, ensuring some element of aesthetic distance. As seen in the example of the Indian story above, the teller has the opportunity to reflect from their particular position as witness to the enactment.

Anthropologists concerned with the practice of healing rituals and performances recognise the importance of creating appropriate aesthetic distance. This is described as 'the balance point between feeling painful emotions that have been repressed in the past and reliving these feelings from a point of safety in the present' (Laderman and Roseman 1996, p.7). While playback does not restrict itself to working through old and repressed material – stories may be joyful, funny, present and future focused – it nonetheless concerns itself with the need to find a balance of intensity and containment.

The ritual dimension

Ritual is an important aspect of theatre, theatre-based therapy forms, and psychotherapy. Most psychotherapists would acknowledge the importance of ritual aspects in their work. The regularity and predictability of time and place is perhaps the most obvious example of this. The way in which a session is begun and finished, the way in which payment is made and absences dealt with are further instances of the ritual dimension in psychotherapy, which helps to provide a clear frame within which the psychological work takes place.

Theatre of all kinds depends extensively on a ritual dimension. Taking western commercial theatre as an example there is the delineation of stage space and audience space; the use of bells and lighting to signal the beginning of the performance; the raising of the curtain at the beginning of a show; the curtain call at the end of the show; the performers' bow and the audience's applause. All these elements together help to define the performance–audience experience as a whole as theatre. At one level they may be seen as 'empty ritual', habitual devices that might usefully be challenged. At another level they have a function which is psychologically sound in terms of the nature of theatrical experience. In particular they take care of the transition phases of the experience by providing form. Theatre involves an invitation to the audience to suspend disbelief, to participate in a portrayed world whose reality is not of the same order as offstage reality, but has the capacity to affect us profoundly. The ritual elements of the experience are familiar devices, which support us in preparation for and disengagement from the theatrical process.

In the theatre-based therapy forms ritual structuring of the work is part of the training and is seen as an essential part of the safety of the methods. When using any group method based on the dramatic or theatrical arts, that is, one that involves movement, gesture, physical and vocal expressiveness, and perhaps most importantly play, we invite a high degree of risk. To play is to open ourselves up to spontaneity and the possibility that we may expose some of the many potential identities beneath the social personae we construct for everyday interaction. The attraction is that this might be a liberating experience, but the danger is of embarrassment and shame. I shall first explore the ritual elements of dramatherapy and psychodrama and then look at the particular case of playback theatre as a theatrical form with a therapeutic interface. The ritual dimension is present in all these theatre-based groupwork methods, but is significantly different in each.

Within the dramatherapy tradition emphasis is placed on ritual as a safe container. It provides a reliable and familiar frame to the work, a doorway into and out of the liminal space of the 'as if', where serious play can take place. Sessions are constructed in a tripartite form reminiscent of transformation ritual (see Van Gennep 1960). The safe journeying between levels of reality (the everyday, liminal and a transformed everyday) is analogous to the process of travelling by plane (Chesner 1994). Attention must be paid to the process of checking in and taking off at the outset, and to landing and picking up any luggage at the end. The phase of the journey that moves us from A to B is in the air, the liminal phase of the flight, but the safety and success of the journey is dependent on each phase being fulfilled. The clients' ability to risk spontaneity and personal/group exploration through play and metaphor is understood to be dependent on a feeling of containment, which is expressed through the growing familiarity of the ritual session structure.

Like dramatherapy psychodrama uses a tripartite session structure: the warm-up, enactment, and sharing. Particular attention is played to the moments between the phases of a psychodrama session. Out of the warm-up, which involves the whole group, a protagonist is chosen whose personal work becomes the focus of the enactment. Sociometry (see Moreno 1978) is used to ensure that the protagonist chosen best represents or carries the concerns of the group at that moment. The group expresses its resonances and choices visibly and concretely, for example by each group member moving to stand behind the person whose work as protagonist would best meet their own need. After the psychodramatic enactment the sharing brings the focus back on to the individual group members, who have the opportunity to acknowledge their lines of identification and differences with the characters and perspectives portrayed in the enactment. The process rests on the understanding that there is a subtle and important interconnectedness between the individual and the group; and that the enactment itself takes place in a trance-like state, not only for the protagonist, but also for the other group members. Whether they have participated as auxiliary egos or audience, they too have been part of a shared process, which takes place in the liminal space. The *sharing* constitutes the coming in to land, and a preparation for the return to everyday reality.

Playback theatre at its best fulfils a threefold function: an aesthetic, a social, and a ritual one. These interconnect and enhance each other, indeed Fox suggests that the realm of good playback theatre is where these zones intersect (Fox and Dauber 1999, p.127).

The ritual dimension in playback theatre acts as a known and reliable container for the unknown, spontaneously arising stories and enactments. It facilitates the flow between audience, conductor and performers (see Figure 2.1); between the individual and the group; between the here-and-now dimension of the social event and the artistic dimension of the 'as if'; between the personal and the transpersonal; the individual and the collective.

There are a number of rules which conductor and performers adhere to, all of which support the ritual frame. As shown in terms of psychodrama and dramatherapy ritual characteristically pays attention to transition moments. While the playback performance as a whole needs a beginning, middle and end (giving it a familiar, tripartite structure), the ritual frame in playback must support numerous transitions and enactments within the course of a performance. The words 'Let's watch!' are used to transfer the audience's attention from the conductor–teller dyad to the stage and the enactment of each story. There ensues a brief period of setting up, another transitional moment, which follows a particular form. The actors move from their straight line – from where they have listened to the story, during which time they have moved from a seated to a standing position as their role in the story is allocated – to take their place on the stage for the start of the enactment. Perhaps they take a moment to choose and position a coloured cloth or box to set the stage. During this short time between the invitation to watch and the enactment it is usual for the musician to play, the musical overture acting as a ritual preparation for the enactment and a container for the transition period. The moment between preparation and enactment is also marked by a pause in the music and a moment of stillness on stage, so that the coming to life of the enactment begins clearly and with a certain sense of magic. This is comparable to traditional rituals from other cultures. In the Kaluli healing séance of Papua New Guinea, for example, the moment when the spirits enter the performance is marked by a hissing outbreath and the singing of a particular kind of song (Schieffelin 1996).

The transition period at the end of the enactment is also held within the ritual form, so that its separate elements can be attended to as described below. Within the context of the playback performance as ritual we can usefully regard the telling and witnessing of their story as a 'rite of passage' (see Van Gennep 1960) for the individual teller concerned. As such the tripartite process of separation, transformation and re-integration takes place, not just once as in the case of classical psychodrama but, because there are several tellers in one performance, several times during the performance as a whole. The invitation to the teller's chair is an invitation to a moment of 'separation' from the audience space. The move to the teller's chair involves being seen, a focus on individuality in the presence of the group. The telling of the story is in itself a spontaneous, creative act, the story often emerging in an unexpected way in the dialogue between conductor and teller. The teller's experience of witnessing their own story being creatively enacted can be a moment of heightened awareness for the teller, during which they might be described as being in a 'liminal' and potentially 'transformative' space. The subsequent phase of 're-integration' of the individual into the audience must occur safely and again this transition is held within the ritual frame. The enactment concludes with a moment of stillness and a look of acknowledgement from the actors to the teller. For a moment they remain onstage, ready if necessary to perform a correction or a transformation scene. The conductor checks in with the teller and has the function of holding the moment with the teller. This is the moment during which the experience begins to settle. The teller's trance-state reduces as they begin to focus more on the here-and-now context of the group as a whole. The conductor has the crucial task of maintaining a meta-level awareness, taking care of the individual, the performers and the audience. He or she ensures that the teller is 'dismissed' (Fox 1999a, p.128) from the chair and returns to the

audience at a moment appropriate to the teller and the rhythm of the performance.

I have given only some examples of the rules and traditions that hold the
ritual. There is a correlation between the containment of the ritual and the
freedom of expression that playback theatre invites. All stories are welcome in a
playback event, some of which may be personally revealing and socially deeply
challenging. The enactment unfolds without planning, and has the tendency to
be bold, giving shape to the perceived 'essence' of the story. There is no confidentiality agreement in a public playback theatre performance, and yet these
deep stories are told. What makes it safe to disclose such stories within a
therapy setting is the analytic/therapeutic frame. What makes it safe enough in
playback theatre is the ritual frame, through which comes a sense of respect for
the seriousness of the endeavour. For example, it is a matter of the ritual form
that the actors do not address the teller. They have to trust the conductor to
elicit enough information in the interview. This 'rule' ensures that there is a
boundary in place for the teller. Another example is the procedure of checking
back with the teller after an enactment. This element of the ritual gives the
teller the final word and the space to make a public reflection. It constitutes a
moment of returning the personal story to the person.

From an anthropological perspective ritual and drama have the function of
providing opportunity for 'plural reflection...plural reflexivity' (Turner 1979,
p.94). At its best, the playback theatre event invites what Turner describes as
'spontaneous communitas', a sense of profound connectedness, characterised
by 'a high value on personal honesty, openness, and lack of pretentions or pre-
tentiousness' (Turner 1979, p.45). It has elements in common with Kaluli
séance, as mentioned above. Schieffelin regards these rituals as 'inherently
riskier' than more rigidly formulaic kinds of ritual, where the content is prede-
fined. He writes: 'The element of risk in these types of performances derives
from their improvisational and dialogic construction...' (Schieffelin 1996,
p.80).

We could make a similar comparison of risk levels in terms of traditional
forms of western theatre. A scripted play, while actors do aim to bring a
freshness and quality of 'as if for the first time' to its enactment, falls into the
category of what Moreno calls a 'cultural conserve' (Moreno 1940). The kind
of audience participation found in pantomime, for example, is rendered relatively safe by its reliance on known formulae ('Oh no it isn't!' 'Oh yes it is!').
Playback theatre is dependent on the spontaneously created dialogue between
audience and performers, and there is no rehearsal for the audience as

co-creators. It is a high-risk performance for all participants. The ritual elements of the form provide a necessary containment for the risk – they do not abolish it. There can be casualties, moments of wounding when a teller feels their story has been misheard or diminished in performance. At such moments a correction may be required and an acceptance of fallibility on the part of the company.

Group analytic and dialogic perspectives

The interplay between individual and group is central to group analysis. Foulkes regards the 'social nature of man' as basic rather than secondary. He writes of 'the existence of a constant stream of communication, verbal and non-verbal, conscious and unconscious, indeed of a community of experience' (Foulkes 1964, p.125). The same words could describe a playback theatre process. Indeed Foulkes acknowledges that group analysis has 'features of an action method' (Foulkes 1964, p.129).

In the group analytic setting the focus is both on the individual and the group process. Dalal challenges us towards *Taking the Group Seriously* (Dalal 1998) and thinking in terms of a 'social unconscious': 'As no one is privileged to be outside the social, we are all blind to the structure. It is beyond our ken. Nevertheless, through painstaking analysis, by one discourse testing another, one can catch glimpses of something, only shadows to be sure, but shadows of *something*' (Dalal 1998, p.222).

There is an important role for reflection and analysis in playback theatre. Reflective and critical processing happens to some extent immediately after a performance, and more fully at a later time, when the immediate energy of performance has subsided. Within a performance or workshop the notion of 'one discourse testing another' is a helpful one in considering the process. In the analytic group the discourse is verbal and based on free association within the group. In the case of playback theatre the discourse is one between enacted stories. 'Glimpses' are caught in the interaction between the stories, which can deepen our understanding of the relationship between the 'individual' and 'group' and communicate something of our experience of being in the world. The method and form may be different, but the group analytic task of trying to 'understand how the field is moving the individual, and how the individual is affecting the field' (Dalal 1998, p.222) is similar to the task of playback theatre. The personal stories told inevitably have a social dimension, referring to a wider social context outside the playback performance. They are told within a social context, that of the particular audience and performers who have come together at a specific place and time for the performance. The 'field' in this sense can be understood both as the wider context of life experience from which the personal stories are drawn and also the here-and-now matrix of the participants continually responding to the unfolding network of stories and enactments. It is an active process in which 'text and context are mutually constitutive' (Laderman and Roseman 1996, p.3).

The physicist and thinker David Bohm, in considering the importance of dialogue and 'the nature of collective thought' (Bohm 1996, p.49), suggests that thought is a 'subtle tacit process' and that what is said explicitly is only a small part of meaning (p.15). He suggests that we can change thought by communicating at the tacit level. Fox considers playback theatre a way to achieve dialogue in Bohm's sense (Fox 1999b, p.196) and indeed much of what happens in playback theatre is a celebration of and act of trust in tacit communication. The way in which meanings and details are conveyed between teller, conductor and performers goes beyond what is explicitly narrated. The red thread or discourse between stories manifests at a tacit level. A highly skilled conductor might be able to allude to it verbally at the close of a performance, giving explicit expression to the emerging dialogue. Even without the conductor's naming of the connections there is often a clear if intuitive sense of appropriateness as one story follows another, or refers obliquely to an earlier theme in the performance from a new perspective. To continue the comparison with the ritual performances of the Kaluli tribe, we might also say of playback theatre: 'What a particular performance is about in both its text and all its subtexts depends on the agendas of performers and audience' (Schieffelin 1996, p.65); and that its success as a ritual depends on doing justice to these variables on a particular occasion.

Bohm uses the concepts of 'presentation', 'representation', 're-presentation' and 'collective representations' to discuss how thinking and changes in thinking can happen. Memory, feelings and 'felts' as well as the sensory realm of the body inform the dialogue and play a part in the 'net presentation' (Bohm 1996, pp.55–56). In playback theatre there is a multi-level interplay between what is represented and presented. The story told during the performance by a teller is a representation of an experience. Its enactment is a representation in response to a representation, mediated by the manner of the conductor's interview and the mental representations that arise in the performers' imagination as they hear the story, and in the audience's imagination as they witness the enactment. On the one hand this process has the potential to create distance and abstraction, but paradoxically the enactment also creates a sense of immediacy, through its sensuality and physicality. It is a *presentation*. As we resonate with the story and images on stage, emerging in the here and now, we are in touch with both memory and the present.

Narrative perspectives

Let us now consider three kinds of story: the traditional myth or folktale, the personally created fictional story, and the personal narrative. They all have a place within psychotherapy and personal development traditions. Myths and folktales are understood to be vehicles for psychological and cultural truths. The works of Jung (Jung 1960), Bettelheim (Bettelheim 1976), Estes (Estes 1992) and Gersie (Gersie 1997) are rich in examples of such stories from the collective and their usefulness in personal work. The characters and dynamics of these known stories can be powerful vehicles for addressing personal concerns through action methods in individual and group therapy contexts. The value of the personally created fictional story in therapy is its use of distance and metaphor. These stories can facilitate exploration and allow indirect expression of issues that are perhaps too painful, unclear or complex to be approached head-on (see Cattanach 1997; Chesner 1995). The personal narrative is perhaps the most familiar to psychotherapists. The client tells and explores their story with the help of the therapist. Another therapeutic application of personal narrative is 'journal therapy' and life-story work, used in groups such as Alcoholics Anonymous (Atkinson 1995).

Playback theatre rests on personal narrative, but is enriched by the other two kinds of story. It is rare for the teller to frame their story in terms of a known myth or tale, although it is common for metaphorical elements to enter the narration through their use of language. The players may pick up on the linguistic metaphor and express it physically. For example, in a short enactment, such as a fluid sculpture, the term 'letting off steam', or 'butterflies in the stomach' may be portrayed literally, thus intensifying its impact and creating a new expressionistic perspective to the story.

In a longer story the players may notice a relationship between the teller's story and a known story or mythical figure, and use this connection to frame the enactment. For example, a young man tells about his continual attempts to get a job in his chosen profession. He talks about his regular scouring of the newspapers, the numerous job applications he has written, the sense of hope each time that *this* application will be successful. He describes the string of dis-

appointments he has suffered, when no letter comes, or when, after an unsuc-
cessful interview a letter of rejection arrives. He is wondering if he should give
up hope. The story could be played naturalistically, but this may not add a
great deal to what the teller and audience have already heard. If a connection to
the myth of Sisyphus is made, the players may structure the whole enactment
within the physical frame of repeatedly pushing a boulder up a hill, only for it
to roll down. The cycle of effort, hope and disappointment expressed in the
personal story can be shown through the mythical metaphor. From an
aesthetic point of view there is the advantage of the simplicity of the image.
There is an element of surprise in the shift of setting, and the interplay between
the mythical and everyday. The mundane is shown in its mythical dimension,
and the young man's endeavour takes on heroic proportions.

By attempting to highlight the implicit message of the story, the mythical
framing serves not only the teller, but also the dialogue between stories.
Perhaps this story might inspire other stories about life's challenges, expanding
on the theme that life is hard; or it might trigger a very different story on the
theme that persistence sometimes pays off. The possibilities in any moment are
limitless and unpredictable. 'In the life story of each person is a reflection of
another's life story' (Atkinson 1995, p.4). There is an element of mystery and
surprise as one story evokes another in the context of a performance, and a
sense that the unique combination of people present at that moment somehow
contributes to the necessary conditions for that story to be told.

The urge to narrate a personal story is deep. Coles (1989) writes of the 'call
of stories'. The nature of the urge is multi-faceted. There is the challenge and
need to give form and coherence to personal experience. There is a desire to be
heard and understood by others, to search for connection, acknowledgement
or approval. There may be an element of the confessional, or a plea for help in
coming to terms with something difficult. There may be the impulse to
challenge the status quo to take account of difference. The impulse may be
about inclusion or about affirming distance. In each case there is an implicit
invitation to a response. The narration in the context of performance is based
on the 'dialogical principle' that 'what is said is incomplete until it has met a
response in the other' (Bakhtin 1979).

In any narration an audience is implicit, whether it is an audience of one, in
a private journal or individual therapy session, or an audience of many in an
autobiographical book. For the playback audience, there is also an urge to hear
personal stories. The performance aims to provide a respectful environment,
where each teller and story is honoured. The desire to hear another's story in

this context inevitably includes and also goes beyond the question of curiosity or voyeurism. It has to do with a desire for connection, an impulse towards self-knowledge, in which 'self' is understood not only at the individual level, but also as a social phenomenon. The audience needs to hear itself speak, to bear witness to itself. It particularly needs to hear its quieter, perhaps repressed voices, the voices of the sociometric isolates, the minorities and outsiders. A skilful conductor will have an eye for the sociometry of the audience, and will often devote the early part of their dialogue with the audience to finding out what sub-groups and hierarchies are present. Even in the naming and recognition of these sub-groups something palpable begins to happen in the group as a whole. Each statement of identity suggests the presence of a multitude of stories, some of which will be told during the performance. Many conductors use the technique of asking audience members to turn to a neighbour for a few minutes and share a story briefly. The buzz of a multiplicity of stories being told *a deux* acts as a warm-up to more public telling.

The audience's desire for stories also involves a readiness to take a risk as listener and witness, to be open to the possibility of irritation or transformation: 'To speak is one thing, to listen is another. To listen is potentially a very frightening process, because to hear the words of another is literally to let their words and meanings into the self – it is to let a stranger into the home' (Dalal 1998, p.223).

For the performer–teller–audience group as a whole the emergence of a variety of stories from different sub-groups draws attention to our interdependence and is an invitation to investigate that interdependence. Stories reveal our similarities and our differences. One of the challenges of playback theatre is to do justice both to the mythical dimension, which emphasises commonality, and also to the element of difference that has to do with our uniqueness as individuals and the particularity of our experience as members of cultural sub-groups. Atkinson, writing about life-story work, suggests that a connection is established between those present when a life story is told that remains, independent of whether those concerned ever meet each other again (Atkinson 1995, p.15). My own experience of playback theatre suggests that this is true of playback too. Many of the stories told lodge themselves powerfully in the memory of the audience. This may be as a result of the themes, the telling, the enactment, the ritual setting, or a combination of all of these. Their resonance may continue for a long time and potentially broaden our understanding, or transform our previously held view of the world by incorporating a new sense of the other into our perspective. Fox gives a particularly powerful example of such a story. He describes the impact of a story told in Israel in which the teller disclosed acts of terrorism he had committed in another country. The audience was challenged to look at the issue of terrorist violence from a terrorist's own perspective (Fox 1999a, p.124). This is a striking example of the audience 'letting a stranger into the home' (see Dalal above) and of the desire of the 'stranger' to be witnessed. It is a moment of dialogue in the sense of the 'emergent friction between contrasting values' (Nichols in Bohm 1996, p.ix). Risks such as these are dependent on the playback performance embodying a culture of 'mutual acceptance', which Zinkin defines as not meaning agreement, but as including 'the acceptance of difference' (Zinkin 1998, p.201).

The playback company

Western theatre as it originated in ancient Greece may have grown out of choric ritual events, in which the chorus were skilled representatives of the community (Arnott 1989, p.30). The playback theatre company can be seen as a modern-day chorus, facilitating group dialogue within the ritual context of the performance. As suggested in Figure 2.1 the performers, like the original Greek chorus, are both part of the larger group and separate from it. Similarly the audience is both separate from the performing group and participant in the performance ritual.

The process of becoming a playback company is complex. It involves learning the skills and forms of the method, its philosophy, culture and spirit, as well as developing into an ensemble at artistic and interpersonal levels. I have been involved in the founding and training of two companies, the Munich Augenblick company, and the Findhorn Playback Company in Scotland, and am currently involved in the founding of England-based Playback International. In considering playback theatre as a group method it is helpful to distinguish two interrelated aspects of company process. First, the company itself is a continuously evolving group, independent of whether it is involved in a performance. It has to deal with the same kind of challenges as other groups as it matures and as individual members' personal commitments change. This is the inward-looking level of company process. Second, the degree to which a company can serve its audience depends on the skills and capacity of the company, and this is an outward-looking level of process, where there is always some sense of a future audience or community. However, the distinction is blurred. During rehearsals group members use their own stories as material for practice, and skills development. This is not simply a technical exercise, and over time company members become familiar with each other's life struggles and stories in a way which is not dissimilar to the process over time of a therapy or personal development group. The Findhorn company speak of a particular weekend in their first year together when they 'gelled', in terms of recognising their interdependence and a deepening of mutual trust. The Spiegelbühne company in Frankfurt who have been together for several years report many such shifts in their developing process (Arping and Feldhendler 1999, pp.91–111).

Playback techniques may be the primary language of the work as a group, but it is not the only one. Inevitably group dynamic issues arise over time, which require reflection through discussion and supervision processes as well as playback. There is also a recognised place for socialising in the group. The sharing of food and leisure time contribute to the bonding of the group and to the kind of familiarity which is seen as supporting its capacity for spontaneity and risk-taking. This is in contrast to a group whose task is primarily therapy, where abstinence from socialising is the norm.

In my description of playback in performance I have focused mainly on the flow of stories from audience to performers. There is also a subtle flow in the other direction. Although the performers do not tell their own stories in a performance it appears that at a tacit level their process invites and inhibits stories of a certain kind. When the time came for the first public performance of the Findhorn company there was a feeling of nervous excitement amongst the group. Until that point we had only performed amongst and for ourselves, and now we were to expose ourselves to the public gaze, albeit to that of an invited audience. It was a transition time for us, a coming of age. There was no overt thematic agenda for the performance, but the first two stories told from the teller's chair mirrored our own adolescence. The first story was about a young woman whose trousers split during a date at the opera. The second story was about a twelve-year-old boy and his embarrassment in a social situation. He was a guest at the house of a schoolfriend's family. He arrived with a cold, but felt unable to admit to his illness. He furtively used and hid toilet paper to blow his nose on. His dilemma was what to do with the hoarded used toilet paper and the painful climax of the story came when he tried to dispose of it in the toilet, which got blocked. As well as reflecting the neophyte company's embarrassment issues, the telling of these stories was also an act of tremendous trust, mirroring the company's leap of faith into public performance mode.

Another example of this mirroring of performers' and audience concerns occurred recently when Playback International performed for the anniversary celebrations of a psychodrama training school. In our private group warm-up prior to the performance each group member checked in verbally with the group. One group member told us of a dream she had had that night in which she encountered her ex-husband at the home they used to share. Later that day as the performance took place our first story from the audience was a dream involving the same themes of revisiting the marital home after a break-up.

The tacit communication from performing group to audience also blocks the telling of stories whose content is too deep or challenging for the company at a particular time, so it is important for a company to develop a sense of its own changing capacities over time. An example of this is given by Arping and Feldhendler (1999, pp.98–100). The Frankfurt Spiegelbühne company during a time of change and challenge in their group recognised that it was not appropriate for them to perform as part of a Holocaust Memorial project on the theme of Holocaust and Reconciliation. The task was too challenging for them in the light of the company's vulnerability at that time.

Applications

Playback theatre can be used to enhance group communication through both workshop and performance approaches. In a workshop the whole group is introduced to some of the practice exercises used by companies in training and preparation. The games, songs, and short structures used here have value in their own right, bringing benefits such as a shared experience of fun, the development of spontaneity, physical and vocal expressiveness, listening skills, trust and a sense of connection within a group. These qualities have relevance to team building and the development of emotional intelligence and so have application in various work settings. In a workshop situation participants get to try out a variety of performing roles and to share personal stories.

Workshop vignette

A recent experience of playback theatre as a workshop method: a group of mental health service users in London has received a grant to create a play. The project involves a drama project worker and a playwright. I am invited in early on in the project to facilitate a day of playback theatre with the focus on creating an environment where personal stories are generated, shared and performed, as a warm-up to the wider project.

The morning is spent on games, spontaneity exercises and fluid sculptures. In the afternoon two stories are told and played. The first is told by a woman with learning disabilities, who recounts a 'peak experience'. This is a school trip involving an adventurous journey to the top of a mountain by cable car. The teller particularly remembers leaving behind a less able school friend who is unable to enter the cable car. The second story is a man's memory of his adolescence – the time when he is apparently introduced to cannabis by a friend. The friend gets stoned, while he feels nothing. Later they find out they have been sold oregano.

In the closing discussion of the day what emerges strongly in the group is an assertion that any play they produce must go beyond the confines of their labels as mental health service users. The workshop experience has put them in touch with the wealth of stories they possess as human beings independent of those labels and the strength of their desire to represent themselves in that fuller light.

Performance vignette

I have recently been involved with a performance for Asian people living in London.

The performance team is white, but performers and conductor identify themselves in their introductions to the audience as having had the experience of living and working in other cultures. The performance is hosted by Tamil members of a Catholic community in the East End of London (a relatively deprived part of the city); the audience are highly motivated to get us to portray the difficulties of living in London as an immigrant – it is cold, expensive, unfriendly, difficult to travel around. There is a sense of collective pleasure in this audience group being actively heard in their criticisms and complaints of the dominant culture. The only positive perspectives of life in London are elicited from the children, who describe the pleasure of playing together. Subsequent longer stories that are told include the story of one woman's struggle to be accepted as a professional in this country. Having trained as a teacher in India, when she came to London to join her husband the only work she could get was as a worker in a box factory.

Fox describes some of the contexts in which playback is practised whether as a workshop or performance method (Fox and Dauber 1999, pp.13–14). I use his description as the basis for the following.

Playback in therapy

It is used as a resource for spontaneity and role training; I have used it also in therapy training; as a creative activity providing a change of intensity and as a means of reflecting on group process during a training weekend. During a recent weekend of training in creative approaches to supervision a playback exercise provided an excellent closure for a day's work. Standing in a circle the whole group played back each person's two-word summary of how they felt after the day's work.

Playback in supervision

In group supervision playback can be a useful tool whereby the therapist-supervisee-teller gets first to recount a process and then to have the benefit of seeing it played back from a slightly different perspective informed by the perceptions of the supervision group members. Unlike some other applications it seems that this kind of application needs to include subsequent verbal reflection and dialogue.

Playback in education

Here it is used to facilitate children and older students telling their stories. It can be a tool for validating their feelings and benefiting the school culture. As a workshop method involving the body and senses its structures are helpful in imparting listening and communication skills and for active learning. It can be linked to the curriculum, and is becoming an object of study in its own right. The first international symposium on playback theatre was held at Kassel University in 1997 and there are research projects in progress across the continents.

Playback in social service

Here it is used in many settings to enhance communication skills and for witnessing a personal story. Its non-therapy but therapeutic status means that it may be perceived as less threatening than some other group methods.

Playback as community theatre

Companies give regular or occasional performances aimed at a wider or local community. This is in contrast to the following, which usually represent specific commissions.

Playback and the marking of transitions

It is used for celebrating birthdays and anniversaries, and as a memorial form. In conferences it is widely used at openings, closings, and to mark processes of change during a longer event.

Playback and organisations

It is used in training events around particular themes; for conferences and consultancy at times of change; to help create a balance of the cognitive and emotional in team development.

Conclusion

I have discussed playback theatre in the light of the other group methods that are part of my own groupwork repertoire. As a method of communication in a group context it has elements in common with all three (psychodrama, dramatherapy, group analysis), both in terms of an underlying philosophy about people, groups, and community, and as regards its use of ritual structure. At the heart of the method is a process of dialogue in the context of the group. As a psychotherapist I am interested in the question, 'Where do our stories belong?' The growing use of playback theatre in a wide range of cultures and settings suggests that one answer to this question is that to some extent our stories belong in the wider group, where they can contribute to a process of dialogue and the development of community.

References

Arnott, P.D. (1989) *Public and Performance in the Greek Theatre.* London: Routledge.

Arping, M. and Feldhendler, D. (1999) 'Practical aspects from the life of a playback theatre ensemble.' In J. Fox and H. Dauber (eds) *Gathering Voices.* New Paltz: Tusitala.

Atkinson, R. (1995) *The Gift of Stories: Practical and Spiritual Applications of Autobiography, Life Stories and Personal Mythmaking.* Westpoint, Connecticut: Bergin and Garvey.

Bakhtin, M. (1979) 'The problem of text in linguistics, philosophy and the other human sciences.' In *Estetica SlovesnogTvorchestva.* Moscow: Bocharov.

Bettelheim, B. (1976) *The Uses of Enchantment.* London: Thames and Hudson.

Bohm, D. (1996) (edited by L. Nichol) *On Dialogue.* London: Routledge.

Cattanach, A. (1997) *Children's Stories in Play Therapy.* London: Jessica Kingsley Publishers.

Chesner, A. (1994) 'An integrated model of dramatherapy and its application with adults with learning disabilities.' In S. Jennings *et al. Handbook of Dramatherapy.* London: Routledge.

Chesner, A. (1995) *Dramatherapy for People with Learning Disabilities, A World of Difference.* London: Jessica Kingsley Publishers.

Coles, R. (1989) *Stories and Theories, the Call of Stories.* Boston: Houghton Mifflin.

Dalal, F. (1998) *Taking the Group Seriously.* London: Jessica Kingsley Publishers.

Estes, C.P. (1992) *Women Who Run with the Wolves.* London: Rider.

Foulkes, S.H. (1964) *Therapeutic Group Analysis.* London: George Allen and Unwin. Reprinted 1984, London: Karnac.

Foulkes, S.H. (1974) 'My philosophy in psychotherapy.' In (1990) *Selected Papers.* London: Karnac.

Fox, J. (1999a) 'A ritual for our time.' In J. Fox and H. Dauber (eds) *Gathering Voices*. New Paltz: Tusitala.

Fox, J. (1999b) 'The journey to deep stories.' In J. Fox and H. Dauber (eds) *Gathering Voices*. New Paltz: Tusitala.

Fox, J. and Dauber, H. (eds) (1999) *Gathering Voices*. New Paltz: Tusitala.

Gersie, A. (1997) *Reflections on Therapeutic Storymaking*. London: Jessica Kingsley Publishers.

Grotowski, J. (1975) *Towards a Poor Theatre*. London: Eyre Methuen.

Henderson, J. L. (1967) *Thresholds of Initiation*. Middletown, Conn: Wesleyan University Press.

Hoesch, F. (1999) 'The red thread.' In J. Fox and H. Dauber (eds) *Gathering Voices*. New Paltz: Tusitala.

Jung, C. (1960) *Collected Works, Vol. 8*. London: Routledge.

Laderman, C. and Roseman, M. (eds) (1996) *The Performance of Healing*. New York: Routledge.

Moreno, J. L. (1914) *Einladung zu Einer Begegnumg*. Vienna: Anzengruber Verlag.

Moreno, J. L. (1940) 'Spontaneity and catharsis.' In J. Fox (ed) (1987) *The Essential Moreno*. New York: Springer.

Moreno, J. L. (1978) *Who Shall Survive? Foundations of Sociometry, Group Psychotherapy and Sociodrama*. Beacon, N.Y: Beacon House.

Moreno, J. L. (1983) *The Theatre of Spontaneity*. Ambler: Beacon House.

Moreno, J. L. in collaboration with Moreno, Z. T. (1975) *Psychodrama Volume 2*. Beacon, N.Y: Beacon House.

Schieffelin, E. (1996) 'On failure and performance, throwing the medium out of the séance.' In C. Laderman and M. Roseman (eds) *The Performance of Healing*. New York: Routledge.

Turner, V. (1979) *Process, Performance and Pilgrimage*. New Delhi: Concept.

Usher, R. (2000) 'The magnificent seventeen.' *Time Magazine*. 24 July.

Van Gennep, A. (1960) *Rites of Passage*. London: Routledge and Kegan Paul.

Zinkin, L. (1998) 'Is Jungian group analysis possible?' In H. Zinkin, R. Gordon and J. Haynes (eds) *Dialogue in the Analytic Setting*. London: Jessica Kingsley Publishers.

CHAPTER 3

Getting to the Heart of the Matter
A Jungian Approach to Social Dreaming

Peter Tatham

What is social dreaming?

The activity known as Social Dreaming™ is not a therapy, nor does it take place within a therapeutic group. In this chapter I will describe the process as it is done and make suggestions about its nature, from my own perspective as an analytical psychologist.

First 'discovered' by W. Gordon Lawrence and colleagues, in 1982, social dreaming has since been developed by himself and others, around the world, the first major paper about the method, 'Won from the Void and Formless Infinite', (Lawrence 1991 in Lawrence 1998), being published nine years later.

In that paper he described the construction of social dreaming as a 'discovery' rather than an invention, quoting the physicist Roger Penrose, who has suggested that there is always more to come from any discovery than was first put into it, whereas an invention does nothing other than what it was brought into being to do (Penrose 1989, pp.96–97). This has certainly been the case with social dreaming, the nature and applications of which are still being explored and extended.

By naming it 'the social dreaming matrix' – 'matrix' means 'uterus' in Latin – Lawrence deliberately suggested that its nature was as 'a place out of which something grows', with the implication that no one can ever know exactly what will arise from within that place, just as with any pregnancy.

Used in this way, the word 'matrix' could refer to the dreaming group itself as well as its social unconscious, from within which any such meanings will arise. The root of the word is from the Latin, *'mater'*, meaning mother, with the added female, agential, ending, *'-ix'*. So a matrix is not just a place for containment that fosters growth, but will also, like any womb, actively produce its fruits into an outside, waiting, world. The same word, matrix, is also used to describe the rock mass surrounding a fossil or gemstone, as well as being the name of a blank sheet of type metal into which lettering can be stamped by a punch (patrix). Both of these images might be seen as metaphors for social dreaming.

Foulkes was the first to use the word 'matrix' in relation to the psychology of groups, writing that it

> ...is called 'matrix' because it is the mother-soil in which all dynamic processes take their place. I cannot enlarge on the concept of matrix, beyond saying that it is possible to claim a firm pre-existing community or communion between the members, founded eventually upon the fact that they are all human. They have the same qualities as a species, the same anatomy and physiology, and also perhaps the same archaic traces of ancient experiences. (Foulkes 1971. p.212)

Earlier than that, C.G. Jung had described the unconscious mind as 'the matrix out of which all consciousness grows' (Jung 1923 in C.W.17, par. 102). This theme runs as a leitmotif through all his work, being mentioned in his first book, *Symbols of Transformation* (1912). In this, the word 'matrix' refers to a 'mother-symbol' pointing to the unconscious as 'creative matrix of the future' (Jung 1959 in C.W.5, par. 459); and although the word 'matrix' is not used in the first English translation of this work, the implied meaning is clearly the same (Jung 1919, p.185).

Allied to his notion of a 'collective unconscious', Jung is clearly referring to the matrix as more than just the property of a single individual. As Jung understood it, individuals can relate directly only to their own personal unconscious, which is always contained by, as well as within, a collective unconscious mind, made up of archetypal forms. This transpersonal realm, a mental deposit of archaic experiences, is the matrix to which Jung referred, and with which Foulkes seems to agree, by mentioning 'archaic traces of ancient experiences'.

The nature of social dreaming

Social dreaming usually takes place as an integral part of the gathering together of a number of people for some other overall purpose, for example, a group, an organisation, or as members of a seminar. In this way it reveals the unconscious activity generated by their coming together. There is therefore both a shared, conscious experience, as well as unconscious activity (the social unconscious). And these will include also the reflections of each individual upon his or her reasons for being there, reactions to the experience of being a part of that gathering and so forth.

These insights concerning the process have emerged over the past twenty years, during which time matrices have taken place around the world, in such different projects and situations as conferences or congresses, educational settings, and seminars of various kinds, as well as in action research, organisational consultancy and so forth.

If not a therapeutic group process, what is it then? In his description of the matrix, Foulkes uses the words 'community' (a quality pertaining to all) and 'communion' (social intercourse), both of which also have their own specialised meanings, although as far as Foulkes was concerned they described aspects of the therapeutic group.

For myself, I now prefer to say that social dreaming takes place within a 'commonality', which the dictionary defines as 'a body of people organised into a social unity'. It seems to me that this term is sufficiently neutral for the purpose, not being 'loaded' with any baggage culled from any other particular or specialised usage.

A matrix will last from one to two hours, its use also being limited in time to a day, a weekend, or else forming a regular, integral activity of any organisation and its members. The number of people participating in any matrix can vary; and I have myself worked successfully with as few as three other people and as many as a hundred.

Such diversity of practice reveals itself in the recent book, edited by Lawrence, *Social Dreaming @ Work* (Lawrence 1998). The papers that it contains clearly show that by taking part in such a matrix, whatever the setting, individuals may feel more in command of themselves as members of a community or organisation, especially when faced with the sometimes contradictory demands generated by an increasingly complex and depersonalising work situation or social setting. Social dreaming fosters 'thought' in individual participants concerning their surroundings and the functions expected of them in that setting, whether a temporary one or ongoing activity. But these thoughts are based upon unconscious processes, deliberately fostered by the matrix. The method also enables participants to explore, in depth, the nature of their involvement with current social realities, whatever those might be.

Any group meeting to dream socially represents the social context in which the process will take place. It is made up of individuals, each having their own psychic make-up, as well as being a part of the whole, which is the commonality itself, possessing its own individual nature, form and rules.

So how is it done?

Participants do not sit in a circle, for this would foster the establishment of a group dynamic. Instead the chairs will have been placed spirally (Lawrence 1998, p.17), in a 'snowflake pattern' (p.32), or else in some other random, chaotic form: the intention being that no person is directly in front of, beside, or behind, another. Sometimes, participants may even find themselves seated back to back. When such a commonality, made up of individuals, has been formally opened by the convenor(s), one person will start proceedings by telling a dream. Another member's association to the shared dream will follow; and this may take the form of a comment upon the dream's content, a memory evoked by its images, or another dream. Any association, of whatever kind, is valid and allowed. Some of these may arise spontaneously from the here and now: for example, last night's dream, a casual conversation between partici-pants, or a theme from some previous lecture/discussion or matrix. Other inter-ventions may relate to the more distant past, such as a childhood event, induced emotions, the long-remembered dream or nightmare, as well as half-forgotten memories now recalled. Any intervention is allowable but, most importantly, no dreams are ever interpreted, as might be the case with individual or group psychotherapy.

And so the matrix proceeds, giving birth *not* to a single unified thread of significant meaning, common to all those present, but to a 'multiverse of meanings', in Lawrence's term (p.282), perhaps as many as there are people present.

'Multiverse' is defined as 'an infinite realm of being or potential, of which the universe is regarded as a part or instance' (New Oxford Dictionary of English, 1998). Each expressed meaning carries equal significance, all being directly related to the reason for the matrix coming together, that is to say: the shared work situation, the theme of a weekend seminar, or title of some formal conference. The task of the convenor(s) is to draw attention to the links being made in this way, to any direction in which the matrix seems to be heading, or to whatever themes may be revealed. In one matrix of which I was a member, for instance, it was noted that many of the dreams, recently told, seemed to be about travelling or going away. Some minutes later, the convenor remarked that from what had been shared since he last spoke, it looked as if we were now coming home. Both interventions were relevant and each person hearing them may have made something different of what was said.

Crucially, the dreams, their nature and implications, are always of greater importance to the matrix than the dreamer as are any associations made, as well.

The start of the matter

Many of these matters were forcibly brought home to me when, soon after my first experience of the method as participant, in 1994, I co-convened, with Herb Hahn, a residential weekend that we just called: 'The Social Dreaming Matrix'. Inexperienced as we were, we had, with our title and without realising it at the time, taken for subject matter the 'void and formless infinite' itself. This course of action gave us an exciting weekend, but also led, inevitably, to chaos and confusion, along with much affect amongst us all. Five years later, I am still making sense of some of what went on then.

Early in our first meeting, one participant described a dream of cutting open his wife's chest with a scalpel and then very carefully dissecting his way down through the various tissue layers and ribcage until he reached her beating heart in its pericardial sac. After observing her heart in its natural activity for a time, with awe, he retreated, meticulously sewing each layer back together, until finally closing the skin.

This was quite a dream with which to begin our weekend; but I have now come to understand it, for me at any rate, as an 'initial dream' with regard to social dreaming, which I now see as having contained and implied much that I have since learnt about social dreaming (not that the process of exploration and understanding can, or will, ever come to an end). The term 'initial dream' has been used of the first dream brought to any individual therapy. Much later in the analytic process it may be seen to have encapsulated much of what has now been made plain during the unfolding of the therapeutic relationship.

Social dreaming, so declares this dream, goes right to the living heart of the matter, which is the matrix itself, and does so with the precision of a professionally wielded scalpel. Yet the blade is also plied with care, love and compassion. Layer after layer (or is it dream after dream, or meaning after meaning?) is passed through to reveal another beneath, and yet each is always separate from the next, its integrity remade upon withdrawal. There will be no mix-up of strata, while the purpose of the dissection is merely to observe and to be emotionally moved by what has been uncovered, while the memory of the heart image will remain and inform, long after the surgical operation is complete.

The object of attention, with its living heart, is female, as is any matrix, symbolically speaking. Yet when imaged as 'wife', it is a personal and individual feminine object, relating only to the dreamer. But, since the dream had now become a shared experience and image, there would be as many 'wives' in the commonality or its underlying matrix, as there were members. In Jungian parlance, we would say that for each of us she represented the 'soul complex' (Jung 1935 in C.W.7, par. 296).

Some of the other dreams of that weekend focused upon gender, infants and birth. Much irritation was expressed that, by convening the event at all, two men should dare to think that they could together have a womb and make a baby, as well as giving birth to it.

Later in the weekend, a woman shared a dream of holding upon her lap a child, 'who might or might not have genitals'. At the time, we recognised this image as moving the understanding into another realm, where 'man', 'woman', 'womb' and 'baby' were to be seen as symbolic and beyond gender. It might be said that 'man' enables and dissects, while 'woman' has 'heart' pumping nutrition around as well as eliminating waste, which might symbolise both the 'feeding' power and the interpretive power of the matrix. Both sexes also possess an ability to give birth to what is new, which is 'child' itself; while 'gender' is an image of a difference that implies idiosyncratic skills (see Tatham 1992, pp.234–237). And all of these actions can belong, psychically rather than physiologically, to beings of either sex.

What of the transference?

Each of the issues described above might be viewed through the lens of 'transference', for whenever people gather together to perform a shared task, group dynamics and issues of transference – to the setting, the subject or event and its convenors – will be present. When arising as an integral aspect of group psychotherapy, such projections are grist for the mill of the group's progress, whereas in social dreaming they get in the way, by shifting the focus from the dreams and their dreaming to the dreamers, or convenors. In view of this, it is important that transference be minimised, even if it cannot be totally eliminated. One way in which this may be done is by the deliberate placing of chairs, as described previously, so that no circle is formed. Another action is to regard everything that happens, is spoken of or implied, once the matrix has been 'opened' and even those items that seem to be avoided, as *belonging and referring* to the matrix itself.

For instance, the envious irritation of the women with Herb and I for seeming to usurp the role of mothers should have been further commented upon in this light, as referring not to us personally but to the matrix itself, which had taken over individual creativity. That we did not do so sufficiently was due to our relative ignorance of the method and of how it might be consciously used.

An instance when such an intervention did take place was during the daily matrices I convened with my colleague Helen Morgan at the Thirteenth Congress of the International Associations of Analytical Psychologists, in Zurich in 1995 (see Morgan and Tatham 1998). We had been allotted a ballroom-sized space in which to work, with floor-to-ceiling windows looking out onto Lake Zurich. Not knowing how many of the event's 800 participants to expect, we had put out about 40 metal chairs in the centre, with others stacked against the wall. We also left the heavy door ajar so that any latecomers would not feel inhibited from joining us. As it turned out, about 80 people arrived, some of them very late indeed, so that there was a continuous disturbance made by the banging door and even more noise as chairs were taken from the stack. Clearly this was unsettling for all, including the convenors, both of whom felt responsible. Eventually, one member irritably suggested that in future we should put out more chairs before beginning and lock the door after a reasonable time, since the interruptions made it hard to concentrate. Both of them were reasonable objections, with which it would have been easy to agree and make apologies. But in reflecting on the title of the congress: 'Open Questions in Jungian Psychology', my intervention then became one of wondering if the feelings of irritation and intrusiveness had another dimension. The difficulty with the door might be similar to that of keeping questions open, rather than going for premature closure. And any discomfort at having to accommodate newcomers arriving, when we were fully engaged, could relate to being faced with the intrusion of disturbing questions that we might prefer to avoid, by not allowing them into our minds at all.

A short while later, I announced that the matrix was now closed, whereupon Helen remarked that I had done so 15 minutes too early! Amid much laughter, we all recognised that even a convenor could have difficulty in keeping things open, thereby confirming my previous remarks.

What of dreaming?

Dreaming happens spontaneously, each night and for every person. Jung has suggested that dreams work within us, whether we remember and interpret them or not. The important thing is, so he said, to have them, which in any case cannot be prevented, since dreams are a part of our biological and evolutionary make-up.

However many, theoretical, theories of dreaming there may be, it is generally agreed that the dream connects the conscious 'I' of the dreamer with its unconscious counterpart, of whom the individual is more or less unaware. Jung named this aspect 'the shadow', which consists, in part, of once-conscious material repressed because of its unacceptability to the conscious 'I'. Yet shadow also represents further creative aspects of an individual, of which she or he is unaware. They are, as yet, unacknowledged and unborn, expectantly waiting to be made conscious by the containing mind.

Social dreaming is a container of a different kind, for it does not specify a particular meaning for the dream (neither personal nor collective, not individual or universal), but allows instead for a multiplicity of meanings, each as significant as the other. Dreams used in this way, says Lawrence, assist us in our thinking. And, as previously mentioned, their importance to the matrix lies not with the dreamer, but in their idiosyncratic effect upon members of the matrix, each with their individual creativeness and pathologies.

Although the twentieth-century western world has regarded dreams as individual and personal belongings, it has not always been so. There is a long history of dreams, with their meanings, being of relevance to the social group, however defined, of which the dreamer is a member. There are well-known biblical dreams; Mesopotamian dreams stored upon clay tablets have been found, as well as examples of Egyptian hieroglyphic ones.

Anthropological evidence and historical accounts also exist that suggest the same. Lawrence has commented upon the use of dreams by the aboriginal inhabitants of Taiwan, for telling fortunes and deciding propitious dates for important events (Lawrence 1998, p.13).

Black Elk (1863–1950), a Native American of the Oglala Sioux, had a vision/dream, when he was nine years old, which he knew was to be made into a ritual for his people, as was done later. His visions still have great value and significance to Native Americans and his story has been described as one of the great religious texts of the twentieth century (Black Elk and Neihardt 2000).

An example from Europe is that of Charlotte Beradt, who secretly collected the dreams of ordinary people in pre-war Germany. After later evaluation, she described the dreams as arising from conflicts into which these people had been driven by a public realm in which half-truths, vague notions, and a combination of fact, rumour and conjecture had produced a general feeling of uncertainty and unrest (Beradt 1968 quoted in Lawrence 1998, p.15).

Twentieth-century examples, similarly to social dreaming, do not ask for unified action or response, though they may at times lead to shared attitudes to the setting or its theme.

In April 2000, I led a social dreaming matrix on each of four mornings of a conference concerned with the nature of organisational systems and their connection to theories of complexity, under the title, 'In Charge, but not in Control'. Overall themes of the first day's matrix were concerned with control, in its negative sense of any action that prevents a system from evolving. On the second day, 'chaos' was the flavour of the matrix; while humour surfaced on Day Three, as a means of dealing with, or denying, the understandable fears of any such chaos, with its overtones of destructiveness.

In this context, it is worth remembering that the word 'chaos' has two meanings. The first denotes a complete lack of structure, as was present before any object existed, *Kaos* being the name of the original Greek goddess and parthenogenetic mother of *Ouranos* and *Gaia*, from whom the whole Olympian Pantheon descends. Similarly, the first book of the Bible says: 'The earth was without form and void'. These words are translations from the Hebrew *'tohu va vohu'*, (*tohu-bohu* in English) which is defined by the dictionary as 'that which is formless, chaos, confusion'.

In Scandinavian mythology, *'Ginnungagap'* (the yawning gap) describes the initial chaotic state of fire and ice from which Middle Earth arose.

This state of chaos *is* the matrix, a timeless, ubiquitous and infinite void from within which all is created, to be born. The mythographer Karl Kerenyi has poetically described this space as 'that which remains of an empty egg when the shell is taken away' (Kerenyi 1951, p.18).

The second and more familiar use of the word 'chaos' describes disorder and confusion. Used in this way, it describes a possible conscious attitude to the original 'void and formless infinite', any experience of which can feel so disturbing, as my example from the earlier Zurich matrix shows.

So it was not surprising that, at a conference concerned with complexity, both kinds of chaos should be experienced. We were, after all, 'living at the edge of chaos', an experience that is both disturbing as well as creative.

On the fourth and final morning of this social dreaming, the themes changed to those of 'being in charge'. The last contribution to the matrix came from someone who had not spoken before, though he had attended on each morning, and who had little knowledge of psychology or dreams.

He told us that he had had a thought, in the shower that morning, and had decided to share it with us. His 'thought' was that he was not in control of the hot water that his shower produced, but that he was in charge of mixing it with cold water for his own comfort. He went on to say that neither was he in control of having had this thought, but that he was in charge of deciding whether he shared it with others, as he had now done. So for him, 'to be controlled' was by what I might call an impersonal, unconscious power (the hot water in the pipes or the spontaneous act of thinking), while 'being in charge' allowed him to make a conscious choice (turning the cold tap, as well as speaking out).

In a dream matrix, no one can control the sequence of dreams that are told and associations made. But each is in charge of what they make of the flow of images, which will be unique and individual though shared.

Dreams and the archetypal world

As someone trained in the psychology of C.G. Jung, I believe that dreams are individual, creative, psychic expressions, arising not only from the personal unconscious of the dreamer, but also from that transpersonal realm, called by Jung, 'the collective unconscious' (Samuels, Shorter and Plaut 1986, pp.32–33). By this, he meant that each image within any dream possesses deep, archetypal aspects, knowledge of which can only enhance the dreamer's understanding of, or affectedness by, his or her dream. And social dreaming, whatever else it does, seems to me to reach that realm of collective unconsciousness so as to make its archetypal energy available for conscious elaboration by individual participants in whatever ways they may choose. For instance, we all reacted to the story of the hot water in the shower in different ways.

Jung regarded that which he called the *archetype-per-se* as 'an empty, theoretical form existing universally in the soul of humankind, to be filled out by individual experience'. Such a personification he referred to as the 'archetypal image', which is individual and unique. A person can, from their dream images, track back to the archetypal form, which that image represents for them personally. The image is *not* the archetype.

For example, 'Mother', as archetype-per-se, might be said to represent a universal force for containment, as well as one that encourages and allows inner psychological growth to take place, in addition to a 'bringing forth', in the shape of images. Such a force has probably existed from well before the appearance on this earth of Homo Sapiens. In a shorthand kind of way, it may be called 'The Great Mother', which we find in early images, both painted and three-dimensional, of some Great Goddess figure.

Mother as archetypal image, however, will be personified for me, for example, not only by goddess figures, but also by the woman who bore me, the mother of my dreams, the one I have just read of in a novel, the mother or maternal situation presented to me by a patient, as well as many more. And all of these would be a different set for each individual. The mother in negative guise might also be imaged as witch, gorgon, harpy, or abuser.

Social dreaming presents another such image: mother as matrix, or 'the form into which all experience is poured' (Jung 1938 in C.W. 9 pt.1, par. 187) and 'from which something might be born' as Lawrence has put it.

The totality of all such archetypal forces, animate and gendered, abstract or inanimate, Jung named 'The Self' which is, once again, an empty theoretical concept. He defined this as 'the whole range of psychic phenomena in Man' (Jung 1960 in C.W. 6, par. 789), which is very close to his definition of the psyche, as 'the totality of all psychic processes, conscious as well as unconscious (Jung 1960 in C.W. 6, par. 797). Such similarity exists since all humans are potentially able to realise the Self in consciousness, though despite the work of a lifetime's individuation, this goal is unlikely ever to be reached. Jung's concept of Self is distinct from that of an individual 'self' as the word is frequently used in psychoanalysis today.

The Self also expresses itself, imaginally, not only as the centre of that totality, but as its periphery also (see Samuels, Shorter and Plaut 1986, p.135). Archetypal imagery of the Self therefore is that of wholeness, singularity, or completion, such as the sun, the transcendent god, and other such images that are accompanied by experiences of transcendence, feelings of numinosity or of unlimited power. Synchronicity, defined by Jung as 'an acausal connecting principle' may happen in connection with Self experiences (Jung 1952 in C.W. 8, par. 816–871). That is to say, two events occur together, as if by chance, yet they can be seen as linked not by causality but by shared meaning: as when I think of someone, or something, for instance, and they turn up, or it happens. A dreamed-of symbol may also unexpectedly appear in real life, which establishes a co-incidental link between the psyche and the physical world.

Negative Self experiences can also occur, which may include the certainty of imminent dissolution and destruction, feelings of terror, or of absolute chaos – in its cataclysmic sense.

Archetypal dream motifs of all kinds are frequently presented in social dreaming. It would be surprising if they were not, since experience confirms that the process is a highly affective one.

At a conference in Denmark, in the spring of 2000, entitled 'Jungian Psychology and the Millennium', I led a social dreaming matrix each morning before the day's programme began. On the first day, almost all of the dreams that were shared concerned trees, which reflected the subject of the previous evening's opening talk, when a Brazilian analyst had described the disfigurement, by an indiscriminate hacking off (not careful pruning) of the tops of many street trees, in São Paolo, because they got in the way of the power, or telephone lines. The speaker saw this as a concrete sign of the unconscious social neglect present in that city in favour of the 'technological fix'. São Paolo is now the third largest city in the world, with massive slums and huge social problems reflected in an astronomical murder rate.

But trees are also potent archetypal symbols of growth: an image that is rooted below ground, as if in the unconscious from which it draws up energy: one that flowers and fruits in its middle range, while providing home and sustenance for living creatures, and which then reaches up into the heavens to draw down and make use of the sun's rays and necessary rain. Trees also connect a human world with the divine heavens.

The many mythological 'World Trees', including the Scandinavian Yggdrasil, were also mentioned as powerful images of the Self. The deaths of many mythical figures on trees, Christ crucified, Tammuz both born from and hanged upon a tree, or Odin who survived his upside-down hanging in Hell only to reappear infused with knowledge, were not spoken of. Nor did we discuss the lopping of the trees as a symbol of castration. In retrospect, I realise that I should have drawn attention to these omissions, for feelings of impotency mixed with hopes of survival by means of increased awareness represent the universal fears of destruction, as well as yearnings for a benevolent future, experienced by many at the Millennium-tide.

Social dreaming and synchronicity

Synchronistic happenings or coincidental events, mental and physical, linked not by causality but by shared personal meaning also frequently occur around social dreaming. In Zurich, during one of our meetings, someone thought that he saw, through a window, Jung himself walking past the building. He then realised that it was another senior analyst, though one who had, in fact, been trained by Jung himself. This event was not surprising, for one of the themes that arose at the congress (significantly from within the dream matrix) was about how we could be 'true' to Jung, in keeping his work alive, while at the same time 'killing him off' so as to keep the nature of analytical psychology alive, 'open', and able to evolve (see Morgan and Tatham 1998). On this occasion, participants remarked that for most of our time in Zurich we concerned ourselves upstairs in the lecture hall, with intellectual and political matters, while down here 'in the basement', as they liked to call the ballroom in which we worked, our concerns were with addressing the 'unconscious mind' of the congress.

A further example of synchronicity comes from the first Jungian conference in Denmark, in 1998, entitled, 'Jungian Psychology on the Modern World'. A shared dream concerned an upstairs bookshop in Copenhagen, filled with old books. Among a string of associations made by participants was one about the Russian Czar, Peter the Great, being 'a bit of a cowboy', and on one occasion riding his horse into an upstairs room. Another person then revealed that on her flight to the conference city, she had found on her airline seat a complimentary copy of the comic book, 'Fantomen' (the Phantom), which is very popular in Scandinavia. In this story, Fantomen was dressed as a cowboy and became involved in an adventure with Peter the Great.

A different and highly significant theme was addressed in the second part of the same dream in which the dreamer was standing next to me in a public toilet, both of us urinating. I suggested that this represented a 'Peter the Wee', the word 'wee' meaning 'urine' as well as 'small'. The act of urination can be an image of personal creativeness, here performed individually, but together, in the dream matrix.

My original relationship with this Danish group had been as a seminar leader and supervisor, while it was working towards membership of the International Association of Analytical Psychology. The dream suggests that in the 'modern world' of Jungian psychology in Denmark, neither I, nor any of the other ex-seminar leaders now present, were 'Czars' any longer, with access to esoteric knowledge, upstairs in the head. Instead, we were now all equals, our wee penises being no bigger than anyone else's, while their organisation was no longer one of 'cowboys' riding up into the big boys' bookshop. Or at least that is one meaning, as far as that commonality was concerned.

'Self' and the implicate order

As already noted, the Self can be experienced in images that are central, unitary, and whole – like the godhead, or the sun. Paradoxically, it may also appear in multiples, such as a swarm of bees, an infestation by cockroaches, or the starry skies. What is usually thought of as a single unit is, at the same time, a multitude. Such facts as these, as well as Jung's belief that the physical and psychological worlds would ultimately be recognised as two different descriptions of some, at present unimaginable, unitary state, led the late Louis Zinkin a group analyst as well as analytical psychologist, to reflect upon the work of the physicist David Bohm and its relevance to Jungian psychology (Bohm 1980; Zinkin, Gordon and Haynes 1998).

Bohm likened the universe to a hologram, the photographic image of which can, by the use of polarised light, still be seen three-dimensionally in each and every fragment into which the photographic plate might be broken. The underlying unitary state, which he called 'the Implicate Order', can be seen to 'unfold' itself into external reality, there to be seen as various 'explicate orders', that can, equally, become implicate again, by re-enfolding. He went further to state that what was most fundamental to both states was the unfolding/enfolding process, that he named the 'holomovement'.

The wholeness of the implicate order is, Bohm insisted, still contained within each and every explication, just as the whole image is present in every fragment of the photographic plate. The world *is* contained within each grain of sand: the gods *are* in all things, while the Self is both unitary and implicate, just as it is multiple and explicate in all conscious endeavours, as well as being expressed by the holomovement between those two states.

All of which suggests that the implicate Self must be holographically present in every dream image, explicate through dreaming and shared in social dreaming, while a holomovement is primary, allowing for passage in either direction. Lawrence has implied as much with his description of the matrix as a place out of which something can be born (1998, p.267). Just as this something must contain the matrix itself.

Social dreaming and organisation

Lawrence and colleagues have already explored the relevance of Bohm's ideas to social dreaming (Lawrence, Malz and Walker 1998, pp.169–181). They suggest that what is increasingly becoming explicate in the world today is an 'information society' as opposed to the past industrial one. And they see social dreaming as a valuable tool for exploring and explaining the current nature of organisations in a novel way that is more appropriate to the 'acoustic, imaginal space' implied by such a societal trend.

The vertex of their chapter is organisational consultancy, which is not my main interest, except in so far as we are each members of some organisation or another, from 'the family' upwards. Indeed, the act of organising – the formation of an unitary state out of independent elements – is an essential biological activity, whether it be the grouping together of various intracellular processes; the union of cells with similar function into organs; or the interrelatedness of those organs to make up an organism itself.

Through the evolutionary process, humankind has taken this a step further with the formation of the non-substantial organ that is called 'mind' and which has made human beings pre-eminent within the animal world. In addition, we humans have learnt to group ourselves together, for safety's sake or common purpose, whether such groupings are called a troop, a band, tribes, the nation, or one of innumerable organisations of different kinds and with various intentions of the present time. Lawrence has advocated the servicing of such organisations by means of a consultancy that includes social dreaming for the purpose of allowing each individual access to 'the unthought/known' (Bollas 1987) contained by that grouping together. The similarity of this term to the notion of archetype has already been recognised by Zinkin, though he preferred the phrase 'unimaged/known' (Zinkin et al. 1998, p.101).

The commonality of social dreaming

Even if the occasion for social dreaming does not happen as part of any organisation, or consultancy, but represents instead a temporary coming together of individuals for some other purpose, such as a seminar or conference, there is a common, shared purpose to that setting and its purpose, of which social dreaming is only a part. Until now I have explored the nature of social dreaming as if it were only the concern of each individual participant, putting her or him in touch with their inner psychological structures for the purpose of a deeper relationship to, as well as personal experience of, the overall theme of the gathering. Taking a Jungian viewpoint, individuation may also be inferred by means of this process.

On the other hand, there is no getting away from the fact that the process can only take place in the company of others, whatever we call that temporary state of organisation that is not a 'group'. As already mentioned, I have chosen to call it a 'commonality'. It would therefore be possible to describe the process purely from the point of view of the commonality, without reference to any unconscious, underlying structures of any individual member of the matrix.

This would be a valid approach, but since that is not the purpose of the present chapter, I return to the 'initial dream'.

Back to the heart of the matter

In an anatomical or physiological sense, the heart is nothing but a muscular pump responsible for a circulation of the blood, that enables the carriage of oxygen and nutrition to all tissues in the body, as well as eliminating all waste products through lungs, liver, or kidneys. It is central to living.

For Jung circulation was an important image representing, as he saw it, the endless movement and progression (as well as regression) of the human psyche, whereby consciousness is formed (or lost), or broken down only to be re-formed in a nature that is more inclusive. Likening this to the old alchemical process known as the *circulatio*, he regarded this as a basis of the individuation process. This notion of a circulation between consciousness and the unconscious could also be a metaphor for Bohm's holomovement.

Yet the heart is also a symbolic expression of centrality and depth, as in 'getting to the heart of the matter', as well as a 'heart of darkness'. In both these respects 'heart' provides an image of the Self that is central, essential and whose nature is available as a source of psychic nourishment to each and every part of the body or psyche. It is at the heartland.

The heart is also filled with vigour, that word denoting among other things a liveliness of the mind or faculties. Heart lies behind courage as well, from the Latin word *'coraticum'*, whose meaning implies 'that which pertains to the heart'. It is the driving force behind all people of good heart, as well as those with hearts of stone, or the evil-hearted; and much more besides.

Another set of profound images comes from James Hillman who, while relying upon the work of Henry Corbin, comments upon a fact of primary importance, which is

> ...that the thought of the heart is the thought of images, that the heart is the seat of the imagination, that imagination is the authentic voice of the heart, so that if we speak from the heart we must speak imaginatively. (Hillman 1984, p.2, with reference to Corbin 1969)

He goes further to say that the intelligence of this heart is an intelligence of images, which implies a simultaneous knowing and loving by means of images. The love of another person implies imagination, while such an exercise of the imagination so as to bring about its desires was, he says, always at the heart of psychoanalysis, from that initial moment when the first patient, treated by the new method, fell in love with Joseph Breuer, to that good doctor's terror (Hillman 1984, p.4). All of psychoanalysis rests, therefore, upon the human imagination of both patient and practitioner. Another name for it would be transference.

Jung, for his part, discovered and promoted what he called 'active imagination': a process by which individuals explore and take further through fantasy, which may be expressed by means of painting, writing etc., the symbolic images that fuel their lives.

Imagination is therefore all around us, as well as within, for anything made or discovered by humans and that now exists in actuality was once a fantasy.

Back to beginnings

The initial dream of these explorations into social dreaming described a man and wife, images of the 'I' and its soul – an organisation of two entities related by love (and therefore imagination). It also pictured the tender and painstaking dissection of the layers of protective coverings that prevent the individual from seeing, in depth, those central and Self-induced activities. This heart denotes imagination itself, or that human activity upon which all of its organising as well as its institutions and civilisations, its scientific or artistic endeavours, as well as all else including technologies, can ultimately be seen to rest, as suggested above. 'Heart' is the centre of each universe that makes up the multiverse.

The 'implicate order' was once an imaginal fantasy (now explicate) within the heart and mind of David Bohm, as was Jung's Self. (In Chinese script, a single character is used to denote both heart *and* mind; see Cooper 1975).

Social dreaming too was once a fantasy in the hearts and minds of its begetters: a fantasy, now made fact, that attempts to unlock the secrets at the heart of matters which are also, synchronistically, within the mind. This process awakens an imaginal view demanding imagination, whatever factual events – inner, outer, or interpersonal – it arises from. And, having taken a person to the heart of these matters – which once seen are never forgotten – it allows them back again to rest within and among their surface commonalities, yet with their relationship to centrality forever changed.

References

Beradt, C. (1968) *The Third Reich of Dreams*. Chicago: Quadrangle Books.

Black Elk, N. and Neihardt, J.G. (2000) *Black Elk Speaks*. Lincoln and London: University of Nebraska Press.

Bohm, D. (1980) *Wholeness and the Implicate Order*. London: Routledge.

Bollas, C. (1987) *The Shadow of the Object*. London: Free Association Books.

Cooper, A. (1975) 'Chinese evidence on the evolution of language.' In R. Gregory (ed) (1985) *The Oxford Companion to the Mind*. Oxford: Oxford University Press.

Corbin, H. (1969) *Creative Imagination in the Sufism of Ibn Arabi*. Princeton: Princeton University Press, Bollinger Series.

Foulkes, S.H. (1971) 'Access to unconscious processes in the group-analytic group.' In *Group Analysis 4*, 4–14.

Hillman, J. (1984) *The Thought of the Heart*. Dallas: Spring Publications.

Jung C.G. *Collected Works*. Edited by G. Adler, M. Fordham and H. Read. London: Routledge.

Jung, C.G. (1919) *Psychology of the Unconscious*. Transl: B. Hinkle. London: Kegan Paul. Trench: Trubner.

Kerenyi, K. (1951) *The Gods of the Greeks*. London: Thames and Hudson.

Lawrence, W.G. (1998) *Social Dreaming @ Work*. London: Karnac.

Lawrence, W.G., Malz, M. and Walker, E.M. (1998) 'Social dreaming @ work.' In W.G. Lawrence (ed) (1998) *Social Dreaming @ Work*. London: Karnac.

Morgan, H. and Tatham, P.H. (1998) Chapter 5. In W.G. Lawrence (ed) (1998) *Social Dreaming @ Work*. London: Karnac.

New Oxford Dictionary of English (1998) Oxford: Oxford University Press.

Penrose, R. (1989) *The Emperor's New Mind*. Oxford: Oxford University Press.

Samuels, A., Shorter, B. and Plaut, A. (1986) *A Critical Dictionary of Jungian Analysis*. London: Routledge and Kegan Paul.

Tatham, P.H. (1992) *The Makings of Maleness*. London: Karnac.

Zinkin, H., Gordon, R. and Haynes, J. (eds) (1998) *Dialogue in the Analytic Setting*. London: Jessica Kingsley Publishers.

CHAPTER 4

Helping the Helpers

Herb Hahn

Odi et amo, quare id faciam, fortasse requiris?
Nescio, sed fieri sentio et excrucior. (Catullus)

(I hate and I love; why do I do this, perhaps you ask? I do not know, but I
feel it happening and I am in torment.)

Introduction

This chapter is about developing ways of working with and supporting groups
of professionally trained helpers. It gives an account of how I came to start this
work, explores the aspects of the dynamics of the helper role, and provides
illustrations. The approach has developed from therapeutic work with members
of the helping professions and from my own experience as a member of that
profession. Over the years I have found that my commitment to working as a
psychotherapist is refreshed and enhanced by applying what I am learning to
related contexts. When I extended this interest to offering 'facilitation' to
groups of people working in the helping professions, the initial results were
encouraging. New requests trickled in, and working with such groups has
become a regular part of my practice. It provides a degree of variety, which is
both welcome and thought provoking. The process of learning from experience also continues, so the reader who is seeking a ready-made formula will be
disappointed. However, in writing the final version of this chapter I have
attended to the comments and suggestions as to what might be useful, made by
colleagues who kindly read earlier drafts.

Groups of helpers whom I have engaged with include general practitioners,
health visitors, occupational therapists, social workers, voluntary workers,
shiatsu practitioners, psychiatrists, organisational consultants, psychotherapists
and counsellors. They have sometimes belonged to specialist teams serving particular sub-groups such as the blind, inmates of a secure unit, AIDS sufferers,

victims of sexual abuse, drug abusers, and couples wanting to adopt children. The work has also been extended to working with the core staff of a counselling and a psychotherapy training course, professionals in training, groups of organisational consultants, a group of regional managers, and a theatre company. The time scale has ranged from two half-day sessions, to regular (fortnightly, monthly, annual or even bi-annual) meetings over several years. Participants variously name the task, depending on context, as 'sensitivity', 'support', 'role consultation', 'facilitation', 'development seminars', 'team building', 'conflict resolution' or an 'experiential group'. The experience of growing up in a Jewish immigrant family in racially charged South Africa gave me a gritty grounding in the dynamics of intergroup relationships. Later, after qualifying as an individual psychotherapist in England, the following experience was a catalyst in my decision to learn more about groups.

At a child guidance clinic, the educational psychologist, social worker and I (the child psychotherapist) departed from our normal practice of working with clients individually and arranged to meet jointly with a family in crisis. At the initial meeting with the family (comprising the parents and their teenage daughter), the psychologist was late and we started without her. The father began by berating his daughter for failing at school. She started crying. He ordered her to stop. She cried more loudly. Her mother also began cry. The father then turned angrily on the social worker and me for upsetting the family. The social worker hastily left the room 'to get some tissues' and did not return for several minutes. During this time mother and daughter joined forces and began to attack the father, while they also sided with him in blaming the clinic for what was happening. By the time the social worker returned, and the psychologist had arrived, I felt angry and confused about how to work co-operatively with my colleagues. When the family were eventually ushered out with an offer of a further appointment, we professionals stayed behind with the intention of discussing the case. In fact we launched into an unseemly outburst of mutual blame. It was only when we sought the attentive help of a colleague that we were able to think about what had happened. We could then see how the client family's difficulties had spilled over and affected us. Armed with this insight we were able to offer something new and useful to the family at our subsequent meetings.

I also realised that my individual training, thorough as it had been in relation to treating individuals, had also done more to foster a climate of interprofessional rivalry, than to prepare me to work co-operatively with colleagues of related disciplines. Additionally my own early history, and subsequent adult life away from the country of my birth, has fostered the mixed blessings of marginality which have been both modified and accentuated by engagement with, and subsequent leadership roles in, Tavistock group relations conferences, Foulkesian group analysis, and social dreaming matrices (Lawrence 1991). These experiences have influenced my way of thinking about and working with groups of helpers. Reciprocally the groupwork with helpers has influenced my clinical practice, particularly with regard to supervisory work (Hahn 1998).

Dynamics

There is almost daily evidence in the press of the way in which helpers are sandwiched between societal expectations that the 'ill' be made 'well', and the limitations on how much help is available, even if possible. Helpers frequently experience their own and other people's disappointment and their own guilt about the fact that they cannot always be helpful. It is also a common experience among helpers I have spoken to, to receive more formal expressions of complaint and anger than of gratitude and appreciation for services rendered. Some of the negative responses relate to perceived and actual poor service and instances of professional malpractice, but others seem to be about unrealistic patient and client expectations based on wishful phantasies, which can nevertheless lead to litigation. Helpers may then feel driven to diverting some of their energy away from the therapeutic task to having to watch their backs for their own survival.

While such internal and external oppression of helpers is not ubiquitous, what all helpers share is the effect of the continuous process of being receptive to the pain and dis-ease of others. The effects of this are cumulative and become toxic in the absence of appropriate opportunities for the dis-ease to be metabolised or dispersed. By listening empathetically to a multitude of accounts of pain, stress and emotional trouble, the helper vicariously experiences a never-ending sequence of mini-traumas which lead to 'compassion fatigue'. The accumulation of toxicity in the helper can be healthily dealt with in a variety of ways. These include engagement in 'normal' relationships, enjoyment of outside activities, finding peer support, and drawing on the specialist services of others including therapists and supervisors. Participating in a variety of workshops and training and development opportunities, such as those elaborated in this book, are also useful, important and health promoting. Unfortunately many practitioners fall through the net, either because such opportunities are not available or because they are not considered necessary.

In the light of the above, it is not surprising to learn that doctors have higher suicide rates than their patients (OCPS 1986). More generally, researchers have found above average levels of stress and burnout (chronic stress) among doctors, dentists, vets, nurses, social workers and speech therapists (Felton 1998). The list could be longer. Chris Johnstone (1999) writes of the way in which his commitment to becoming a medical practitioner was eroded by the relentlessly long shifts which were required of him. He reached the point where, tired and drained, he felt that his life was turning sour. In a similar vein, Ron Wiener refers in his chapter in this book to being 'exhausted' after five years of work in a therapeutic community. Freud himself (albeit over a period of three decades) shifted from early enthusiasm about the 'transformations' which psychoanalysis could achieve, to doubts about the efficacy of his talking cure (Freud 1905, p.260, 1937, p.228).

This souring of hope may relate to the wear and tear of unremitting direct exposure to the pain of others. A metaphor often used among colleagues when I worked as a child psychotherapist was that in addition to our child patients coming to us for symbolic nourishment (understanding), they also often used us as (psychological) toilets for their 'shitty' feelings. Adult patients can be similarly experienced as conveying, communicating and/or ridding themselves of unwanted or unbearable mental pain by a powerful process of psychic evacuation. This is often not transmitted directly in words, or even via obvious body language, but in subtle and complex ways, which are known through their effects. Thus the clinical encounter may end with the patient feeling better and the helper feeling worse, without either being clear about how this has transpired. The mental pain has been transmitted and received by an invisible process, which is often referred to in psychoanalytic circles as entailing projective identification. Yet the detail of what happens remains wondrous and mysterious. Whatever the specifics of the mechanism, in practice the helper is left with detritus, which needs to be disposed of. If it is not somehow composted or recycled, it fulminates and contributes to feelings of 'stress' and 'burnout'. Where it is disposed of in an unprocessed, raw form, it promotes disturbed or destructive relationships in those contexts. Healthy processing can be promoted in dialogue with an internal or external therapist, supervisor, mentor or peer in dyads or groups. In the latter instance, the involvement of an external facilitator can be useful. As the toxicity may be passed on to those who help the helpers, they also need access to appropriate facilitative resources.

If there are so many negative aspects to the role of being a helper, why do so many people take it on? The benefits include opportunities to satisfy interest in and curiosity about the nature of dis-ease and conflict; the socio-cultural value derived from belonging to and identifying with the helping professions, and the personal satisfaction of being experienced as someone who promotes health and eases pain. Furthermore the work, based as it is on intimacy and trust, provides opportunities to pass on to others the helper's own experience of having been helped; and may sometimes manifest inspiring occasions of transformation, even moments of enlightenment. There is also an aspect of working as a helper which attunes to the deep emotional satisfaction of participating in the archetypal mother–baby nurturing couple. The health providers can also vicariously enjoy the bountifulness of what their patients are receiving. For many, the foundations for taking on the helping role are already laid down in childhood. In my own work with helpers and healers, it often emerges that as children they took on the role of parenting their own parents. Sophie Clark learned from her facilitative work with general practitioners that many were trained in childhood to regard their own needs as secondary to those of other members of the family (Clark 2000).

Considering this dynamic across two generations, it seems that once an emotionally neglected child becomes an adult helper, the helper's own children may in their turn suffer as precedence is given to the needs of patients. I am thinking here of the eagerness with which some mother/doctors I have worked with leave their infants and return to work. For example some helper/parents I have worked with were more concerned about getting back to their clients and patients than with the needs of their new-born infants. It is conceivable that such patterns of functioning are passed on transgenerationally to the point where a stereotypical picture has a grain of truth. The Jungian psychologist Guggenbuhl-Craig in exploring this theme, proposes an archetype of the helper. He draws on the Greek myth of the wounded god Chiron, who could even bring the ill who died back to life, but also suffered from an unbearably painful incurable wound himself (Guggenbuhl-Craig 1971). In our current society, helpers, especially doctors, may be blamed for failing to keep someone from death's door, as if at an unconscious level the doctor is expected to have Chiron's powers. This phantasy is also succinctly implicit in the last four lines of Menna Elfyn's poem:

Standing By (in a doctor's surgery)

> You wait – for a door to open,
> And we stand by – though we're sitting.
> That's how it goes with mortality,
> every moment, an eternity.

Wilfred Bion maps the way in which our society as a whole disposes of its responsibility for those who are 'ill' by delegating the task to a designated sub-group of 'health' specialists (Bion 1961). This societal avoidance of direct responsibility may leave a residue of (unconscious, collective) guilt, which can find popular expression in an eagerness to criticise the limitations and faults of those who take on the role of helpers. Perhaps such critical societal attitudes towards members of the helping profession is also a displacement of angry feelings about the way in which those who are ill impose their needs on the rest. The overall effect is that professional helpers find themselves tightly squeezed between societal and patient demands and expectations.

Illustrations

The following accounts illustrate work with four different groups. The first is with a multi-disciplinary team who staffed the Halburton clinic in the grounds of a large hospital complex. The second, by contrast, relates to a single week-end and involves the partners of a GP practice. It is followed by an account of work with a group of health visitors and a subsequent follow-up. Finally there is an excerpt from an international workshop for health workers.

1. The Halburton staff team

This multi-disciplinary group worked with me for a considerable period of time. The initial contact was on the basis of a word of mouth recommendation. It soon appeared that the members of the group were properly trained, experienced and committed to their, regularly supervised, clinical work. However they also conveyed a feeling of being besieged by the hospital management system and, for the most part, alienated from other hospital staff groups. For example, in the staff canteen, the group tended to sit together and did not mix with 'the rest'. At our meetings, I became aware of the group's style of humour which was reminiscent of that I had experienced among oppressed minority groups in that they shared jokes which were acceptable among themselves but would have been considered offensive if expressed about them by outsiders. For example, 'This would be a great job if there were no patients!' was good for a laugh and taken with a pinch of salt among themselves, but would have been taken as an attack if repeated about them by 'outsiders'.

Recurrent themes at our sessions were the pressures the group members felt under from the management who were spoken of as not providing adequate support, recognition or reward. External referrers were also sometimes described as being demanding and lacking in insight as to the nature of the work. It was as if the group's external organisational environment was experienced as uncaring at best, hostile at worst, and not amenable to change or even influence. In contrast there was a spirit of camaraderie among the team members and a general feeling of goodwill and concern towards the patients who were currently in treatment.

Their clinical manager did not attend the facilitated meetings apparently because she felt that her seniority made her participation inappropriate. She was however not infrequently referred to as the protector of the team and strategic role model. It was said that she provided good clinical supervision and support. She fended off the more unreasonable demands of the hospital management by careful procrastination and by drawing out issues so that the next re-organisation or change of management superseded them.

Gradually as trust grew at our group meetings, the defensive cohesiveness of the group lessened, as did the relative anonymity of its individual members. Some tensions surfaced. In particular anger was expressed by one or more of the women members (who were in the minority) about incidents and instances when one or more of the men had been experienced as lacking in emotional sensitivity. In the group itself, with some facilitative support, these complaints were listened to, thought about and discussed. A member of the team then shared his frustration about being paid less than was his due in the light of the relevant hard-won further qualifications he had invested a great deal of time and money in and had achieved. His efforts to negotiate an increase had been stalled for months and he was thinking of leaving. Not everyone in the group had known about his struggle and they were all now concerned and supportive. Encouraged by this, and by some relevant advice, he renewed his efforts and was successful this time.

On another occasion, a group member shared her feeling that in addition to clinical overload, she also felt dumped on by the group in other ways. For example, though she knew she was being petty, she had come to resent the fact that it was taken for granted that she was responsible for replenishing the supplies of coffee and tea. Furthermore the empty milk bottles were simply left to pile up unless she dealt with them.

In this atmosphere of more open communication among team members, there were also signs of some readiness to engage more co-operatively with the demands, requests and expectations of the management. This included a readiness to offer to help staff a satellite clinic and even consider the whole relocation of the team which the management had been mooting for a considerable period of time.

At a subsequent meeting, two members who had become 'secretly' entangled in some personal difficulty with each other brought the problem out into the open. We learned that some, but not all of the team members, had already been in the know, and it was a relief to all to be able now to address it together. There were also indications of the group taking professional initiatives in relation to other hospital staff by offering seminars, supervision and training opportunities.

At about this time, an experienced practitioner who was on 'placement' temporarily joined the group. He welcomed the group meetings as something new, which he had not encountered elsewhere, participated energetically in them, and successfully undertook to encourage the clinical manager to join our meetings. Her attendance and participation softened the hierarchical nature of her previous relationship with the rest and seemed to encourage a generally less dependent and more interdependent team culture. It also provided an opportunity to address a specific item of unfinished business of her own in relation to the team.

In due course, the clinical manager moved to take up another post. The group sessions then became a focus for the emotional process of separation to be addressed including the concerns and anxieties about the team's future survival. Practical ideas were also forthcoming. In the event, the team was left in limbo for some time after their leader left, and worked hard to keep going. During this time the hospital management, with immediate effect, withdrew funding for the group sessions due to 'budget constraints'. The team brought this information to a meeting as a *fait accompli*. I wrote to the hospital manager stating that it was unacceptable and potentially destructive to staff motivation, and therefore clinical service, to end so suddenly. He replied by agreeing to fund a few final sessions. At the same time the team decided that they would like to continue with the group after the funding dried up by personally sharing the cost.

After an uncertain wait, the leader's post was advertised and filled. Soon after the new leader's arrival, he came to a group session and expressed his doubts about the potential usefulness of this group to the work of the team. He explained that he had had a bad experience of a facilitated group in a previous post. However he wanted to attend now to check this group out for himself. In the event he supported the continuation of the group and suggested, to general agreement, that we meet less frequently but for longer sessions. He thus both made his mark and gave the group his blessing. It also soon became clear that he had a sense of purpose and direction in relation to the future work of the team. As the team was unused to such a clear positive leadership style and had been through a period of self-management, his initiatives were met with some ambivalence at first. Gradually most of the team rallied round. Some of this was worked with and worked through during group meetings helped by the fact that the leader gave the group meetings a high level of priority in his increasingly full timetable. The following account is of a group meeting a few months after the new leader had taken up his post:

As the participants walk into the room, they are much engaged in conversation. One person also mentions to me that they are all *very* busy. They sit down and the usual silence ensues as they change gear and allow themselves to be *present*. A brief message of apology is passed on by one of the group from their leader and is accepted without comment. The silence continues a little while longer. The newest member of the team bridges it to say that she is thinking about 'the office'. (This is the single shared room in which staff do their non-clinical work. The team leader has a separate personal office.) Gradually others join in on this theme:

It is good to share a space.

But it is a bit cramped when everyone is present.

Is it supposed to be for writing up notes and formal conversation only, or is it all right to talk to each other less formally in it?

The big cupboard takes up so much space.

What's in it?

Christmas decorations!

A burned-out kettle!

Bits of crockery!

Old files!

Whose files are they?

Is anyone using them?

The new team member: 'I thought they belonged to some of you!'

'No, they are from long ago!'

It becomes clear that no one has a feeling of ownership for the cupboard or its contents.

Listening to the group, I have a sense that there are underlying themes relating to membership, hierarchy, freedom, power and authority. It also seems that the team itself can be symbolised as a cupboard into which the patients deposit and try and get rid of the bits of themselves they do want or do not find useful. However the group seems actively engaged in their task and I decide not to intervene.

After a pause, one member of the group comes up with an ' idea': 'What if we empty the cupboard completely!'

The proposal evokes general approval and stimulates a surge of energy:

Yes.

The bits that are 'junk' can be 'chucked'.

What about the old case notes?

The secretary can be asked to arrange for them to go into the archives.

The cupboard can then be used for current storage needs.

Then one member says she has just had a 'radical' idea: 'Does a use have to be found for the cupboard? Is it actually useful? What if it is removed? This will give us all more space.'

This idea is well received. Action plans are explored: consulting the hospital storeman and their leader, liasing with their secretary, etc.

There is a general feeling of something having been achieved and the group relaxes into a silence…

A new member of the team then tentatively comments that she has noticed that 'some people' have made the effort to personalise their part of the office space. Sensitively tuning in to her tone of voice rather than the content of what she says, one of the others encourages her to say more. She then 'confesses' that she feels envious of the way in which Jem (a long-established team member) has personalised his space by hanging a picture of his choice on the wall behind his desk. She also hesitantly adds that she does not 'particularly' like the picture.

To everyone's surprise, Jem then comes in with: 'I don't like the picture either. It was there when I joined the team and I felt that I had no right to move it.'

This releases a buzz of conversation with various ideas being mooted about ways of further making the room their own. The space is now being spoken of as 'our room' and not 'the office' as it had been when the session began.

I say that it is time to stop. They leave quietly and with what appears to be an enhanced sense of experiencing each other as people rather than just as busy professionals.

As facilitator, I had said little during this session, and nothing significant that I could recall when writing this transcript. Yet I was also aware that my presence was important to the group task. It gave them 'permission' and encouragement to engage and reflect with each other. In this session the group also drew on the capacity for co-operation they had gradually established with each other over a long period of time. As the work they were paid to do was essentially the same as it had always been, the observable changes could be attributed to a change in the group culture.

I reflect to myself how different the culture of the group is now to when I originally began to work with them. They have become lively and confident. Now that the new leader is established in post, the cobwebs of resigned help-lessness seem to have been well and truly dusted away. At the same time there are hints about an ongoing underlying conflict about finding the optimal balance between addressing their primary professional tasks, and maintaining and developing their socio-professional connections.

The following is an overview of a subsequent session at which the whole team was present.

The group begins with a member sharing his reaction to a baby defecating in the swimming pool at their holiday resort. This is thoughtfully and associa-tively taken up in a variety of ways not only in terms of far-away places but also various aspects of personal and organisational life back home.

A much-liked colleague is leaving and this is her last group meeting. The group makes it clear that she will be missed. She acknowledges this and recip-rocates their feeling. She also reminds them that her departure will land them with more work to do. This paves the way for feelings about this to surface, and the theme of shitty feelings comes to the fore. They extend to a concern that the person replacing their colleague might contaminate the culture of the team. Her replacement would need time to find his feet. The group is clearly aware that this is an expression of feeling, not of conscious opinions. I refer back to the baby shitting in the pool and suggest it also as a metaphor for their work – clearing up the psychological messes their patients cannot contain. If this is projected onto their new colleague, it may prejudice the way he is received, particularly as he is also felt to be replacing a colleague the team is attached to.

That group ended with warm expressions of goodwill to and from the person who is leaving.

What particularly remains with me after this session is the group's capacity to be aware of and work with its own projections and engage with both its loving and hating feelings. This seems to augur well for the way in which the new team member will be received.

2. No problem

In contrast to the extended time scale of the work with the Halburton clinic, this contact with the partners of a GP practice comprised an initial meeting and a subsequent residential weekend at a conference centre. The initial approach came by telephone via the senior partner of the practice. He spoke about wanting to do some 'team building' over a weekend 'away'. When I asked whether his partners were all in agreement, he replied that he had mentioned the idea to them and that there was 'no problem'. He was however in full agreement when I proposed a preliminary meeting as a way of preparing the ground. In the event this meeting broadly confirmed what I had already been told. After we had introduced ourselves, the doctors spoke positively about their work and about wanting to develop further as a team. It seemed that theirs was a prestigious and successful practice. Their lists were full and there were patients waiting to take up any vacancies which arose. The partnership met regularly, and the senior partner was very efficient at keeping them to 'the business' so the meetings did not need to take long. This suited them, but they supported the idea of giving up one weekend to strengthening their connections, and having met me they thought that it would be useful to have me there 'to facilitate'. The plan was to begin on a Saturday morning and end after lunch on the Sunday.

Everyone arrived on time and we worked through until the afternoon tea break in what seemed like a constructive series of group sessions. Various aspects of the practice were explored both in terms of how things were going and ways in which they might be 'fine tuned'. Possible new initiatives and some of their implications were also explored. On the surface the day was going well and doing just what had been asked for. However, during the afternoon tea break, I took myself off for a stroll in the grounds and thought about the work so far. I felt that something was out of synch. For a successful and enterprising group of service professionals, there was a lack of spontaneity. On further reflection I realised that although everyone was participating actively, the contributions usually followed a lead from the senior partner and tended to keep fairly closely to his themes. I then wondered about how best to support a more interactive group dialogue. Mindful of my impression of the transference and countertransference dynamics so far, I decided against offering a verbal intervention. Instead, when the group re-assembled, I reflected aloud on the importance of allowing time for stocktaking and review in a weekend of this type. I added that one way to foster this would be for us to take a break from our groupwork to allow a little time for each member to have an individual session with me. This idea was unanimously welcomed and it was decided to allow twenty minutes for each person and to extend the tea break there and then to accommodate it.

The sequel was surprising. At some point during each of the individual sessions there was a reference to a problem about Jason, the newest member. The senior partner had felt it would be unfair to use his authority to single 'young' Jason out in front of everyone, especially as he liked him and he was a good clinician. However, there was a problem about 'fit' and he wished one of the others would bring it up. The others also referred to some kind of difficulty around Jason while also tending to convey respect for clinical skills. One partner felt Jason should leave, and others also raised this with mixed feelings. Time did not permit going into more detail but when I saw Jason, who was last, things became clear. When I asked how things were going, he hesitated, then suddenly became tearful, and told me he did not have another job but was thinking of resigning. He liked the practice, and he and his wife had also settled in the area. The problem had to do with various administrative and timetabling tasks he had 'inherited' from the person he had replaced in the practice (and 'stupidly' agreed to at his initial interview). He loved the clinical work but had a specific learning disability and was hopeless at sorting out rotas, on calls etc. He had not spoken up at the selection interview because there was a lot of competition and he had badly wanted the job – his first. At the time, he had felt confident about his clinical skills and hoped the rest would sort itself out. They had not and things were getting worse. He spent hours on the paperwork, was losing sleep, felt it was now too late to 'confess', and that it might be best to leave. I explored the possibility of bringing all this to the group. He replied: 'No way. I couldn't possibly.' I then asked if he could imagine some way in which it might be possible. He replied that he *might* be able to if I could somehow help him. We discussed this a little more and ended with his decision to 'think about it'.

In the event, and to everyone's relief, he did bring the whole issue to the group, drawing on my support. Much dialogue and discussion followed over the rest of the weekend, the outcome of which was a re-allocation of the tasks which Jason found so difficult and an agreement to have longer regular staff meetings, and to rotate the chairmanship, to allow for a more facilitating style. Thus the team had used the weekend to grasp the nettle of facing its difficulties in communication by making use of its facilitator to enable a focal problem to surface which they could then deal with constructively. They also took steps to insure against the recurrence of similar problems by modifying their leadership structure.

Reflecting on the work, I found myself having to justify to myself my reason for having so actively initiated a change to the programme. It was not my normal style, yet it still felt appropriate. It was as if I had found some way of breaking through my internalised professional boundaries in a way which was suited to this particular set of circumstances.

3. The health visitors – a failure of continuity

A health district found that it kept 'losing' health visitors from a clinic serving an estate which had as a matter of policy been filled with disturbed families. Things came to a head when a series of staff resignations dominoed to the point where there was no one left. Word spread by the grapevine and it was difficult to find people to fill the vacant posts. When the posts were eventually filled, concern about a repeat of the previous resignations led to a management decision to provide an external facilitator for a period of eighteen months.

The regular sessions became a place where the health visitors could listen to and support each other in relation to painful and disturbing aspects of their work. This included having to hear about, and sometimes witness, cruelty by men towards their pregnant partners, and the serious neglect, exploitation and abuse of babies and young children by one or both parents or elder siblings who were sometimes left in charge. Our group sessions often contained explosions of anger and floods of tears. Peer support also flowed freely. The group listened to and helped each other with practical suggestions and also learned to work as a group in order to gain more suitable work space and equipment, dealing with a demanding doctor, and a new, initially obstructive, practice manager. As we worked together, a feeling of solidarity was built up in the team, which also became known for its pioneering initiatives. It was a red-letter day when we learned that a newly qualified health visitor had specifically sought to work with this team. When my contract expired we were all confident that the good work would continue in self-facilitated meetings. Unfortunately the story does not end there.

A couple of years later, I was approached by a new manager of the team. She told me that the team had again become 'stressed out' and that my services were again required. Because of budget constraints, 'just a few top-up meetings' were expected to suffice. When I met the team, there were several new faces and only two of the original team members. At the second session, the newest member of the team brought a difficult case and found herself weeping profusely as she went into some of the painful details. We had started our meeting late due to teething problems about co-ordinating timetables and securing the venue, so we ran out of time. But I expected that we would be able to pick things up and follow through at our next meeting. I was wrong. When the person who had brought the case on the previous occasion remarked on how useful she had found that meeting, the other members rounded on her and took her to task. They advised her that she needed to toughen up if she wanted to survive in the job. There was no room for sentimentality. The work was difficult enough without also spending time 'getting upset' about it. I felt shocked and my heart sank as I faced the fact that in the absence of ongoing facilitation and with a considerable degree of staff turnover, the carefully built-up staff culture of supporting each other in working through painful feelings stirred by the work, had completely collapsed. Defensiveness was now in the ascendant and that was what new members of the team were being initiated into.

4. Excerpt from a European workshop

The following vignette comes from an international workshop for health professionals entitled 'Caring for the Carers'. After a welcome and general introduction, three colleagues who were from a country which was at the time in turmoil and who worked together to treat victims of torture volunteered to talk about their work. Initially they gave a rather dispassionate account as if their task was an ordinary one to them. The rest of the group listened attentively and asked some careful questions. What emerged, all too clearly, was that this group felt isolated from the larger professional community and had minimal official support for their work. Encouraged by the interest and support of this group, they began to share some of the harrowing details of the terrible things they were told. Then one of the three began to cry. He apologised, wiping away his tears. Then one of his colleagues said that she felt a great sense of relief when

she saw him cry because she cried often at night when some of the accounts of
the victims came back to her mind. She had, until now, felt too ashamed to tell
her colleagues. At the end of the workshop, the three workers thanked the
group and also said that they planned to find some regular support for themselves on their return home. The group of three workers then said that sharing
these feelings at the workshop was very important to them – they now felt a
stronger sense of connection to each other in their work.

The theme of the workshop and the supportive and empathetic approach
of the group as a whole had provided a facilitating environment for the three
workers to connect with and share some of the painful feelings generated by
their work.

Dumping, difficulty and collusion

Unhealthily for others, helpers can seek relief by endeavouring to dispose, in its
raw, unprocessed form, of the emotional detritus with which their role burdens
them. The recipients may include other professionals, partners at home, or the
facilitators themselves. Three illustrations follow.

1. Take that!

In supervision, Marion told me dispiritedly that her consultation to a family
guidance clinic staff team had become 'impossible'. The clinic had sought her
out to provide facilitation after they had themselves been assessed by their
executive committee and told that they were failing and that they needed
external help. They sought out Marion, and the work seemed to start well
enough, but at the third session two of the staff did not turn up and two of the
others spent the session complaining that the facilitator was 'no good' as she
was not producing 'improvements'. At a subsequent meeting, Marion was
accused of 'incompetence' and threatened with a 'formal complaint'. Marion
told me that she felt 'awful' – and at a loss. When we explored her last two
meetings in some detail, it became clear that Marion was working well, but that
the group had a different objective: to give their facilitator a hurtful sample of
the pain they had experienced at the hands of their management. When she put
this idea to the team at her next meeting with them, it seemed to produce some
relief, and paved the way for a limited degree of enhanced co-operation.

2. The dysfunctional captain

A multi-disciplinary team of carers were so consistently critical and rejecting of what was offered that it seemed impossible to continue to work with them. I could see that part of their anger towards me related to fury with their boss who kept letting them down but was also very fragile and skilful at avoiding confrontation. The boss also kept promising to attend the group but always cancelled because of 'other commitments'. The group used the sessions to act out transferentially their hostility to their boss. There was no evidence of insight or learning. Our sessions soon folded. It seems to me that this type of failure may be unavoidable, because of the difficulty in predicting how things will develop once the facilitation has started. However I may have spared us all the wasted time if I had insisted on a proper meeting with the manager at the outset.

3. 'It's you!' 'No, it's you!'

During a facilitated awayday, a group of general practitioners complained about the insensitivity to patients' needs which was evident in the management group, which controlled access to additional funding. It was unanimously agreed that the management group's main concern was to spend less money. However when I met a member of the management group, he complained about the insensitivity of the doctors to the needs of patients. He said that they had no real interest in providing a better service to patients. They were only out to get more money for less work. I felt that I was in the presence of parents (professional managers and caretakers) who are so busy blaming each other that the needs of their children (the patients) are ignored. Both sides needed to feel supported in a way that recognised the pressures they felt under and enabled them to acknowledge their own need and greed.

The heart of the matter

Humphries (1998) points to research purportedly showing that while 'burnout' has features of maladaptive coping in the short term, it is paradoxically protective in the longer term. My reading of this is that once the helper reaches the point of pervasive unprocessed psychic overload, he or she becomes emotionally disconnected and may manifest a robotic type of efficiency, which gives the illusion of coping. This emotional blunting may already have been established in childhood as a response to early emotional deprivation and trauma as discussed earlier in this chapter. Indeed Clark gained the impression that emotional distancing was an established pathological feature of many of the doctors she worked with (Clark 2000). Thus helpers who in their own childhoods were deprived of enough healthy opportunities to express their feelings, may become helpers who do not take other people's feelings seriously. In such a context there is an ethos in which, as Wolheim puts it, emotions 'die of the lack of interaction, of the lack of narrative' (Wolheim 1999, p.224). Those helpers who were emotionally starved in their own childhood may then set up methods and systems of treatment in which their patients become objectified and depersonalised. In this process it is the helpers who make the helped ill. At an institutional level, such pathologising practices used to be common in children's hospitals, where the doctors and nurses would pack the parents of screaming child admissions off as quickly as possible, so the child would 'settle down'. Several of my adult patients bear the psychic scars of such traumatic separations. In her classic and seminal research into the nursing system at a large hospital Menzies Lyth refers to a nurse who wakes a sleeping patient in order to give him his sleeping pill (Menzies Lyth 1988). Menzies Lyth addresses this systemically in terms of unconscious institutional defences against the emotional pain of continuous exposure to ill and dying patients. It can also be looked at from the perspective of the individual nurse who may have already been so adapted to having her own feelings ignored in her own childhood, that she is all too ready to bypass her emotional intelligence again and simply follow orders. She may also be giving her patients a dose of the 'treatment' she herself experienced as a child.

The potential value then in working with groups of helpers is that those whose emotional pain has become frozen, may, by having their own feelings listened to, thaw sufficiently to begin to experience both their own and their patients' needs differently. In this sense, those models of helping or rather enabling others which focus on empowering the client, seem psychologically healthier for the providers than those which take responsibility for making those in need 'better'. The helper as co-participant does more sharing and is less cluttered by the pain of the client. The limiting factor may be that some supplicants lack the inner resources to grasp the encouragement to be self-enabling. They may need instead to have someone else carry the weight of their dependency needs, before any development can take place.

Secrets

Just because helpers are meeting in a facilitated group, it does not mean that they are telling their truth. The climate of trust that is fostered in such groups is always in some degree of conflict with what each individual, as well as the group as a whole, considers it safe to talk about. Groups often establish ground rules at the outset in which they agree to keep what is said 'confidential' to the group, and not to talk about members of the group behind their backs. While these are formal attempts to dispose of fear and mistrust, they do not replace individual viewpoints about what it is safe to talk about. More specifically, if a member of the group is doing something they know is wrong, they may choose to continue to keep it secret either because they want to continue doing it, or, even if they have already stopped, because they fear the consequences if the group finds out. Most frequently this relates to 'forbidden' erotic relationships between practitioners and patients and between senior practitioners and those they manage, though other forms of deceit and malpractice also occur. The relationships between carers and those they care for often provide opportunities for sexual and aggressive exploitation.

From a psychodynamic perspective, it is not only a question of actual sexual behaviour, but also of the way in which erotic feelings and erotic and eroticised transference and countertransference dynamics permeate all groups. An ongoing facilitated group can encourage (but not guarantee) a climate of trust and safety in which such desires can be communicated and struggled with rather than be acted on. This may help to protect clients and patients from being harmed by their carers. It also may provide an opportunity to air complex feelings which are impacting negatively on team co-operation such as those which may arise when there are sexual relationships between co-helpers, who are not 'official' couples in the outside world. When the erotic dimension is brought into the open in the facilitated group, the impact on the team as a whole of what has not previously been spoken about can sometimes be addressed and worked through. The surfacing of these issues is often a relief, although working with them can be painful.

Helpers are in some ways more vulnerable to secret sex with their patients than other professionals. The intimate nature of the work is bound to stir erotic feelings, the requirement for privacy is built in to the professional task, and the strict prohibition against such behaviour can stimulate the appeal of 'forbidden fruit'. The challenge for the group is to create an atmosphere in which temptations can be spoken about before they are acted on. For example in one established group a practitioner, with considerable difficulty, spoke of his sexual desire for one of his patients. She was, he said, also encouraging him to have sex with her. It was clear he had found it very difficult to bring this to the group, and only managed to do so because he felt he could trust the group to help him. In the event he found it a great relief to have told the group and said that he found that it was subsequently easier to maintain his professional boundaries. It is less likely that group members will talk about current or previous transgressions, but when a member finds the courage to come clean, he or she becomes free of the burden of cover-up. It then becomes the task of the group and especially the facilitator to work sensitively, carefully and ethically with the many issues that then surface.

I have sometimes found that the sharing of one or more dreams can enable a motivated group to address issues at a deeper level. In doing so I have drawn on Gordon Lawrence's approach to social dreaming matrices as elaborated by Peter Tatham in this book. Drawing on dreams in this way provides an opportunity to access unconscious material and so shift the style, content and spirit of the group's verbal communication. For example, I was asked to do some brief work with a staff group who felt they had become stuck in their task. About half-way through the time we had together I introduced the idea that sharing and associating to (not interpreting) each other's dreams can illuminate possible blocks in a group's relationship to its task. The most senior practitioner present then narrated a dream of the previous night in which he had been playing a game of tennis with a difference. The game had seemed normal enough until he noticed that his opponent was stark naked and he was wearing shorts. He felt that the shorts had something to do with 'holding back'. The dream released a flood of associations in the group, which related to sexual desire, rivalry and exploitation in general and in the group in particular. This served to clear a block within the group and they were able to address the issues of common concern with renewed energy.

In another group of helpers, there were persistent concerns about group and organisational prejudice that were equally persistently denied. One member then brought a dream about a baby who was conceived by a white father and black mother. When the child was born, neither parent then wanted to claim the child as theirs. The subsequent associations enabled the group to discover and uncover ways in which prejudices were being enacted both in the team and in their wider organisation. This awareness led to a change in the culture of the group, which allowed for a greater sense of membership by all.

The member who had complained then said that she had come to feel more at home in this group than in any previous group she had belonged to.

I have also found that social dreaming can help to contain enactment in a group. The following example relates to working as a group facilitator in South Africa, shortly before the first ever democratic elections, with a group of professionals from the helping professions. There had been an eruption of violence among our membership: our only white Afrikaans male participant had physically assaulted our only female white Afrikaans member. The woman was distraught and the group in uproar. For his part, the man said he was at a loss to understand what had come over him, as he had never before in his life hit a woman. It emerged that in informal conversations outside the group sessions, the male member of the group had felt severely scapegoated by others including his female compatriot as if he was personally responsible for the evils of the apartheid era. His anger and frustration had spilled over into action. While this made sense for some of the group members, the ominous atmosphere, which had developed, remained and the viability of the rest of our workshop was in question.

Then an older woman quietly gained the attention of the group by saying that the previous night she had dreamt for the first time in her life. Her dream comprised a single image and related to a very large old oak tree which actually stood in the courtyard of the premises where we were working: the oak had been completely uprooted and its canopy of branches now rested on the earth while its roots now reached for the sky. Many associations were produced in response to this image. These did not include direct reference to the fact that the branches of the Boabab tree, a tree prevalent in the myths of black African people, look very much like roots. Nor was it explicitly said that the oak was not an indigenous tree but was introduced by the English 'settlers'. However it was clear that the image spoke volumes to all present as a symbol of the enormous uprooting changes which were sweeping through the whole country. The last and most arresting association which was offered reminded us that as the pupil of the eye acts like a pinhole camera, at birth we all see things upside down. Our retina then takes on the task of putting the images right. The links between this image and what all present felt about what was happening in their country did not have to be spelled out. The silence which followed had a quality of awe or enlightenment. Before anyone was ready to speak, a member pointed to the corner where a field mouse could be discerned in the shadows. The mouse ventured out, scampered under our chairs, and found its way out through a gap between the door and its frame. One of the participants then ended our silence with the surprised exclamation that this was the first time in her life she had not screamed when seeing a mouse. By now the angry and disturbed feelings which had engulfed us earlier seemed to have dissolved. A reparative atmosphere became manifest and the workshop moved on to its conclusion.

Professional intergroup dynamics

The final section of this chapter explores aspects of intergroup dynamics of organisations which lay claim to psychoanalytic work. All organisations which purport to work analytically would agree that the unconscious is unknowable and that whatever they offer is by its very nature incomplete. In theory then each approach might also have something to learn from and teach the others, but this hardly seems to be taken into account in practice. The organisations representing different and possibly complementary approaches seem relatively impermeable to each other. Thus there seems to be institutionalised groupism among organisations which support one-to-one analytic work. Couple, family and group approaches also seem to have little to do with each other.

Hopper writing as a psychoanalyst and group analyst asserts that 'the study of the social unconscious is neglected in the training of group analysts, and is utterly ignored in the training of psychoanalysts' (Hopper 2001). He also bemoans the fact that professional trainings in psychotherapy are characterised by an 'unacceptable degree of religiosity' (Hopper 2001, p.23). The senior British training analyst, Nina Coltart, states that during her psychoanalytic training she learned to value nothing about unconscious processes in groups (Coltart 1996). She was already in her sixties when, suspending her prejudices, she joined an Institute of Group Analysis introductory course. To her surprise, in just one year in an experiential group, with the interactive help of her conductor and peer group, she felt she gained deep emotionally effective insight into a central emotional trauma of her childhood, in a way which complemented her previous own personal weekly dyadic analysis.

Writing as an anthropologist and psychoanalyst, Mitchell takes her colleagues to task for missing out on the dynamic importance of sibling relationships (Mitchell 2000). She reminds us of Freud's own pathogenic sibling history and points out that he largely failed to engage with this in his self-analysis. She also details the way in which he acted out these problems with sibling figures such as Jung and Ferenczi to the detriment of the co-operative development of one-to-one psychoanalytic work. Furthermore, from a theoretical perspective, Freud's founding of psychoanalytic theory exclusively on the Oedipus complex, fails to give the necessary *equal* weight to the importance of actual and phantasised sibling relationships from birth onwards.

Reflecting on the above views, and the innovative ways in which psychoanalytic work has developed over the years with couples, families, groups and organisations, it seems anachronistic to call dyadic analytic work 'psychoanalysis' and other approaches 'applied psychoanalysis'. All the approaches share an aspiration to offer helpful ways of exploring unconscious processes, but they have crystallised into separate organisations which tend to have little, if any, creative connections with each other, somewhat like rivalrous siblings who each do their own thing. Each organisation maintains a degree of hegemony in relation to its product and it is left to individual practitioners to establish peer connections across organisational divides. In such peer networks, with regard to group relations, for example, it is well known that group relations work engages meaningfully with power and authority, but also tends towards phallocentricism. It does so by emphasising the director's power and top-down interventions by staff members, while downgrading maternal receptive and nurturing functions, and the creative power of peer relationships. In contrast group analysts 'conduct' in a receptive way which encourages the self-expression and development of group members, but minimises opportunities for robust developmental engagement with authority. It seems that the way in which the psychoanalytic sub-specialisms tend to marginalise each other includes an element of transgenerational transmission of Freud's unresolved struggles with his siblings (and theirs with him). Creative advances can be resisted by narrow forms of followership.

Conclusions

Those who take on the function of being the helpers in society can also be thought of as wounded healers. It is therefore important to promote, refine and develop ways of helping helpers. What is especially important is that helpers have good enough opportunities to process the painful emotional feelings which are generated by their work. As the motivations for taking up the role of helper are complex, selection and training are of particular importance. Transgression and exploitation of patients by helpers, while being the responsibility of each individual wrongdoer, is also evidence of organisational and societal failure. Thus to the extent that the focus is on blame, we all share an element of culpability. It is a mistake to discharge this responsibility only by searching out and punishing or rehabilitating wrongdoers. We also need to aspire to achieving creative and effective preventative care for our care-takers. In helping helpers, we are also helping them to help us, and so also helping ourselves.

References

Bion, W. (1961) *Learning from Experience*. London: Tavistock Publications.

Coltart, N. (1996) 'Two's company, three's a crowd.' In *The Baby and the Bathwater*. London: Karnac Books.

Clark, S. (2000) 'Why do people become doctors and what can go wrong?' *British Medical Journal*, April, 2–3.

Elfyn, M. (2000) 'Standing By.' Translated by J. Clancey (2001) In *Cusan Dyn Dall/Blind Man's Kiss*. Bloodaxe Books.

Felton, J.S. (1998) 'Burnout as a clinical entity – its importance in health care workers.' *Occupational Med. (London) 48*, 4, 237–50.

Freud, S. (1905) 'On psychotherapy.' In J. Strachey (ed) *The Standard Edition of the Complete Psychological Works of Sigmund Freud* (Vol.7, pp.255–68). London: Hogarth Press.

Freud, S. (1937) 'Analysis terminable and interminable.' In J. Strachey (ed) *The Standard Edition of the Complete Psychological Works of Sigmund Freud* (Vol.23, pp.209–253). London: Hogarth Press.

Guggenbuhl-Craig, A. (1971) *Power in the Helping Professions*. New York: Spring Publications.

Hahn, H. (1998) 'Super vision: seen, sought and re viewed.' In P. Clarkson (ed) *Supervision: Psychoanalytic and Jungian Perspectives*. London: Whurr.

Hopper, E. (2001) 'The social unconscious: theoretical considerations.' *Group Analysis 34*, 1, 9–28.

Humphries, G. (1998) 'A review of burnout in dentists.' *Dental Update 25*, 9, 392–396.

Johnstone, C. (1999) 'Strategies to prevent burnout.' *British Medical Journal Classified 1*, May.

Lawrence, W.G. (1991) 'Won from the void and formless infinite: experiences of social dreaming.' *Free Associations 2, Part 2, No.22*, 259–294.

Mitchell, J. (2000) *Mad Men and Medusas*. London: Allen Lane.

Menzies Lyth, I. (1988) *Containing Anxiety in Institutions*. London: Free Association Books.

Office of Population Censuses and Surveys (OPCS) (1986) *Occupational Mortality, 1979–80, 1982–83: Decennial Supplement*. London: HSMO (Series DS No.6.)

Wolheim, R. (1999) *On the Emotions*. New Haven and London: Yale University Press.

CHAPTER 5

Working with Words

Angela Eden

As I planned this chapter a question played on my mind: why do I do this work? I thought back over different pieces of work, and tried to unlock the excitement I feel when the task is going well. I realised that this feeling is based on a series of magic moments when the words that are said, and the thoughts expressed, become shared ideas. At the same moment, I slip into a different space and time frame in which I hear and see an additional set of transactions. Some of these are a set of themes that are part of the client's world. They link together and change the way I perceive their world. At that moment, I feel excited, but have schooled myself to choose the method of sharing my feelings, and when it works it is magic. I realise that it is a function of experience, and the use of skills. I know it is a moment of real engagement, of kinship between myself and the group, and even a moment in which I too can change. My thought is that I want to offer a space for change, a space that will be creative enough to make a difference to the way people work.

In this chapter, words and forms of dialogue will be my focus as this helps me to understand the deeper levels of organisational dynamics. I will explain why those words work for me, and give examples about the impact an intervention can have on the work of a group. I will start with some ideas about those interventions, then move to the wider organisational context for both the individuals and groups in the organisation. In the final sections, I will consider some frameworks for the languages I use when consulting to organisations.

The context for interventions

Learning how to achieve those moments of effective consulting can take hours of reflection and supervision. Offering an intervention is the key moment in a consultancy relationship. It is the time when a word, a tone, the pace, or an underlying nuance can make or break a working relationship. How words are used is a matter of judgement, discipline, training, experience, and the conceptual framework and perspective of the practitioner. Part of that perspective will come from the journey the consultant takes in developing their competence. That journey will also inevitably influence the professional language used in their work.

The first moments of the client and the consultant meeting is a significant fragment of time that frames the ongoing stages of the working relationship. In analysing my records of some initial sessions, I realised that they gave me the metaphor or language for the rest of the engagement. The client's original request should be reflected in the consultant's proposal in the appropriate language for the task. There is a similar practice in product management, where the 'client requirement definition' has to capture perfectly the whole project, which can succeed or fail on the turn of a word. The complexity of designing a technical product entails hours of research, design, testing, instructions, marketing and launch. The work takes place over a number of months, and even so, at a final stage the customer might notice that the product is square when they had specifically asked for a circle. Although it was a basic requirement, it was not noticed, and hours of work were wasted. It is essential therefore that the original request must be framed, and heard as a shared concept by both the client and the contractor. The following story is an example of the right intervention in the wrong language and time frame.

Faster than a speeding bullet

A group of project managers asked for help in the design of a training programme. They had already commissioned an earlier diagnostic phase, used to identify skills and then design an integrated set of models that would develop those skills. During the meeting and listening to the issues I formed a possible proposal for their problem. I put the idea forward, and was met with a blank response. The team wanted something much more detailed and complex, which I should have realised. I had believed that speed would be helpful, but missed a clue that 'more equalled better'. I stayed connected with the project for a year, without being very effective. Finally, after another expensive set of psychometric tests and programmes the same proposals were suggested which I had made a year earlier. I could not understand why I had been ignored for a year, and then found out that the team had not believed I could come up with a useful solution after one short meeting. It was a tough but excellent lesson in pace and use of language.

The organisational context

A current focus for organisations, theorists, consultants, strategists and operational managers, is the pace of change. The changes are coming faster and faster, because of technology, the environment, or social changes. The pace is so fast that it can feel like an experience of 'change whiplash'. Before one change is implemented another starts and there is no time to catch breath, or enjoy a moment of stability. There is a plethora of papers about the effects of change on individuals in their work. I will summarise the debate by saying these changes, which we all experience, are a function of innovation. This has encouraged the exponential changes in technology and communications, when every new product forces a reconfiguration in the way we work. People tell me they are overwhelmed by these changes, stressed by the amount of work that comes through the electronic media, and too pressured to respond at a reasonable pace.

It is interesting to compare an historical benchmark against current employment patterns. Set against the work environment of twenty years ago, technology systems were less ubiquitous. We wrote letters with a pen or on manual typewriters. When a word needed to be changed or erased, whole pages had to be rewritten because there was one mistake. Copies were kept by using carbon paper, and letters were sent using envelopes with stamps. However, human ability has triumphed again and we have adapted to technology and now use it with fluency. We have learnt to live with the speed of messages that are written, sent and read within minutes. Senior managers tell me they receive two hundred messages a day, as a norm for a large company. We are changing the way we understand those messages, even the tone and style of written communication has radically changed. For example, I attempt to write a simple statement, which from my perspective is written with economy and immediacy. Yet on receipt it is read as a brusque instruction, and is experienced as offensive. In consequence, we can be misunderstood as we try to respond speedily to our e-mails.

Another consequence of being technologically competent is the increasing number of people who work remotely. Being hardwired through the technology can limit the need for face-to-face interpersonal connection. However, people outside the organisation's walls can become too isolated. In extreme circumstances, I can imagine groups of workers developing 'institutionalised autism'. Another consideration is the way reward systems have been developed. As technology skills become more valuable, so organisations increase the amounts of remuneration. People are rewarded for spending hours isolated on the web and being immersed in oceans of web surf and e-mails. Electronic patterns of communication become virtual ephemera rather than real-time interactive communication. Now we are connected electronically to the world and have the ability to communicate with hundreds of unknown people. We can join communities, buy commodities, be entertained, and manage financial affairs, with ADSL in our homes.

Another unplanned consequence is the disappearing employment opportunities for clerical and secretarial roles, as desk workers become increasingly technologically self-reliant. Additionally some people, who have no company intranet to access the internal systems, are losing out on corporate communications. As they have limited opportunity to be informed, they become a new phenomenon of an underclass. We are beginning to recognise the health issues in the new working environments. We know that hours sitting at a computer screen can generate health problems, repetitive strain injury (RSI), back injuries, and ocular migraines. We have a new anxiety about computers 'crashing', losing precious data, and experience a sense of catastrophic expectations about being uninformed or unavailable. I hear people saying, 'I need to know what's going on all the time, and if I am not constantly available, what will people think of me?' It can encourage repetitive obsessional behaviour as people try to stay in touch with multiple communication channels.

I have recorded many examples here, as they are critical symptoms of new communication patterns. In large open-plan offices, I see people sitting in their individual area, not talking to each other, but writing and replying to e-mails from their colleagues in the same room. The experience of talking to each other, face to face, is becoming an exception. This misuse of technology can undermine both productivity and relationships. As a consultant in that system, I have to identify those issues, and it becomes even more essential to find interventions that will help. I need to find a language that will make sense, and be heard. I experience that the individual people, who could make decisions, are often so caught up in the practicalities and politics of organisational life that their ears are closed to an unpopular truth. Often so much time and money has been invested that pointing out any downside can be seen as a disloyal act. I can explain this more clearly by describing part of a change process as a vignette.

Shouting louder does not work
A newly appointed senior manager wanted to make a difference to the culture of his large unit. He decided that themes for the unit would be 'Bold, Buoyant

and Brave'. These words were branded as the 3B. He took the advice of design consultants who suggested ways of promoting his image as a strategic leader and having his philosophy adopted by everyone. A communication programme was designed, and logos printed on products, pens, and desk ornaments. All of these were designed to embed the message into people's daily work. A training programme was put in place, but people never managed to find the time to attend. After some investigation, part of the reason was discovered. It was their confusion with this programme and another, different organisational message about 'Productivity + Performance + Price' branded as P3. These two imperatives were seen as divergent. I was part of a team of change consultants who were allocated to this project, and were asked to implement the message of the 3B. However, we knew that the two different messages needed to be re-aligned, linked, or certainly not conflictual, with the other messages inside the organisation.

Reflection on the case study

The task of the consultant was to help the 'culture change' message of 3B, yet we were in a dilemma as knew about the wider context and the conflicting messages of P3. The consulting team tried to alter the programme, and make it more possible for the managers to understand. However the consultants' intervention and suggestions were not heard, or appreciated. Maybe the language was not tempered to the thinking of the senior manager, or the time was not right. The consultants spent some time reviewing their role, and tried to think of a better way of framing their intervention. The consulting team failed, because they could not be heard. My argument is that the consultant's main task is to create a dialogue, and to find the language that can be understood. The organisation may be hard of hearing, but shouting louder will not make a difference. The task is to find a language or medium that can make a difference.

The individual context

For the individual, trying to survive inside the turbulence and flux of constant change is an unsettling and destabilising experience. In the past, and more stable world of work, people had networks of like-minded colleagues. They used well-integrated information channels, and had ways to access intellectual capital. People were able to achieve consistent productivity, feel confident and able to contribute to their objectives. People knew where they worked, with whom, why, and their place in that schema. Unfortunately, the commercial world is moving too fast to allow that organic growth that enables a working community. The shifting structures and sub-systems are in ever increasing confusion. Organisations are learning to re-shape themselves either through policy, political decisions, or environmental influences. They have to re-form and then begin again a re-stabilising process. The new culture is reinforced by productivity targets, management style and reward systems. As the new networks establish productive connections, people in power realise that the new form is only partially effective, and make new changes. So the cycle is iterative and demoralising for some. I will describe people's reactions to change by quoting part of a research paper.

Changing perceptions of change

It became increasingly clear in one company setting that people found it stressful trying to re-adjust to new commercial imperatives. Yet some people seemed to enjoy and thrive on those changes. I noticed that when any organisational change was announced different managers reacted in different ways. By collecting their experiences, I hoped to inform and advise others about a range of strategies as well as creating a feedback loop into the organisation. I interviewed a range of managers who were not only survivors but had prospered through many organisational changes. The questions covered their experiences, behaviour, feelings and ideas. The data was collated and their behaviours fell into four different types of reactions to change, *The Initiator, The Advisor, The Implementer* and *The Recipient*. However, no one person fell neatly into one type of response, as the respondents switched their strategies over time according to their formal role, their own value system, beliefs, experience, and personal history. I wrote the following descriptions to share with others, and as an intervention in the organisation. I specifically recorded the words used by people, written within quotation marks.

The Initiator has formal authority to instigate and initiate change. They have experience through working in many change processes. They recognise themselves as at the front of any change. They feel confident that they can influence or lead a new reality and are uncomfortable if they cannot lead. If they know something is about to happen they make sure they are in the middle of the chaos. They say it was because they could 'remember having no control' and did not like it. Therefore, they take proactive steps to be involved and integral to the change process. They are able to engage in the work, at the centre of the storm, leading from the front.

The Advisor, instead of rushing into the centre of the storm, is more adaptive to the environment. They 'read the signs' and are adept at using their network to find out who the key people are. If they are confused, they 'trawl for data' and watch the direction of the decision-makers. They collect ideas and create various alternatives. As a new path is chosen, they are there, as part of the project. They enjoy an influencing role 'behind the scenes'. They feel comfortable with ambiguity, and adjust their models as they find new data. They are able to manoeuvre into the centre of the process by engaging in 'political courtship' and they have the ability to hold paradoxical data in their mind.

The Implementer finds an essential job within the change process by implementing someone else's decision. They are valued for their experience and ability to translate a broad idea into achievable goals. They are skilled in managing people. Their survival is based on having access to, and being included by, more influential people. They gain that patronage through loyalty and hard work in delivering change programmes.

The Recipient holds a strong memory of being on the receiving end of someones else's decision, which generates a feeling of being 'threatened, ignored, anxious, devalued, bewildered, and personally worried'. They find it 'very stressful having it done to me', disabling, and resent not being involved. They try to avoid that passive 'them and us' situation as it borders on their being infantilised and undermines their professional self-image.

With this data, I was able to make some recommendations to the organisation as a whole, and to senior managers who might instigate large-scale changes in the organisation. I am including the last section of the report (below) as an example of language, which I chose to make an impact on the decision-makers and the employees' experience of change.

CONCLUSIONS AND APPLICATIONS FROM THE RESEARCH

The well-spun cliché that 'no one likes change' is not true. Some people love it, thrive, look for it, and get bored if things stay the same for too long. Others even create change just for the energy of it, and others tolerate it. Evidently, some do not like it. The other variable has to do with control; if a change happens because of your own individual influence, then it is welcome. If it is at the instigation of some other person's decision then the individual's sense of self is defined by someone else. People are forced to recreate a sense of identity in a new space, with new people, new culture and new ways of doing things. There may be a timing issue, how often people have to shift, or whether it fits in with their life pattern. It may be a space issue, geography, and journeys, having a different workplace. It may be a professional issue, learning new skills, disregarding hard-won expertise, re-proving oneself with new colleagues, earning one's stripes, and learning to be trusted.

- *Culture of war*: During the research people used metaphors of warfare. They described the people in the organisation as 'foot soldiers, troops, casualties, cannon fodder'. It is a dismissive way of thinking about employees, yet it may be a way to manage the anxiety of being at the head of a social system. During times of war it could be helpful for individuals to limit their emotional attachments to their comrades as so much loss might be difficult to handle. However, this begs the question of whether it is appropriate in a business context. How can we consider other metaphors that contribute to a less destructive culture? Hypothetically, for those in charge of change, staying emotionally involved with individuals is too difficult. Being a proactive leader (e.g. in an army) also means being distant, especially if the complexity of the decision-making is too great.

- *Culture of communication*: It is difficult to involve and include everyone at all stages of an organisational change process. However, it is also clear that a way out of being passive is to be involved. Therefore, we need to find better ways of giving people access to information that would encourage the continuity of work. This is critical as so many people experience a lull in their work between organisational change announcements. Organisations do not yet have a way of measuring that 'down-time', and it carries a huge cost; people need to be informed and involved. Leaders of change always want to be informed, but forget other people have the same need for information.

- *The Passive/Active paradigm*: The organisation works with a paradox, a double message about being proactive or passive. There is an unspoken ideology that proactivity is good, and reactive-passivity is bad. Yet, there is also a culture of 'don't tell them till it's fixed'. Managers think that the period of uncertainty should be limited, as it decreases performance. So, it is considered to be 'kinder' and better for the organisation to tell people only when the options are agreed and decisions made. This position implies that people should be passive. Conversely, proactive people thought, 'if you are passive you are a casualty'. Calling people 'casualties' implies that they have brought it on themselves: passivity was seen as self-inflicted pain. The double message is an example of an ambivalent culture about the power of hierarchy.

- *Culture alignment*: The ideas in this report could be used as an indicator of where the organisation's culture could be adjusted, not just for individuals' ability to survive the changes, but also for organisational health. If momentous decisions are made, they will undoubtedly affect the well-being of individuals. If the organisation as a whole wants to do more than survive, to thrive, then the needs of individuals, teams, productivity and values have to be aligned to optimise the ways of surviving change.

Reflections on the case study

I have used the results of this research with individuals who came for coaching about their career. The language of the report was familiar, and it included quotes from their own colleagues. They found some useful pointers to their own behaviour, and identified new behaviours they could adopt when presented with change.

The group context

It is an obvious statement that organisations form themselves into groups. Whether they are a hierarchy, or in project-based configurations, everyone is aligned to a group context. People identify with their department, unit, team, professional groups, or rank. Thus each group has a relationship to the whole system and can be identified by classification, function and lines of account-ability. Groups may wish to develop or improve their collective productivity and request some consultancy work in order to facilitate their intent. Requests for help come in distinctively different ways, and for diverse reasons. A new manager may have the foresight to spend time getting to know his/her colleagues by planning a review day. The consultant's role is to structure a day in which all the issues and personalities can be seen and heard. A useful method is to collect the ideas from the team before the agenda is set and present the issues back to the senior manager, with a structure that will move 'elegantly' through the issues that were raised. This method works well because the agenda is framed in the language of the team, not imposed from an external source.

A new team with a specific task may want to define and then plan their work programme. Again this is a time for debate and discussion, formulated around the skills and needs of the new team. Some groups want to go on structured 'team-building' activities. Companies provide sailing boats, mountain treks, survival exercises, and simulations in the form of games. These activities are used as a way of getting to know the team under different pressures, away from the work issues. Whatever they learn can be brought back to the formal task and roles. In these cases, the different language of the external activity is seen as a creative way to build alliances and knowledge. Using a systemic model to understand this type of intervention seems to indicate that the work has to happen twice; once in the external world, and then translated back to the work setting. The consultant's task is to question the intent of the team, the output from the task, and to check the validity of the intervention. Is it genuinely cost-effective to do the work twice, once in the external exercise and then reformed in the work setting?

A well-established group can find itself in a difficult phase of work. It could be that the project plan has gone off course, the requirements for delivering a project have changed, or the team is not working well together. It is always a vulnerable time to ask for help, and the consultant has to respond with sensitivity. In this scenario, it is essential that the 'root cause' of the difficulty is recognised and worked on. There are different ways to tackle the issues. Some organisations find it easier to work over a longer period, and meet regularly for 'non-managerial' supervision. The group dedicates one or two hours on a regular basis to explore their work. The consultant's job is to create a safe enough environment for the group to engage with each other and find the words to express their concerns. I have used the following story to highlight this method and it has resonance with a number of chapters in this book.

Caring for carers

This case study describes a team of professional care-workers who had clients with a chronic and sometimes terminal health condition, visiting client's homes regularly and helping with medical and personal needs. The team was very diverse in terms of age, experience, ethnicity, religious beliefs and culture. They shared some of the clients, and worked individually as 'key workers' over long periods. Their work was stressful, emotionally and physically draining, and undervalued in terms of pay and conditions. The team felt overwhelmed by their differences, and could not agree with each other's ways of working. They were full of animosity and mistrust for their colleagues, and the team was fragmenting. There were a few deeply held beliefs, based on religious, sexual or political commitments, which divided the team. I was employed as an external consultant to help them reconnect to each other. The task was agreed as 'to find a way in which each person's skills and style would be both respected and valued by the others'.

The group met regularly over nine months, in the same room, with a consistent time boundary for every meeting. As the consultant, I needed to defuse the vitriolic accusations, and make space for real dialogue between the team members. Ideas and hypotheses were shared and explored, initially through my interventions, as a lone voice, but increasingly by the team. The group as a whole gradually built a grudging respect for each other. They said they felt valued by the regularity, the professional concern, and the open acceptance of their work at first from the consultant, and then by their colleagues. My early notes of these meetings show how I was initially drowned by the words they used. Then gradually as I acclimatised to their world I was able to intervene and join them. A further example is explored in the following case study.

The absent father

A senior team of ten experienced, highly qualified managers met monthly for a board meeting. They had different roles, but all addressing the same departmental objective. Each member of the team had worked together over many years, so they knew each other well. However the team meetings were disliked, even dreaded, and the decisions they made were not high quality. I was asked to consult to the team and find ways of working better together. I was asked to attend their team meetings and was given permission to intervene if the debate was wasting time. At the first meeting, it was obvious that the senior manager had a style of chairmanship that annoyed and repressed the team. He interrupted discussions, and made autocratic decisions about the issues. He asked for reports about progress and was then inquisitorial about the results. He lost his temper and challenged individual members of the board in an embarrassingly unpleasant way. At the third meeting, he was absent, and the rest of the team relaxed into a humorous, light-hearted mood. They went through the agenda in a desultory way, and were not able to work, or tackle the tasks on the agenda.

This reminded me of basic assumptions theory (Bion 1975) that describes some barriers to the work of a group. Wilfred Bion's observations of groups created a hypothesis that groups did not work when they behaved in any one of three 'non-work' modes. One pattern is the hope for a leader, a Messiah, to save them from failure. A second is allowing two members of the group to form a pair, that would 'give birth' to a new way out of their dilemmas. The third pattern is based on an assumption that the group could fight (within or external to the group) or flee from their problems. This third pattern was evident in my group of managers. It was my task to point it out, in a way that might shift the group into a productive working mode. Eventually a moment came, after a particularly silly joke; my intervention was 'we seem to have such fun when Daddy is away'. Their response was loud, open laughter, and then they settled down to productive work. After this episode I had an individual meeting with the team leader, and asked what he thought of the meetings. His sharp mind could see the issues and solutions quite quickly and he found it unbearable to wait for the whole group to catch up. It was evident that the problem was his impatience and he was then able to identify the moment at which he started to get enraged. He agreed he would try to notice that moment, before he lost his temper, and then explore the solution with the team, rather than dictate his opinion. There was a shift in the next meetings, when the whole board felt they could be part of the decision and their professional expertise had a place in the debate.

Reflections on the two case studies

Both situations had the same element of disrespect, and dismissive behaviour. Both groups were able to find the space to hear and speak. The words were theirs, and the interventions were made within their context, around their specific issues.

The consultant's context

This section shifts focus into the practitioner's perspective. In my experience, there are two levels of intervention. The first is usually a request to support the individual to remain productive, despite any emotional and social confusion during periods of change. The second is at a deeper, less obvious level, where help is needed for the organisation to be both reflective, and remain productive. These moments link to the times when individuals, or family groups seek therapeutic help. However, within an organisational role I am clear that I work in a commercial setting, not a therapeutic community. I am not asked to be a psychoanalyst, a psychologist, or an organisational doctor. I am asked to help in situations that feel uncomfortable, non-productive or untenable. People in industry are less likely to say their team is 'unhealthy or dysfunctional'. People usually come to a consultant with a simply phrased expectation: 'I want to build

a good team'; 'The project has got in a muddle'; 'We have to clarify our objectives'; 'X is not a good team player'. Though there might be deeper, more interpersonal issues, I choose to work with those after the initial request is resolved.
By that time, a level of trust will exist, and only then can more difficult issues be
explored.

These requests from clients raise another question for me about the consultant's task and responsibilities. I wonder how they choose a specific consultant.
Our clients have the luxury of an extraordinary choice of interventions. They
can choose to work with big consultancy firms, who can deploy hundreds of
graduates to work on prestigious contracts, or they can choose a smaller
company who can employ a single professional who works as their main
supplier. The field of choice is now so broad that I notice a new market niche
for helping the buyer to understand the supply side, as a broker of consultancy
interventions. Training agencies are filtering potential suppliers, organising the
recruitment sessions, and taking commission for a successful contract/supplier
agreement.

On the supply side, consultants need to be clear about their rationale for
doing the work. Why are so many consultants engaged from outside organisations, working on the periphery, thought of as mercenaries brought in to fulfil
limited functions? Being external, the relationship to an organisation is
temporary, less intimate, less invested in the survival of the organisation, and
the consultant has to find a role that has personal satisfaction as well as professional results. Their reputation as well as economic drivers make those
temporary relationships work. However, I wonder if the shorter intimacy of
these relationships has a wider resonance in the relationships between
employer and employee. Maybe the words we use to describe this relationship
need to change, from 'contractor' to 'mercenary', from 'client' to 'commission-
ing agent'. How can we describe our work and what we sell? As the employment market changes, so we need to pay attention to the words we work with.

There are also a range of moral and ethical issues that need attention. We
need a benchmark for the style, content and the language of interventions.
What does it feel like to do a piece of work that does not need to be done? The
objective consultant will ask, What role do I have? Do I feel responsible for
some wider perspective and knowledge? How can I translate what I see into a
language that can be understood? An example of these issues is described in the
following story.

Language of leadership

An organisation recognised that it had to lift itself from a slow bureaucratic process-driven system to a snappy, e-culture of fast decisions and speedier results. The management team was inundated with demands for better results, higher productivity, less cost, fewer workers, while maintaining its image of quality and good service. Each team had a series of stretching targets, productivity imperatives, new products, and re-engineered processes. Attempting the struggle to become more efficient combined with the struggle to be an even better manager was stressful. People wanted to do well, be better, solve their problems, and have a happy team. The question was how to encourage people to achieve more, take on more work, and find time to address the interpersonal aspects of the work. What sort of intervention, and what language, would help, rather than overburden a full diary?

A senior manager discovered an intense immersion into leadership training designed and implemented in the USA, where the concept was sold to an organisation. The UK company agreed a budget to import this external West Coast American company to explain about good leadership behaviour. The programme stipulated a four-day residential meeting, for each senior team to establish a complete focus on the workshop. The messages were delivered through simple games, and lengthy conceptual teaching sessions which where encapsulated with simple words:

- Be here now, and focus on the moment.
- If you listen you can build rapport.
- People always act with the best of intentions.
- Use all the capacities of your mind to be more creative.

Some people were genuinely moved by the experience; they heard the words with a freshness and simplicity and were able to change their behaviour. Others were bored and wanted to get back to the 'real' world. I watched these reactions with curiosity, trying to understand why some people could hear and respond to the messages. Why did some words work so well? Why did the concepts get through the shell of defences and make a difference? Why were some people so resistant to hearing and appreciating the good intent?

Reflections on the case study

My own experience of working with those concepts was disorientating and too uncomfortable. I tried to listen without prejudice, with an open mind to the possibility of new learning, which was often diametrically opposed to my own intellectual framework. I came to the hypothesis that any concept that is used for organisational or personal development is simply another translation of some universal truths: respect, standards, growth, diversity, care, and concern. These are the translatable words for the tools of the consultancy trade, and can effect a change in some people. In the end, I have to accept that any intervention in any language is 'good enough' if it is offered at the time, and in the mode, an individual can use. In the current fast-moving commercial environment people seem to value quick and easily digested messages. If the intervention has too much complexity and takes too much time, it may not help that short-term focus. This raises another dilemma for the consultant. If the methods of consulting cannot adapt to the pace and language of the client's world, we may be out of a job.

Models

In order to place some of these concepts in a framework, it may be helpful to look at the spectrum of consultancy work, and then consider a model that might suit the current commercial reality.

Psychodynamic model

The classic model of a one-to-one long-term analysis has generated a range of individual and group methods. The principle is that the unconscious world of the patient holds the nodal point of an initial and catastrophic distress. This set of experiences is held as a construct that disables the patient from acting or relating in a healthy way, with intimates, friends or eventually in the world at large. The work of the therapist and the patient is to bring that unconscious into an undefended conscious exploration, which frees the patient to change their personal construct and ultimately their behaviour.

This work within an individual analytic relationship has hybridised into a number of business settings. The language of the unconscious, through translation, has moved into the conscious language in the world of work.

The following are some examples:

- Employee counselling services that work with the individual to understand and make an effective change, usually at a point of stress or change. Such occasions arise due to redundancies, failing a promotion board, mis-matched job placements, tensions between

the individual and their manager, career advice, or interpersonal
issues that cause stress and poor performance.

- Organisational culture change initiatives that try to address the
  underpinning motivation and behaviour of large groups of people.

- Using supervision for consulting roles to understand the projections
  that manifest as either strong feelings or behaviours.

- Team development programmes that encourage people in teams to
  understand the interpersonal dynamics of the group. The following
  story is an example.

CONFRONTING RACISM

A senior team leader became aware of some oppressive behaviour, which was
reported from inside the team as racism. He was very concerned and wanted to
find a way in which the whole team might think about and set standards that
would eliminate racist language and behaviour. He did not want a lecture or a
heavy-handed political polemic, just a way in which the issues could be raised
and attitudes changed. He made contact with an external consultant who had a
psychotherapeutic and 'group relations' background (Miller 1990). After
weeks of research she put forward a proposal for a complex series of
workshops, where people would meet in small groups, talk, reform in larger
groups, discuss and explore their feelings about race and equality. The principle
for the intervention was sound, and offered a structure in which groups would
form, discuss a task, send representatives into other territories and then reform
across newly differentiated boundaries, and in plenaries. Unfortunately, the
report was written as psycho-social theory and with a socio-technical systemic
vocabulary that the client found impenetrable. The intervention was not used.

The manager asked me to prepare an alternative proposal. As a consultant
with the same theoretical perspective, I could see the value of the original
proposal, which I translated into a more familiar commercial language and
which was therefore more acceptable to the organisation. I changed the
structure slightly, and small groups were asked to read and discuss three case
studies. The first addressed the need for a recently disabled employee to find a
more office-based role. The second outlined an industrial tribunal about equal
pay for work performed by men and women. The third was a dispute about
promotion of an Asian manager with enormous technical expertise but defined
as having 'communication' problems. After each case study, the group discussed
people's prejudice, assumptions and an alternative strategy to settle the issues.

The programme was successfully delivered to different groups of managers who had similar issues in their own teams. They responded with intelligence and sensitivity to the case studies on the programme.

REFLECTIONS ON THE CASE STUDY

It is both valid and illuminating to have a psychoanalytic understanding of complex interpersonal issues. However, the theory may not be easily accessible to managers in organisations who have a different discipline or organisational construct. Using practical everyday examples allowed the issues to be understood and integrated into the workplace.

Commercial model

An alternative perspective, and consequent language shift, is based on work in the commercial world. Profit-based organisations have to be governed by that commercial imperative. The critical issue is competing for market share, and survival is bonded to economic viability. People know that their previous ways of being successful may not be adequate in the new electronically speeded world. The drive is to find new ways of becoming more efficient, at less cost, for greater profit. There are a proliferation of ideas, fashions, and theories, which are seductive as a way of striving for excellence. The business schools, consultancy firms and management theorists are earning a good living through product differentiation. These products are a response to organisations seeking external interventions to make that essential improvement in their company that will help their survival. There is a sense that the next idea or paradigm will be 'The One' to make that essential difference. Organisations try different remedies, sometimes sequentially, sometimes in parallel.

I can now add another layer of complexity: as the organisation grapples with the enormity of the world markets, the cost of products, and the advances in technology, the company feels it has to reconfigure its structures, boundaries and processes. The impetus for change is collated from huge amounts of data, economic analysis, an intuitive sense of the market, and a vision. This vision can be implemented through a variety of mechanisms, re-structuring, shifting boundaries, and fewer people covering more functions. An added difficulty, especially in large organisations, is the complexity of many systems and sub-systems. Each one has its own specific issues and yet each has responsibility to the organisation as a whole. To effect some corporate changes, a variety of different strategies (from inside the organisations, and from external consultants) are deployed in the attempt to be successful. Each strategy is designed with care and good intention. Each new programme has the hope, an ideal, embedded within it, to improve profitability. However, the main obstacle is often the existing culture, which is reinforced by a whole range of entrenched procedures, like the productivity targets, management style and reward systems. It seems an impossible task to shift all the employees' attitudes, with one universal programme. In all this complexity, what language can a consultant find to make a helpful intervention? I argue that the language has to be based in traditional 'organisation-speak', using words that can be recognised by the client. The following contract is an example.

THE POWER OF PRESENTATION

This way of working can be seen in a piece of work I did with a team of seven managers who were employed to run a newly established region. The geographic area included three different sub-regions that had recognisably different cultures. They had a five-year history of being autonomous and distinctive in three UK areas. The team leader needed to find a way of allocating the new territory in a way that matched the geography, and the team's skills. He knew it might mean giving up some old connections, and he did not want to impose a decision on the group. He contracted with me as a consultant to find a methodology that would involve the team. The company already had a portfolio of team-building exercises, review processes, and task allocation techniques, all using the corporate cultural style. He decided they were not useful in this context as they were too familiar, and contained too many references to an older style of management. I suggested a team / individual profile method, that would help in analysing strengths and weaknesses. Other psychometric tools had been used before but as it was a new team, a new map was needed. I decided to use the HBDI process (Herrmann Brain Dominance Instrument). This produces reports from a questionnaire. The individual profiles highlight work preferences, and the underlying personal style. The reports are visual, colourful, easy to understand, and written in a way that engages different learning styles. A team report maps the individuals to a team profile, and both are used to understand the individual and the team.

On this occasion, the team had a short explanation of the theory, and time to look at their own individual reports. The data was easy to understand, non-judgmental, and informal enough to be spontaneously shared with the rest of the team. They quickly identified their different work styles, management skills, and alliances. A collated team profile made the data even more helpful in re-allocating management responsibilities. The team had fun, laughed about their personal traits and preferences and then shared the new geographic territory in a collective decision. The whole process took three hours, and has stayed with the team as a new shared language.

REFLECTIONS ON THE CASE STUDY

As the consultant, I could have used one of the existing management processes. It would have worked, but not had the freshness and vivacity of HBDI. The language of the method was familiar enough to be accessible, but novel in its presentation. It engaged the group, gave them existing information in a new way, and speeded up the collective decision-making.

Process model

Finally, I want to discuss the framework that has shaped my practice. My work as a consultant to organisations has been greatly influenced by the pioneering work at both the Tavistock Institute and the Tavistock Clinic. This integrates a socio-technical systems model with psychoanalytic concepts. *The Unconscious at Work* (Obholzer and Zagier Roberts 1994) relies on both dialogue and reflection as an intervention into the system. In the introduction to the book, James Krantz draws our attention to the

> emphasis on devoting organisational resources to establishing forums that enable staff groups to articulate and understand their emotional experiences. The idea [is] that through working together to understand their experiences [they] can better 'contain' and learn more deeply from them, and in turn foster their own effectiveness. (1994, Foreword, p.XV)

He knows that the emotional experience at work is important, yet that emotional experience is rarely put into words. Unfortunately, it is only partly acceptable to focus on emotional work as an inherent part of the organisation's well-being. The task is to find the words that work for the client's system. Though managers do not use words such as 'in denial, pathological, depressive positions, fragmentation', they are aware that they experience the fall-out of those emotional states. When they do speak of any feelings or mood in the organisation, they talk of 'motivation, morale, job satisfaction, performance indicators and achievements'. These words work because they are understood, and these are the words I use.

MY PROFESSIONAL MODEL

The platform for my work is to influence the systems, procedures, and processes as a way to improve effectiveness. I have argued that working with organisations we need a range of professional theories and concepts. Inevitably, we will choose the construct that gives confidence and authority to our interventions, one that we can offer a client with some experience of its efficacy. I recognise it is not possible for every consultant to have expertise in all the modes. However, we need to reflect on why we offer one specific theory or intervention rather than another. We need to ask ourselves a number of questions to check our practice.

- Are we exclusive or inclusive in our choice of words?

- Do we explore the possibility that our favoured framework is not the best for that piece of work?

- Are the words we use available/helpful to the people we are working with?

- By sharing a language, do we lose power by being familiar, and become too available for being drawn into the client's system?

GUIDELINES

This chapter considered which language we use to join the client's systems, as well as our theoretical frameworks. I will offer the following practice guidelines as a starter for debate.

- Hold an ideal model in mind which might influence systems, procedures and processes.

- Use reflective comments rather than judgemental opinions.

- Use the experience of being on the receiving end of a projection as information for the client.

- Ask questions that may change a perspective or a way of seeing a problem.

- Use professional judgement to find the right place or the right words to make a 'therapeutically' helpful intervention.

- Avoid burdening the client with the weight of theory.

- Aim to build a mature interdependency between client and consultant.

- Take the stance of collaborative enquiry.

- Find a way to offer a nutritional intellectual diet that encourages people towards health, not indigestion.

- Reconnect with the magic of the good interpretation, through the choice of words.

- Invent a consultancy dialect, near enough to the clients' language to be understood, but different enough to create attention.

- Be partly a translator, and partly an interpreter.

If we are judicious in building a shared language, it might limit the unhelpful countertransference when it becomes unclear who is feeling what, and the consultant becomes part of the problem. It might alleviate that feeling of being caught inside an inescapable organisational vortex. In a previous paper (Eden 1994) I have argued that holding the theoretical framework in mind acts as a lifeline in avoiding the seduction of being totally immersed in the world of the clients we are working with.

Summary

As a final thought, the work is simply finding the optimum way of being in dialogue. My main activity in organisations is working with words. It demands a translation of professional 'consulting' concepts to the reality of commercial experience. Having a different perspective about the organisation's behaviour is of no value if others cannot see that view. Therefore the use of words and the translation to the receiving culture is a practice that needs discipline, intuition and empathy. Additionally, in a professional consulting role, the work entails dialogue in many forms. These activities can be in meetings, debate, discussion, research, reports, recommendations, coaching, counselling, and informal conversation. Each category of dialogue has its function in relation to the task and the context of the work.

So, in a perfect way of working, all interventions would be chosen for their fit. However, in the pragmatic world, people find a tool that is available and understood. If we follow that line of thought we realise this puts some onus of choice on the client. They need the help of a consultant at the time of most confusion in chaos. I would argue that it is also a time when judgement is blurred. This puts a professional responsibility on the consultant, who is being paid to be objective. An elegant discussion about objectivity and choice is given in *The Group Context* in which Sheila Thompson (1999) asks the reader to think about a patient who comes to a doctor with a bad leg. The treatment on offer will be dependent on the practitioner's frame of reference. The leg is part of the patient's system so the choice is how and where to intervene into that system: at a physical, social, or emotional level. I am arguing that the objectivity of any practitioner might be improved if we became conversant with a wider range of interventions. We might then be able to offer not only our own expertise but with generosity and wisdom the skill of other practising consultants. This shifts the role from consultant to 'broker', a model that is used in an assessment meeting for the best psychotherapeutic help. This broker role would have access to a wide range of consultancy models and interventions, as well as a network of practitioners. Recommendations could be made with the benefits and limitations of each method. If we followed this way of offering help to our clients the work would benefit by being flexible, as well as multi-lingual.

Finally, I know my task as a consultant is to maintain a professional objectivity. I try to do this by analysing the experiences of the organisation through the filter of both my and their conceptual frameworks. The second task is to find the best language to suit the culture of the organisation or team. After all the last word is with the client.

References

Bion, W. (1975) *Experiences in Groups.* Group Relation Reader 1. A.K. Rice Institute Series.

Eden, A. (1994) 'Resisting the undertow.' In R. Casemore, G. Dyos, A. Eden, K. Kellner and J. McAuley (eds) *What Makes Consultancy Work? Papers for the International Consulting Conference.* London: South Bank Press.

Miller, E.J. (1990) *Experiential Learning in Groups. The Social Engagement of Social Science Vol.1: The Socio-Psychological Perspective.* London: Free Association Books.

Obholzer, A. and Zagier Roberts, V. (eds) (1994) *The Unconscious at Work.* London and New York: Routledge.

Thompson, S. (1999) *The Group Context.* London: Jessica Kingsley Publishers.

CHAPTER 6

A Sociodramatist Goes to Work

Ron Wiener

'What is the purpose of being human and alive without doing new things?'
(John Sulston (2000, p.9), Director of the Sanger Centre, where they deciphered the book of human life)

'For we can do nothing substantial toward changing our course on the planet, a destructive one, without rousing ourselves, individual by individual, and bringing our small imperfect stones to the pile.'
(Walker 1997, p.xxii)

Introduction

My life during this year has, on reflection, three main themes that run through it. The first was the attempt to integrate better some of my varied work roles. At the beginning they all felt somewhat disparate which is reflected in the style of writing in this chapter. The second theme was to determine what value my life had and how I made sense of this through the ageing process. The last was existing as a survivor of childhood abuse and a dysfunctional family upbringing and how this related to my work and sense of worth.

The start

I was walking down Pen-y-ghent, one of the Yorkshire Peaks, on New Years Day at the beginning of the millennium, on a cold but sunny day, feeling that my life as a training consultant was becoming boring. I had come to exist through my work and it was my work roles which largely defined me – but did they any longer have any meaning?

I had a number of work roles – training consultant, organisational psychologist, team facilitator, mentor, sociodramatist and supervisor. Of all of these, the sociodramatist role was the one that gave me a kick, a touch of danger where the boundaries were looser, where the world was less controlled, where anything might happen. Training was OK, sometimes exciting, and it utilised a lot of psychodrama and sociodrama methodology, what is loosely called 'action methods'.

The structure of the chapter is to begin with some background to help interpret some of the year's events. How did I come to be a group worker in the first place? What was it that I was bringing to the groups that I ran? The chapter then goes on to look at some of the different roles that I played in the first six months of the year. These include: trainer, organisational consultant, the small businessman, supervisee, peer group member, mentor/supervisor and sociodramatist. It also includes an account of a workshop that did not work (the one that got way) because it reverberated with me long after the more successful workshops had been filed away.

There is then a diary account of the middle of the year followed by a reflection on why by the end of the year I came to feel much more positive about the world and my place in it.

Background

Career

A first degree in psychology in Sydney was followed by a year in Tasmania working as a vocational guidance officer. There was an irony, at the age of 20, that my first job involved giving advice to young people as to what path their life should take. I then caught the boat to England to see the world before settling down and, as I later realised, to put some physical and emotional distance between my parents and myself. Six months of odd-jobbing and hitchhiking around Europe ran out of steam and I got myself a job at the National Institute of Industrial Psychology. Again it felt like being called to give advice without always having the necessary experience.

I soon realised that I would have a short career with only an Australian pass degree and after much scouting around found myself at the LSE on a Masters/PhD programme where I finished writing a thesis on drug taking (Wiener 1970). I then did some research on conflict resolution before moving to Holland to work at an international foundation concerned with funding compensatory pre-school programmes around the world. It was here while on a trip to Australia that my eyes were opened to racism through work with the aboriginal community. I learnt for example of how white youths used to come raiding aboriginal settlements on weekends to rape the women. I visited an aboriginal camp in the outback to find them living in shanty huts and old cars while listening, on a clear desert night, to an illustrated sermon from the local Christian missionaries on the dangers of being a rich Pharisee and not getting into the Kingdom of Heaven. This job finished when at a conference I had been asked to organise on aboriginal education, which I had found to my disgust had no aborigines invited to it, a situation which I soon rectified, an aboriginal woman got up and said to one of Australia's more eminent experts, 'White man, every time you open your mouth, you tell lies'.

I moved sideways and spent a few months acting as an educational drug advisor for Rotterdam City Council (Wiener 1971) before being invited to help set up an action research unit in Belfast. This led to a frantic three years working primarily as a community planner (Wiener 1978) with a small group of colleagues concerned with the social and political issues facing people on both sides of the sectarian divide. The work involved forming or facilitating and/or advising community groups. This on occasions meant contact with some of the para-military organisations that had an interest in everything that happened on their turf.

It was a time when American group workers came to town to try to broker some understanding between the two sides. Often this would involve taking so-called 'leaders' from the two communities to a retreat for a few days so that they would get some awareness of each other's position that they could take back with them. This work was flawed in two ways. First, there was no political and economic analysis which showed this as being an appropriate strategy at this time and, second, participants were being undermined, and put in possible physical danger, through being perceived to have consorted with the enemy.

After three years there seemed a limit to what an 'outsider' could do and I returned to London to spend six months writing up the work before accepting a job in the adult education department at Leeds University with a brief to develop community education. I had some notion, based on the degree of political involvement in Northern Ireland, that it would be possible to set up a large number of community classes to understand how the city worked, and from this produce some momentum for change owned by those in the community. This proved over-ambitious but a series of the Worker's Educational Association (WEA) classes on the political economy of Leeds (Wiener 1976; Wiener and The Leeds Political Economy Class 1977) proved to be seminal for a number of community activists and led to the establishment of the Leeds Trade Union and Community Resource and Information Centre (TUCRIC).

Money ran out for this work and I got a job lecturing in community work and then community psychology at Bradford University. I realised eventually that this was not for me, that in learning styles I was more of an activist and reflector rather than a theorist. After a long night pondering my future I applied for a job working in a psychiatric day centre. After a long period of struggle over how it should be organised, I ended up as manager of the centre with it being run on the lines of a therapeutic community.

This lasted for five difficult, emotionally exhausting but challenging years and it was important in seeing how a group could empower its members to act on the world and take some control of their lives. In the end I was burnt out and moved back to a part-time job at the adult education department organising classes in the community and started building up a freelance training consultancy. After three years I went full-time and that has been my life for the last dozen years.

Activist history

I was a late starter, probably in part through my upbringing, particularly in attending an Australian private boys school with all its élitist, sexist and racist attitudes and behaviours. I developed: an awareness of racism through the aforementioned trip to Australia, in class terms via the work in Belfast and in an understanding of gender issues via relationships and being in a men's group. My process continued via trade union activity while running the psychiatric day centre, membership of the Labour party and community activism via TUCRIC and local community campaigns.

However, when I became a freelance trainer, while much of my work was concerned with issues of empowerment, I lost touch with my trade union basis and became disillusioned with the Labour party. This was because of its internal strife and the limited role for local party members as election foot soldiers palmed off with the chance to vote on fairly meaningless motions which disappeared into the party ether. It was clear that real power lay with the coterie who advised (shadow) ministers unless you were prepared to devote your whole life to the cause and work your way up though the party echelons.

About five years ago I decided that political action should stem in part from a material base. The two areas that felt relevant to me were my status as a 'survivor' and my increasing desire to get in touch with my Jewish roots. I ended up as an advisor to the Leeds Survivors Project and becoming involved with the Leeds Jewish Welfare Board. The former finished about two years ago and brought an end to 'survivor' playing a central role in my life. The Jewish role continues through membership of a number of committees.

But when at the beginning of the year I looked at my overall political activity I seemed to have lost my active involvement in wider social change. One of the question marks was whether sociodrama would or could provide an avenue for this, or was it enough to be a well-meaning, *Guardian*-reading, somewhat cynical observer of life?

Personal history

I come from a German Jewish refugee family which in the 1930s was scattered to the four quarters of the globe. I was born in England but my family emigrated to Australia when I was seven. Shortly afterwards my parents were divorced and I was sent to boarding school where I became separated from my brother. My experience then is of growing up in a family of distance. On top of this there were two occasions when I was sexually abused, once by a group of older children, once by a 'family friend'.

Later when I was involved as a trainer in running workshops around issues to do with fostering and adoption I came across work around self-esteem. This argued that self-esteem is dependent in part on feeling, when a child, secure, with a sense of belonging and having a family life and being loved and loving (Thoburn 1985). This was a necessary condition to grow and make new and satisfying relationships as an adult, something I was unable to do during my twenties and thirties.

It was with the advent of three years of individual therapy that I began to recreate in my late forties some of the life conditions that I had not had as a child. I stayed in the one house, having previously had something like 36 life moves, was in a long-term loving relationship, had secure and long-standing friendships and had been in a long-standing peer group.

> So this is what they feel like, I thought: roots. Not the ones we're born with, can't help having, but the ones we put down in our chosen soil, the you could say radical selections we make for ourselves. (Rushdie 1999, p.414)

On a sofa, sat in the street outside an up-market, trendy furniture shop, near Central Park in New York, were carved these words: 'Follow your heart, Kiss and hug, Dream, Know love, Cherish family'. However by the age of 58 it felt that this life task as indicated in the above words had been done and there was a

base on which new things could happen. One of these was trying to make
contact with distant cousins whom I barely knew.

Growing up in Australia I lost touch with my Jewish and Germanic roots.
My parents coped with the trauma of their refugee history by becoming
non-religious, though later in life my father reconnected to his Jewish ancestry.
I was sent to a Church of England school and grew up knowing more about
Christianity than Jewish custom. German remained the language my parents
retained so they could speak to each other without their children understanding.

In 1996 I went to an international psychodrama conference in Jerusalem. I
expected to feel at home. In reality I felt an outsider, these were not my people. I
had no common cultural identity. The only time I felt different was when I went
to Yad Vashem, a memorial site for the six million Jews who perished in the
Holocaust, and tried to look up what had happened to my grandparents. I told
my family name to the custodian of the names and he said that it was no good,
there were over 4000 families with that name. Surprisingly, to me, the people I
got on best with at the conference were the German practitioners. Keeping
contact with them became important.

Two other effects of my childhood abuse were a fear of groups and a need
to be in control. The effects of the group abuse lay within me for a long time
and only shifted during the course of an eight-day gestalt/psychodrama
intensive where I could own up within the group to how my abused child was
feeling. (It is interesting in passing to note that when one goes on residentials
there is an assumption that it is OK for strange men to share rooms together
which mirrors the hidden problem of men as victims of abuse.) The need to be
in control is to a large extent reflected in the way I work as a freelance consultant and occasionally throws up problems when there is a need to co-work.

Psychodramatic history

The last strand is my development as a sociodramatist. The main route came via
my interest in different therapies while working at the psychiatric day centre.
This led to going to psychodrama workshops and eventually coming across
Ken Sprague and Holwell which at that time was the only place offering
sociodrama training in the UK. I came to see that sociodrama, especially when
combined with Ken's enthusiastic activism, was a way of working with groups
which dove-tailed well with my interest in individual and social change.

This was combined with an interest in amateur dramatics primarily as a director and playwright but always enjoying the spontaneity of what could be created in the moment.

At the time I got involved with sociodrama, the British Psychodrama Association (BPA) was primarily involved with the clinical uses of psychodrama. At its general meetings I would feel like the poor kid from next door who had been lucky enough to be invited to the rich kid's birthday do. It felt like a long struggle to get psychodrama in its wider sense including action methods and sociodrama accepted as being part of the BPA's mission. I ran an informal sociodrama training course for a number of years where it often felt I was half a step ahead at the best. This slowly crystallised into developing a more formal course and allies started appearing. I became part of the 'establishment' and joined the BPA Executive and Accreditation Committees.

Physicality

There was also an awareness of growing older during the year. There was not quite as much energy as before. My short-term memory started to deteriorate. I would get to the top of the stairs with no idea of why I wanted to be there. There were more of what Goldman (2000, p.46) calls senior moments, 'the total blank that creeps up and grabs you and you cannot remember what it was you had for lunch that day'. I would write numbers down in the wrong order. The wrong words would come out. Once in a session I wanted to say 'speculate' and the word that came out was 'speculum'. I could hear it coming, knew it was not right but could not stop it.

Summary

So this was me at New Year in the year 2000 wanting to know if what I did still made sense.

The first six months – key roles

Trainer

SUMMARY

In the first six months of the year I ran eight two-day training courses and about 30 one-day courses. The employing agencies include: the police, social services, health trusts, emergency planners, youth offending teams and voluntary organisations. The areas of work cover: team building, groupwork skills, diversity training, delivering training designed by others, challenging behaviour, training trainers and organisational review days.

The sessions drew on a number of methods or techniques from psychodrama such as role reversal, sculpting and doubling; from sociodrama such as role and systems analysis; from action methods such as time lines and from sociometry such as finding connections in the group as part of the warm-up process.

The various sub-roles that I played alongside that of trainer included:

- tired traveller – the average journey time to and from venues is about an hour and a half

- furniture remover – one of the first tasks is normally to arrange the room furniture

- group worker – being aware of the group processes which may aid or hinder the learning

- warm-up artiste – warming up self and the group, to the room, the group, the task, the co-worker etc.

- role play director

- negotiator – each training event requires negotiation before and after with the commissioner.

AN EXAMPLE

A two-day workshop on training 16 local authority first-line managers on how to train others in presentation skills.

I start by asking them to form pairs and, in the role of potential trainers, ask how they would set up this room if it was their training session. We move at their suggestion from a semi-circle into a circle.

I then place them in new pairs, still in the role of trainer and ask what they would do next. We follow up their suggestions and do introductions, people de-roling back into being course participants.

However at the end of the introductions we find that people still do not know each other's names so we ponder what purpose doing introductions has. We agree that it is part of the group forming process.

I then ask the group to stand in a straight line (continuum line) with one end being a lot of experience in presenting information in a group and the other end being minimal experience. We talk about this as an action method for determining the amount of knowledge that exists in a group as a way of finding out where to pitch the session.

The group now feels noticeably safer and people start sharing what it is that they want from the two days. I get the group to reflect on where the safety has come from and introduce them to the idea of 'spider-webbing' – making connections in between members to help hold the group together.

We negotiate a group contract to focus the course on the topic of 'customer care'. Just before tea break people form 'reflective pairs' to write up what they have learnt so far. The pairs repeat this at the end of each session both as part of the learning cycle and to create their own course handout.

After teabreak, people in new pairs consider how they would introduce the topic to a group of workers that they might be training. The majority plump for group discussion.

As an alternative I introduce people to the idea of 'sculpting' – using people as physical images to show for example the implicit power dynamic which exists in a provider/customer relationship.

We then move on to consider how to get people to think about customer care. We explore the use of 'role reversal' – getting people to share from their experiences of being a customer and receiving good or bad service. We experiment how this sharing leads into role plays.

Finally before lunch we look at ways of taking feedback from small groups without losing the energy from the exercises.

After lunch, group members in new pairs come up with a warm-up/ice breaker exercise which we do in turn. This both adds to people's trainer's tool boxes as well as warming them up to Day Two when they will be leading the group.

I then demonstrate to the group the advantages, when using role play to do skills training, of starting with examples of 'how not to do it' – it creates energy and a safety baseline.

Then in new pairs we do an exercise around breathing and non-verbal behaviour in making successful presentations during which participants coach each other.

After tea, people in pairs plan a presentation which they present on Day Two with the rest in the role of 'course participants' after which they receive feedback.

DISCUSSION

What value does training such as this have? This course produces positive evaluation forms and some later feedback as to its usefulness. I am asked to run a further set of groupwork skills courses for an authority because the first set were so well received. The challenging behaviour workshops have been renewed for next year. A voluntary organisation invites me back to do a further review. On the other hand some team building work with the youth offending teams is contracted out to some of my students.

It is the piecemeal nature of this work which lies at the heart of some of the dissatisfaction. I do a day with a team here, some creative training with others there but I am unclear as to what happens afterwards. Was what I did effective, did it make any difference? Perhaps what I need to do is to have more follow-ups after three months to see what changes if any flowed from my intervention with the individual or group.

I attempt to do this where possible. Therefore the course 'Training on Groupwork Skills' requires participants to be running a group throughout the course so that they can put the lessons from the training into practice and the course can also be used to provide supervision of what happens.

On other courses I spend time at the end helping participants to plan how they are going to implement the learning from the course and how to overcome the systemic blocks to change that will exist in their organisation. I do not usually know though what happens when they return. Even when I do know what happens, such as with the police work, I am usually not in a position to be able to influence events when the commitment to change flags. I write reports and letters, which sit on desks for a bit and are then filed.

The training which feels best is that where there is an ongoing working relationship with a group or organisation.

The organisational consultant

I have spent three years working with a police force. During this time I have been involved in two large change exercises – the introduction of problem orientated policing and the development of diversity training and policies – as well as working as a developmental consultant to their trainers. It has been fascinating and frustrating at the same time. In both the change exercises there was the same rush of enthusiasm as a group gathered to sweep a new brush through the corridors of power down to the trenches. By the end the tidal wave had petered out and trickled tiredly under the remaining doors, which were at best half ajar.

The police were hierarchically organised and task driven. People moved jobs frequently because of the short career and the need to gain experience if you wanted promotion. Therefore people were rarely in post long enough to see projects through and the only tasks that mattered were those that one was going to be judged on at the end of the year. The tasks themselves changed from year to year, often being driven by the Home Office agenda.

As a 'civvy' I was often viewed with suspicion. Being under fire at the frontline, it was easy for the police to view all outsiders as potential saboteurs. On the other hand there were those who saw the need to join up with the Labour government's partnership strategy if they were not to be marginalised.

Again it felt difficult to gauge what effect, if any, my own contribution had made.

The one that got away
WHY AREN'T I PERFECT?

> There is nothing worse than feeling responsible for your own misfortunes. You suffer, but you feel you deserve to suffer more. You want sympathy, but you feel too guilty to accept it. (Chancellor 2000)

This was a difficult weekend workshop with a co-facilitator debriefing a large group of people who had been dealing with a case of widespread abuse. At the end the group split and we were on the receiving end of a lot of anger. My co-facilitator felt there was too much of my omnipotent self around making it difficult for her to be fully there and for me to hear what was going on. This might stem from my doing so much work on my own or meeting my childhood needs for being in control.

The first day went 'well' – mirroring how well the participants' work had gone at the start – but my co-facilitator was left shattered and I woke the following morning feeling heavy, both of us carrying the transferences from the day before. On the first day we had identified the need for someone to hold the 'objective ego', observer role, but somehow in our weightiness we lost for a bit the ability to communicate about that.

I worry about why this happened. Why was I so keen to be the 'leader' with the co-worker holding the observer role? Plenty of justifications – the work was contracted to me because of previous work I had done in a similar area; I had a clear vision of how it could go etc. Yet in doing this perhaps I contributed to my own downfall – if I was omnipotent to start with it made it very difficult for anyone to be in a position to tell me to think again. The roles needed to have been negotiated and then re-negotiated. Perhaps what I was really looking for was a live supervisor whom I could turn to if needed or who could point out things I was missing, who was entirely outside of the process. It was made more difficult by the fact that on this occasion our different approaches – group analyst and sociodramatist – clashed rather than complemented each other.

I am aware that my way of working is often quite intuitive, finding a way of being with what is happening and allowing the next step to 'appear'. This means that my cognitive warm-up, which could have given me a theoretical overview of what is occuring, which could if necessary anchor me, is sometimes inadequate. For example, if this exercise is going to work what needs to be happening in the group? My approach means occasionally I can get flooded by the weight of projections and transferences, succumb to projective identification and lose the ability to be outside the process – which is what happened on the second morning when we moved into doing some empty chair work which met the needs of some of the group but not some of the others. I/we did not pay sufficient attention to the 'no' voices. Our own process became entangled with all the issues of power, hidden messages, containment, etc. flying largely unspoken around the room. It also reflected the later stages of participant's work with the 'clients' and the fact that in some cases they were still in the process of finishing off their therapeutic sessions. The debriefing hit against some of their need to stay in control while completing the work. This connects with Herb Hahn's chapter on 'Helping the helpers'; the facilitator was being made to suffer as the team itself had been.

FIVE DAYS LATER

I get feedback from the workshop organiser who says people are angry about the empty chair session on the second day – it put them in a space in which they did not want to be. I am left in more confusion – I have a long debriefing phone call with my co-worker. She is hanging on to the more positive things we did – she feels that what happened had to happen. I am more into how I/we got caught on what felt, in the end, like one of those moving stairways at an airport – you are on it and cannot get off until you reach the end. 'The only people who see the whole picture are the ones who step out of the frame' (Rushdie 1999, p.43). I feel guilty about not being able to get off and watch what was happening. From there, with hindsight, I would have negotiated it differently, used action methods to explore other ways of proceeding such as story telling or running a sociodrama.

My co-worker wants us to have some joint supervision about what happened. I suggest our peer group, she says that is too far ahead. She suggests my supervisor – I feel uneasy – unsure about boundaries but probably it is more to do with my need for me to be able to work it out in private with him – I need space to beat myself up in. I feel happier about doing it with a third person with whom neither of us have 'special' ties.

What am I being defensive about? Why did I decide for this workshop that I needed a co-worker? Apart from the obvious reasons of the size of the group and the subject matter, somewhere in my psyche I probably felt that I might need rescuing during the workshop (a telephone contact suggested that I had therefore created the very situation I wanted to avoid) but I think that I did not fully trust my co-worker to be able to do this and that I then structured our relationship to prove some childhood mantra, about women who abandon. Given the subject matter it is not surprising that my childhood themes are wandering unbidden and unnoticed across the stage. My scattered fragments of frightened child had started to dance with the primitive group feelings. No wonder a part of me, fearing this, had fled into omnipotent self, and had not wanted this level to come out in my pre-session supervision. Also, of course my 'abused' child is still there when I hear the feedback and it knows that it deserves to be punished.

So why the fixation on the empty chair? Whom did I need to speak to? What feels more likely is that it was my inner child, freakily engaged by the emotions flying around on Day One, who needed a space to be heard and if it could not be heard directly then it would be heard through the voices of others who came up to speak. Not surprisingly I felt a lot calmer after lunch, more in touch with the process and able to engage constructively with the group.

In terms of roles, I was 'action man'; I wanted my co-worker to be 'wise supervisor' (but never articulated that clearly enough to her or myself) but she moved over to take the role of 'holder of emotions' so we ended up short of a role and a role holder. Craig Brown, the Scottish football coach, has said that 'the easiest team to select is the hindsight eleven'. In fact people in the group tried to take the missing role but this, for the reasons above, was not appreciated at the time.

We are of course in the land of the drama triangle. I expect to be a victim, call in a rescuer and when she does not deliver, risk turning her into my persecutor. During the course of the workshop my child part becomes a victim, but my over-compensating adult part becomes, for the group, a persecutor, and they become angry victims without a rescuer.

TWO DAYS LATER

We have a one-and-a-half-hour, three-way, post-workshop debriefing supervision. It becomes clear that my co-worker took on the necessary role of holder of the group emotions, which I did not want to have while leading the action, so that the role of objective ego got lost.

Also the size of the group meant that ideally we should have set ourselves the task of acknowledging that an emotional debriefing needed to happen to cope with the feelings engendered by the project work but that this might not be the right place to do it and then we should have discussed where and how it should happen.

THREE DAYS LATER

I am reading a Brazilian contribution to the journal (Batten and Wiener 2001) I am co-editing and it just brings home to me how much I had lost contact with my creativity during this abortive workshop. I had heaviness instead of a lightness of being. We could have done a play, used Boal's (a South American social dramatist; see Boal 1995) structures, anything but what we did. However I cannot rerun the clock; life regrettably is not a video with a rewind and erase button.

TWO DAYS LATER

It is time to begin moving on – 'only those who are asleep make no mistakes' (Kamprad, founder of IKEA, 2000).

People who go about seeking to change the world…are often as flawed as anybody else… But it is the awareness of having faults, I think, and the knowledge that this links us to everyone on earth, that opens us to courage and compassion (Walker 1997, p.xxiii)

The small businessman

I am self-employed. Therefore if I want to work four days a week, say, for 40 weeks a year, then most working weeks I also have to find three or four new pieces of work. So where do these come from? In 90 per cent of cases they come via personal recommendation from people who have been on something I have run. Therefore one is always hoping that the existing employer will invite one back and if the course involves people from different agencies, that someone will pass on to a colleague news of one's skills. It therefore means that one has continually to deliver high quality training especially as we know that bad news travels faster and with greater pungency. It also means that any downturn can turn into a spinning spiral – the less work you do, the fewer people see you do it and the fewer people there are to recommend you to others.

One of the best ways of getting new work used to be via creative training courses that I ran at the local university as these used to recruit trainers who were also commissioners of work. However the university changed its accounting system which meant that all courses had not only to cover costs but also to carry a share of the department's overheads which they calculated at about a £1000 per course. This just ruled out small courses such as the ones I had been running.

Other attempts at getting work – sending out prospectuses on spec, writing books (Wiener 1997) and articles, being on the list of the local Training and Education Council (TEC) providers of training – were a dismal failure except perhaps as background noise so that if my name came up in another context it might ring a bell.

One attempt to increase work was to get together with other trainers and form partnerships to target particular audiences. The first attempt, which was to build on the police work around problem solving policing, ended without a single commission. The second attempt with two new trainers started slightly more successfully, but only just. We set ourselves up as BEYOND SURVIVING and advertised a one-day training event 'Working with Abuse' to be held in Birmingham. Participants were given the option of working with all three of us at different parts of the day. We thought that utilising our three networks we should be able to pull in some 40 or 50 punters. Five weeks beforehand we had two applications. The numbers crept slowly upwards and on the day there were 13. One of the trainers had to pull out in the morning with a virus, which meant that we had to revise the programme. The actual day went well, the feedback was good, the hotel was OK as a conference venue and we made a minimal profit. Overall though it felt like hard work for little return.

We tried to work out why it did not recruit. Wrong topic? Wrong venue? Wrong format? Networks not as strong as we thought? Not as much training money around? At a dinner party I was told that abuse is 'old hat' and we should have gone for spirituality.

I read *The Tipping Point* (Gladwell 2000) which talks firstly about the 'Law of the Few' and the importance in spreading information of using 'connectors', people who are at the hubs of many networks; 'mavens' who are knowledge collectors who pass on good finds to the connectors and 'salesmen' who clinch the deal. As a result of this we decided next time to target individuals that we knew rather than nameless job titles in organisations.

Gladwell's second rule is to do with the stickiness factor, what makes people take notice of something and act on it. We redesigned the leaflet and changed the colours we used. The third rule is to do with context and the implication here is to try to sell the course in a group situation so that peer pressure can be brought to bear on people to come. We also changed the format so that this time people have to stay with one trainer throughout the whole day and we lowered the fees for individuals paying for themselves.

The result was a complete disaster – we recruited only four people, lost a packet on printing and cancellation fees and as a result I cancelled another embryonic workshop based on a combined psycho and sociodramatic workshop about eating disorders.

The other aspect of being self-employed is the loneliness and isolation – potential friends are often also competitors and attempts at partnerships, as seen above, are not always successful and do increase the overheads. Handy (2000, p.11) puts this well:

> At work, our loyalty and responsibility is first to ourselves and our future, second to our current group or project and only last – and minimally – to the organisation that is currently paying us…it makes for a lonely world, one in which the neighbourhood is a jungle.

He also claims that it leads to a lack of commitment and responsibility and that without these 'there is no need for morality. Anything goes'. This does not feel true for me in so far as I have a political belief in liberal socialist values, which underpin whatever work I take on and do.

Continual professional development

The different roles involved in my continuing professional development include:

1. SUPERVISEE

I have two peer supervisors. I see one monthly, one bi-monthly. One is a psycho/sociodramatist, the other a consultant well versed in action methods who is also a gestalt therapist. Sessions last between one and one and a half hours.

The latter and I have been meeting for about eight years at a hotel in Derby, which is roughly half-way between our two homes. We have an ongoing relationship with the hotel which is characterised by different T-shirts we have had printed. The first read, 'We do it Dovedale every two months' (Dovedale is the name of the room we normally use). The second, after they had tried to increase the room rental, 'Save the Dovedale 2' (they did not put up the price).

Both supervision sessions use action methods such as sculpting, role reversal and empty chair work.

One supervision session

We look at a workshop I have run for group workers developing their skills. I am asked to take on the role of being 'my wise counsellor' to give feedback to Ron (myself) of what happened. I then take on the role of the 'disrespectful challenger' to try to understand why this group member was giving me such a hard time. We explore the issues of boundaries, especially as regards confidentiality, as one group member has applied to be in a different group I am running. I take on the role of this member and look at what is needed from her viewpoint and then become again my 'wise counsellor' to give advice to Ron on how he should deal with this situation.

Live supervision

A German colleague sits in on two whole-day sessions that I run. In the first, one of the issues for the group is the role of an external observer or supervisor and we model ways of doing this via a fishbowl format.

I co-run a five-day workshop with a more experienced colleague – learning by observation, discussion and feedback.

2. PEER GROUP MEMBER

I am a founder member of a peer group for BPA psychodrama practitioners and trainers. We meet three times a year in different cities in England and Scotland. The group has a possible membership of about 16 interested people but attendances at each session vary from about 8 to 14. This creates problems sometimes in terms of boundaries such as rule keeping. The group has had a number of aims including: training, helping people to the next stage of BPA membership, support, space to try out ideas and opportunities to be a protagonist. It has been an invaluable space for me – to be accepted in a group; to receive recognition as a sociodramatist and support for developing sociodrama within the BPA; to try out different roles; to get succour through difficult times; to make friendships and find possible partners to try out experimental workshops with.

3. BPA CONFERENCE ATTENDEE

This year was a speedy, somewhat chaotic, affair. I arrived at the conference late, missing an executive meeting, because of running a session of the sociodrama training group. I joined in the whole conference welcome and went to a voice workshop (an interesting space as I have always been told that I cannot sing), then into a round of BPA committee meetings until 9.30pm after which I was too exhausted to sleep properly. Going away to large group events always has traumatic undertones for me because it mirrors one of the times I was abused as a child.

I survived the AGM the next morning. This included a debate on whether the name of the organisation should be changed to include the word 'sociodrama'. I had long been an advocate of this as a symbol of the organisation recognising the non-clinical uses of psychodrama. However this year my position had changed. I felt that the organisation had shifted, sociodrama was on its agenda, the diploma course was up and running and that therefore psychodrama was being used in its generic sense to include sociodrama and action methods. I was happy for the name to stay though I recognised that the name change still had significance for people who had supported me in getting sociodrama onto the BPA agenda. The next development for me was to find a space within the organisation for those interested in using action methods and sociodrama in a variety of different situations to come together and find out how the BPA could help them.

Peter Kellerman then ran a large conference workshop following closely the paper (Kellerman 1998) that went with it. I had had enough by then and fled home for a good night's sleep. The next morning I went to a small workshop on eco-psychology where I became a rock on Sydney harbour's foreshore denouncing all human endeavour, a role not particularly helpful for the director in terms of the direction they had wanted the workshop to take.

I then ran an introductory workshop on sociodrama which I had to change at the last minute as my co-presenter was unavoidably called away. I would have rated myself as 'just passed' in terms of my director's performance. I had not for example specified a safe space in the room where people could go to let go of roles, which resulted in a couple of people being left too long in roles. Other things worked better such as an initial exploration of how roles worked.

Then it was straight into the working lunch for the new BPA Executive and then into the car, having to miss the conference closing session, in order to drive to North Devon to attend the post-conference workshop run by Kellerman on working with conflict.

Somewhere in all of this there were lots of conversations with people, making contacts and talking about the diploma course.

Mentor/Supervisor

My one-to-one work consists of mentoring a senior health service manager, two middle level social services managers and the director of a small voluntary organisation. In addition I supervise a trainer. The sessions are every six weeks or so and last for one and a half hours. Again I use a lot of action methods, such as sculpting and using objects, to lay out and explore the systems and the situations in which people find themselves. Role reversal helps mentees to understand the viewpoint of other people in their social atom or network. The work involves coaching and role training to help people deal better with the situations they are confronting.

The sociodramatist

WHAT IS SOCIODRAMATIST?

Sternberg and Garcia (2000, p.4) say that 'sociodrama is a group action method in which participants act out agreed upon social situations spontaneously...to express their thoughts and feelings, solve problems and clarify their values'. For them sociodramas are always about hypothetical situations reflecting group concerns. Moreno (1993, p.59), the godfather of psychodrama, defines sociodrama as 'a deep action method dealing with inter-group relations and collective ideologies'. Sociodrama is generally a large group event exploring common themes from a social learning perspective. It is at the opposite end of a continuum from psychodrama which has one protagonist working in a group situation to deal with largely therapeutic issues.

What makes my work as a sociodramatist different from countless others who do similar work, using a variety of different titles such as 'management consultant', 'change agent', 'training facilitator' and 'organisational consultant', is that nearly all the sessions use action methods such as role playing, doubling, sculpting and role reversal as well as having a clear structure of warm-up, action and sharing.

While some of this emphasis comes from people such as Moreno its history stretches way back. The ancient Chinese philosopher, Lao Tzu, was quoted as saying: 'If you tell me I will listen. If you show me I will see. If you let me experience I will learn.'

THE WAY FORWARD

The aim, this year, was to see if the sociodrama work could give me added value, could make what I did feel politically relevant and meaningful.

It were, he explained, as if life,

Was a pointless boredom

In which work, marriage,

And the occasional hobby

Filled in the gaping hole of nothingness. (Shepherd 1983, p.120)

If sociodrama is involved with analysing, understanding and moving social situations on, then surely there is no shortage of potential clients. Everything from Northern Ireland (where it was reported that what helped George Mitchell make progress was getting each side to understand better the pressure the other was under – a typical case of role reversal) to drug use. Moreno was said at the height of the Cold War to want to run a session for the presidents of America and Russia. He was concerned with sociatry – changing the whole of society. He saw this as a legitimate goal for a therapist.

There were two concerns. The first was: could I find a way to work as a sociodramatist? Espying a need is not the same as getting someone to recognise that a sociodramatist might have something to offer. The second was whether it made any difference.

By August the first draft of this chapter was written; I had run a small workshop on 'using sociodrama when working with abuse'; I was co-running a sociodrama summer school week (with eight participants – we were working from the personal to the social and back again, spending a lot of time looking at workplace issues and giving people tools to work with) and helping to establish the first diploma/certificate course in sociodrama and action methods in this country, which by August was set up and ready to go, depending on how many people wanted to do it. It is interesting that once it was designed I already wanted it to be something different. Talking about it in peer supervision with my co-trainer I realise that what we are after is multi-modal practitioners who are comfortable with action methods, psychodrama, playback, storytelling, music making, art etc. and who can move appropriately from one to the other within one group session. (See Anna Chesner's chapter in this book.)

Also three large-scale events happened during the first six months.

The first of these was a morning drama workshop on the environment with 230 final year school children. I worked initially with a group of a dozen children where we agreed to focus on the impact of the motor car. We decided that a Boal forum theatre was not an appropriate way of working and decided that each of the dozen would act as a director for a group of about 20 young people. We agreed the scenes and the warm-up we would use with the big group. Each group had about 20 minutes to prepare their scene and the scenes were then shown one after the other with my role being master of ceremonies and link person, a bit like a joker (Schutzman 1994, p.147) in Boal's terms.

The second was a review evening for a large Jewish welfare organisation where after a getting-to-know-you warm-up, we had 90 people sitting around in a circle. We sculpted the structure of the organisation in the centre using chairs and then had people speaking to each other from different roles that had been identified in the script. After refreshments there were small group discussions. The letter to all members of the organisation, after the event, from the president of the organisation said:

> Many people have described the event as having a buzz of excitement with people busy networking at all levels, staff having access to Board members and volunteers having access to staff. Some described it as a family *simcha* with the usual amount of '*broigus*', '*kvetches*' and '*kvells*'.

The third large-scale event was an open evening in Sheffield to run a sociodrama on asylum seekers.

> To begin, we draw our chairs into a circle and, after a brief introduction from the Director, say our names, the places we currently live and our place of origin. Some sociometric connections are made overt and then we split into small groups saying what has brought us here. In new groupings, we then share one personal experience of crossing frontiers or moving countries, either for ourselves, family members or people we know.
>
> Back in the larger circle we call out titles for the stories we have told (Denial, Betrayal, A Big Welcome) and name one of the key players in our drama: parents, other family members and, in one case, a brown envelope.

Enactment: Scene One

The Director asks for two volunteers, who he invites to stand in one corner of the stage space. Through interviewing-in-role (e.g. about where the main groups of asylum seekers to this country currently come from) and encouraging the wider group to co-create the roles ('where do these two

come from?'), the central roles of two refugees from Kosovo are established. (Adderley 2001)

This ran on the evening of the last session of the year's sociodrama training
group. It was successful in the sense that people came and said they enjoyed it
and learnt something about themselves, the issue and about sociodrama. It felt
necessary to do something public as part of Moreno's philosophy was about
trying to change society. The question is whether a small workshop like this has
any impact on the asylum seekers' debate. It was in competition with
newspaper articles, television programmes and teach-ins – a group meeting,
often with invited key speakers, to learn about a subject. This raises the
question of how useful one-off events, which are not tied into some structure
which can take forward any outcomes, are. The same thoughts apply to the
school session and the work with the Jewish organisation where a year on there
is still talk of restructuring and little seems to have changed.

On the other hand:

> All my reporting life, I have thrown small pebbles into a very large pond,
> and have no way of knowing whether any pebble caused the slightest
> ripple. I don't need to worry about that. My responsibility was the effort. I
> belong to a global fellowship, men and women, concerned with the
> welfare of the planet and its least protected inhabitants. (Gellhorn 2000)

The middle months – a bridging section

21 June

Evening meeting wearing BPA executive hat to discuss European money applications with these brokers we have found. Decide to revise an existing bid for
role training and then we get talking about other applications for European
money. Suddenly it becomes clear that we might be able to get money to fund
some of the action methods work that we have being doing. However what
grabs and keeps me awake is the idea of doing some community theatre –
there's a buzz I haven't felt for some time. I think of possible partners, such as
the local Councils of Voluntary Service. I'm engaged by the immediacy, of
creating something, there's an awareness of the piecemeal nature of much of my
existence, of coming in and out and rarely being around to see the end product
of my work. Memories of other bits of community theatre I have been engaged
in come flooding back – a day in Birmingham using forum theatre with a group
of people and then putting on a show with audience participation for a crowd
of 90 plus in the evening looking at housing and environmental issues.

23 June

Birthday blues – 58 and it's passing me by. A not so successful workshop has shaken my confidence; I phone up about the community theatre and am told there is already a drama company in the area doing exactly this. The person I speak to has used my services a lot in the past but now it's 'we're doing very well without you thank you'.

The phone doesn't ring with new work offers. I go to see the accountant who informs me that my income was down last year by a third and asks why that might be. I immediately feel inadequate and flounder around for a rationale, though there is a bonus of a tax rebate, which is a nice birthday present. The accountant offers to pass my name around her contacts. My partner's career is spreading tentacles in many directions which is great and we're off tonight to celebrate, but leaves me feeling stagnant. Discuss this with my neighbour who comments 'behind every cloud is a silver lining'. A gardener down the street says 'we have to keep on going' – I'm tempted to ask why but don't. Have resorted to reading my horoscope which says basically the same thing. My glass however remains half empty.

29 June

Phone call from ex-mentee who was a senior social services manager who phoned to say how much I had helped her – nice warm glow.

1 July

Dinner with a German colleague, same age, similar work structure – but he is angst free, comfortable with his family, his income, his sense of himself as a good therapist – no questions of whether this is enough. For him it is. Perhaps the phone not ringing is in itself a communication to slow down, enjoy the work you do, stop worrying about the future, be with the moment more. He was saying a life strategy for survivors is the need to make a positive mark on the world. An old therapist said – how many certificates do you need on your wall before you accept your competence? Perhaps it's the same with the marks – if I need to keep making them, there will never be enough.

19 July

More at ease with the world – or as it says on my kitchen wall – flow, go with it – and as soon as one stops hunting, the quarry appears – new work offers, a possible invitation to help lead a multi-media event for 250 community representatives.

Reflection

It is October – I am in a train in Germany, travelling to Heidelberg, and I am aware that much of the New Year's angst has dissipated. It is a feeling that stays with me right through until the end of the year. There are a number of reasons for this.

The sociodramatist

I have grown into my role as a sociodramatist. It is somewhere I feel comfortable. I have overcome the hesitancy that came from being the first sociodrama graduate in the UK. I arrived, newly capped, aware that I had not followed any comprehensive recognised training course. Therefore when I was given practitioner status I was unsure whether I was worthy of the title. I had no peers to compare myself to. My trainer said 'all graduation means is that you are on the first rung of your ladder of learning'. This uncertainty was compounded the following year when I came back from a New Zealand psychodrama workshop feeling very deskilled.

This all changed during this year. I had a peer in Francis Batten, a senior trainer from Australia who came to live in England. During the year we became co-supervisors, joint trainers of the first formally recognised sociodrama training course in the UK and joint editors of a special edition of the BPA journal on sociodrama and action methods (Batten and Wiener 2001). There was a gradual sniffing around as we sounded each other out and decided that we quite liked working together. This came to fruition in a sociodrama summer school we ran together.

I am on this train because I have just finished 'running' (an inappropriate word in one sense as it implies a facilitator working at full speed struggling to keep up with a group) a weekend sociodrama workshop for the trainers at a German psychodrama institute. In exploring their future they have had to build a boat out of objects in the room and work out who was the captain, who the crew, whether they needed a map or even whether they needed to know where they were going. It has gone well, especially as we finish working mainly in German, which I do not speak, and I have to sense what is going on in the group. This workshop feels like another validation of my role as a sociodramatist.

Throughout the year, sociodrama and action methods have continued to make themselves a home within the BPA. There is now a suffcent mass of people that it does not feel that I personally am needed to ensure its survival. I have helped to run a day for BPA members who are interested in this way of working and now there are others ready to take on the mantle.

Editing the journal brings me into contact with an international group of peers and this gives me an awareness of the richness of the Morenian method and how narrow its interpretation has been in England.

Now my sense of being a skilled trainer is matched by my feeling of being a competent sociodramatist.

The trainer

My life as a trainer seems to have become more varied. Over the last three months, in addition to the bread and butter training sessions, I have run: a management development course using action methods for senior managers and directors of a hospital trust; a creative visioning day for 150 'movers and shakers' of a northern town; with a psychodramatist, a day on 'mid-life: crisis or opportunity' for the British Association of Group Psychotherapists; a two-day creative training event for family placement officers and an event helping to close down a children's project team.

The work also seems to be more creative, for example using film/song titles ('Hard Day's Night', 'I Can See Clearly Now') as a way of taking feedback on a basic groupwork skills course. In another course on reviewing discharge policy for a hospital we map out and explore the system using sculpting and role play.

The work also seems to have become more effective. I am asked to run a series of workshops for a children and adolescents mental health team on the recommendation of a similar team I worked for in the previous year. These new workshops go well – sculpting the team as a family and using this metaphor through a number of sessions to help the team both understand and work through some of the issues they are confronting.

Also the police trainers ask me to run an ongoing series of workshops incorporating group supervision and the development of their training skills. I am working here on an ongoing basis with those who are committed to change within the police rather than confronting the reactionary tendencies. I am asked back to a police team with whom I have not worked for a year – this time it is possible to see a change with a lot of the bubbling anger absent (due as much to a change of personnel as to any influence I might have had). Before this workshop I have a dream which clearly carries my anxieties about the day but unfortunately it is not a safe enough team to explore the significance of dreams (see Chapter 3).

I am also invited back to work with another team of trainers involved in child protection. This has become an annual affair, a celebration of their success as well as a skills development day. We finish with a sharing of both individual and team New Year resolutions. It is a pleasant change to work with a high performing team and a feeling of privilege to share a day with them.

The organisational consultant

I have for the past 18 months been working with a small voluntary organisation. I started running a series of 'developing skills in groupwork' sessions. When these finished I ended up running six weekly team support sessions for the workers exploring in detail the need for their roles to change as the organisation grew and developed. These were well received. One group member wrote in a letter:

> the sessions have been extremely useful in developing relationships and a sense of belonging to the organisation… Ron expertly guided us to look at our organisation, the past, where it is now and where it is going in the future… I felt it was a relaxed and safe place to be where we could discuss our roles openly.

In addition I facilitated awaydays for core team members as well as appraisal sessions. This successful ongoing work with one organisation helped to give a continuity to part of my working life, which was lacking in the one-off training sessions.

The wise reflective friend

I have grown to value this role over the last few months. It is as if there is an accumulated wisdom to impart which is just as valuable as being on the 'front line'. This became clearer to me when I was challenged in the peer group that I had become uni-dimensional because this was the role this person always saw me in. On reflection I decided that I valued this role and it was a relief to have less of the 'wounded child', the 'would-be escapee' and other similar roles that I had carried with me from group to group.

As this role developed I felt less competitive with my trainees in looking for work and I gained an acceptance that this role would involve a slightly slower pace of work and a possible reduction in income.

One way this role has grown is through my work as a mentor to professionals in the health, social services and voluntary sectors as well as business people. This work has been very varied touching on areas of: race, sexual orientation, harassment and the meaning of 'success'. A further expansion of this role has been through the roles of: trainer, supervisor and tutor to certificate and diploma students on the sociodrama and action methods course. I have felt less isolated when some of them come to help on training workshops.

Of course there is not that much difference between being a 'wise reflective friend' and being 'an opinionated boring old fart' offering platitudes about the 'good old days'!

The family

As was mentioned earlier I grew up in a family of distance. During the year I conceived the idea that for my sixtieth birthday I would see if I could get all my cousins and their families together. This involved making contact, going on visits in England and to Holland and beginning to realise that this family was another home, another place in which I existed, had roots and shared common experiences.

Conclusion

The interesting work looks like it will continue into the new year. One of the apparently defunct training arrangements has burst into life with organising a partnership workshop on behalf of the police for 170 delegates. I am also mentoring staff who are planning a workshop to be facilitated by young people in care for professionals who work with them. I am involved in designing a post-conference workshop for the BPA on working with diversity where I will run a workshop. I am also engaged in a series of workshops to help users and carers make better use of partnership groups.

The year feels like a journey from isolation to acceptance, from not knowing to having a place, from losing roles to gaining roles. In the wider context it is been a journey from troubled adolescence to wanting to change society and finding a groupwork method and style which meets this desire. The activist role is now being complemented by that of the wise old friend helping individuals and organisations to travel down their road and using action methods as a way of getting there.

It has also been a journey away from the isolated warrior to becoming a member of groups including my extended family, the Jewish community, the psychodrama circle, German friends and my own immediate family. Having a series of worlds in which I am accepted makes it easier to accept who I have become. This has weaved together some of the broken strands of childhood.

References

Adderley, D. (2001) 'Asylum seekers.' *Tele*, BPA, February, pp.5–8.

Batten, F. and Wiener, R. (eds.) (2001) *The British Journal of Psychodrama and Sociodrama 16*, 1.

Boal, A. (1995) *The Rainbow of Desire*. London: Routledge.

Brown, C. (2000) *Radio Interview*, 24 June, Radio 5.

Chancellor, A. (2000) *Weekend Guardian*, 24 June.

Gellhorn, G. (2000) Reported in *The Guardian, G2*, 26 May.

Gladwell, M. (2000) *The Tipping Point*. London: Little, Brown & Co.

Goldman, W. (2000) *Which Lie Did I Tell*. London: Bloomsbury.

Handy, C. (2000) *The Guardian, G2*, 20 December.

Kamprad (2000) Reported in *The Guardian, G2*, 26 June.

Kellerman, P. (1998) 'Sociodrama.' *Group Analysis 31*, 179–195.

Moreno, J.L. (1993) *Who Shall Survive?* McLean USA: ASGPP.

Rushdie, S. (1999) *The Ground Beneath her Feet*. London: QPD.

Schutzman, M. (1994) 'Brechtian shamanism.' In M. Schutzman and J. Cohen-Cruz (eds) *Playing Boal*. London: Routledge.

Shepherd, B. (1983) *'Dave' The Barefoot Therapist*. Preston: Community Press.

Sternberg, P. and Garcia, A. (2000) *Sociodrama:Who's in Your Shoes?* Westport USA: Praeger. Second edition.

Sulston, J. (2000) Reported in *The Guardian, G2*, 26 June.

Thoburn, J. (1985) From a paper read to the 'Planning into practice: social work with children and families' BAAF conference, Derbyshire.

Walker, A. (1997) *Anything we Love can be Saved*. London: Womens Press.

Wiener, R. (1970) *Drugs and Schoolchildren*. London: Longmans.

Wiener, R. (1971) 'A report on a drug education programme.' *Journal of Drug Education 4*, 305–315.

Wiener, R. (1976) *The Economic Base of Leeds*. Leeds: WEA.

Wiener, R. and The Leeds Political Economy Class (1977) *The Social Base of Leeds*. Leeds: WEA.

Wiener, R. (1978) *The Rape and Plunder of the Shankill*. Belfast: Farset Press.

Wiener, R. (1997) *Creative Training*. London: Jessica Kingsley Publishers.

CHAPTER 7

Group Merging and Splitting
The Case of Europe and the Quest for Identity

Antonio L.S. Fazio

Introduction

What has drawn me to this topic can easily be traced back to some autobiographical elements. I was born in Sicily, right on the edge of the southern border of Europe, to a Sicilian father and a half-German mother. I spent several years at university on the other side of Italy, on its northern border with Austria, right in the middle of Europe. I have since lived a large part of my life on yet another border (and another island), on the northern flank of Europe, in the UK. The UK might not only be regarded geographically as beyond the so-called Continent of Europe, but also for many other historical and cultural reasons has always felt quite proud of its being so. As the joke goes, when the Channel is foggy, the Continent gets isolated…!

I could in this context argue that I am 'European' enough to respond to some stimuli that have appeared on this part of the world scene so intensely in the last few decades.

Questions might legitimately be raised as to why reflecting and writing about Europe should be included in this book at all, and as to what creative novelty and relevant connections can be found between all the vicissitudes Europe has been going through, and the daily work of the clinician.

The point I will be trying to make is that the changes that have taken place in our post-modern era in the world political climate, as well as within Europe itself, have dramatically modified the perception of the old Continent in many people's unconscious and collective imagination. The area I would like to explore is how such changes may be linked with equally great changes in the sense of identity of a vast number of individuals, including the clinicians and their patients, as well as national groups.

We are now witnessing in Europe a very new situation whose importance cannot be over-emphasised. Some of the western European countries that had been fighting against one another for centuries are now trying to overcome their historical differences and their conflicting interests and rivalries. Through the formation of the European Union (EU) they are striving in an unprecedented manner to reach out for a common goal and aim, instead of being at war with one another. We seem to be confronted with a very exciting and interesting new phenomenon. Its consequences in psychological, political and social terms are bound to be long-lasting and far-reaching, and to have a very considerable impact on all the people involved.

These dynamics seem therefore to deserve the full attention of the group psychotherapist and the psychoanalyst, as much as that of the politician and the social scientist.

The pros and cons of psychodynamics when related to political life

The flourishing literature which is available today on this topic has examined the problem of Europe from various perspectives, but mostly focused on the historical-political and socio-economical approaches. Lately, however, there have been a growing number of psychoanalysts and group analysts who have published works on socio-political themes and issues, where they have applied models borrowed from their clinical practice and experience.

Talking about the widening range of interests of psychoanalytically minded clinicians, Rangell describes how psychoanalysis has been used to describe 'art, psychobiography, psychohistory, war, cultural events, social mores and psycho-political phenomena', stating that 'the wide political or socio-cultural world becomes a subject of the analysis…when it is sufficiently pathological to attract analytic thinking on its own account' (Rangell 1996). Alford, supporting the view of the usefulness of clinical experience of small groups to throw light on the functioning of large human institutions, has emphasised how 'it makes sound conceptual sense to apply the experience of the small group to large group-like entities, as I shall call them, like nation-states'. He continues by saying that small groups 'are enough like texts that it makes sense to read one in order to better read the other' (Alford 1994). In a similar way, but extending the concept further to include individual mental functioning, Volkan has underlined how politics 'cannot be understood except in terms of groups', adding however that 'groups' psychological processes reflect certain operations and functions of the individual mind' (Volkan 1994).

Applying our professional models to fields other than the clinical one is not without risk, however. Rafael Moses has warned us about the dangers of using such a methodology 'applying and transferring to large groups and society as a whole, the knowledge we have acquired from…dyadic treatment…[and] small therapeutic groups' (Moses 1995). He has pointed out how important it is to be aware of and alert to the possible 'rescue fantasies' that whoever engages in this task may be subject to. There may be the wish to be able to provide a valid-for-all interpretive key, without giving the necessary attention to the full complexity of the political phenomenon. This could escape the clinician's understanding and go far beyond his clinical capacities.

Moreover, in this peculiar observational setting there are other important differences as compared with actual clinical practice, such as the impossibility of making use of a therapeutic alliance with the object of our observations, and the lack of a transference relationship. The tool that is still available to us and that could function in a compensatory way, however, might be our own 'societal countertransference', that is our reactions to and feelings about all the things which occur around us. In this sense, he advocates the role of the analyst as participant observer of the same environment of which he is part.

I am therefore bearing in mind all the risks of venturing as a clinician into a field that is not my own, and I do not claim to be particularly knowledgeable about politics, or, at least, not any more so than any other citizens who are exposed to the events that occur around them, and who are affected by them, whether they like it or not. Having said all that, I would still like to take such a risk and share a few thoughts in this paper, trying to integrate some sociological observations and some reflections arising out of my clinical experience as a psychoanalyst, working with individuals and groups, both here and in Italy. In attempting to do this, I will draw from my personal experience, very much according to what Moses has said concerning the role of the analyst as participant observer. I shall be looking at some of the major political changes that have occurred in the second half of the twentieth century in Europe, in a very broad way, and from a psychodynamic and group analytic perspective. For the reasons outlined above my focus will be the UK and Italy.

The origins of 'Europa'

'Europa' in Greek mythology was a very attractive nymph, the daughter of Sidone's king. She caught the attention of Zeus, who transformed himself into a seductive white bull in order to get closer to her and take her away with him. From that liaison several children were born.

The tale is reminiscent of the theme of Beauty and the Beast, where there seems to be a sort of combined parental image, made up of strength and power jointed with grace and beauty, as well as fertility. The bull has often been used throughout history as a mythological symbol to represent sexual power and strength. Its whiteness may add another dimension to it, making it lighter and more peaceful. These two different aspects may well represent how this part of the world was probably perceived in those ancient times.

The name 'Europa' may be a composite of the word 'Euro', from the Greek verb 'eurisco' meaning 'to find', and 'ope' meaning 'where'. It seems to refer to the idea of a newly found place, a sort of internal 'mainland' which was quite different from what was better known to the southern Mediterranean world of that time, then limited to Asia and Libya, and with very different climatic and morphologic features (*Encylopedia Britannica* 1978, p.1033). The very high mountains, the rivers, and the very cold temperatures of Europe might all have been associated by the Greeks with powerful and strong male elements. Presumably the newness of this world helped make it exotic and attractive to them.

The present position of Europe in the world scene: a parent's revolution against its offspring?

While Europe may have become interesting to the ancient population of the Mediterranean world because of its being different, nowadays there may be various other reasons, conscious and unconscious, that contribute to keeping it such a lively and charged topic, capable of mobilising intense and widespread feelings and emotions, in so many people's minds and perceptions.

Undoubtedly, to many people all around the world Europe cannot but represent some kind of parental figure. Many new countries and cultures, from the Americas, Canada and South Africa, to Australia and New Zealand, sprang from European roots. The situation that has ensued has been that the overseas offspring that Europe produced have grown up very quickly and far too well. In little more than two hundred years, the USA has become one of the leading countries in the world. It can be said that the 'children' have done even 'better' than the European 'parents' they originated from. The latter have been left behind, mostly to carry on fighting with and against one another, much like a very destructive and enraged old parental couple.

It would seem that the European parents have realised only lately, and for the first time in a very long history, that while they were so preoccupied only with their self-destructiveness, their children were handling their own affairs much better than them, and that perhaps it was time for the parents to stop this nonsense and get together again. Having decided to do so, there may be a component of rivalry and competitive envy of the 'parents' against the 'children', envy of their success, power and wealth.

Some have underlined how one of the reasons for the establishment of the EU was protection from and reaction against Anglo-Saxon values (Connolly 1995).

At least some of the leading members of the EU such as France, for instance, never made a secret of their wish for independence from the transatlantic super-power. General De Gaulle not only kept his country outside NATO, but also delayed for a long time the admission of the UK into the EU. I will mention below a similar underlying rivalry towards Europe felt by the USA, which may be the other side of the same coin. We see this nowadays in the constant checking of and comparison between the state of the euro and the dollar, and speculation as to which one is eventually going to be the best.

In this sense then we could say that there seems to have been a consistent shift of tension from the old European parental couple to the transatlantic intergenerational level.

The tensions within Europe: pro-Europeans and Euro-sceptics

Talking about Europe in the media has become an almost daily occurrence. There is a daily update about European issues in most newspapers. This has produced another arena where people can easily identify themselves in quite distinct bipolar terms, as pro or anti-Europeans, according to their own stand-point and personal perspective.

Within this international debate Italy and the UK could perhaps be taken, in broad terms, as representatives of these two groups of countries and the two different schools of thought.

Whereas some people talk quite openly about the not-so-secret agenda of aiming to move gradually towards the ultimate goal of an actual political union between the EU member states, others seem to feel absolutely terrified of such a possibility, with all the consequent implications in terms of potential loss of national autonomy and self-rule.

The ambivalent attitude to the EU in the UK

In order to understand more clearly the uncertain position that the UK seems to occupy within the EU and to identify some of its unconscious components, I will consider first its special relationship with the USA and the radical changes the country has had to endure in its international role in the last century through the loss of the British Empire. I will then try to suggest how some of the rituals and myths of everyday life and popular tradition, such as 'Guy Fawkes' night and Remembrance Sunday and even hooliganism, may have something to do with and be expressive of people's underlying phantasies and mental attitudes related to our theme.

There has always been some degree of ambivalence in the way the UK has dealt with the issue of joining the EU. The decision to stay out of the European Monetary Union (EMU) and the euro is only the most recent evidence of it.

Tony Blair has underlined such mixed feelings several times in his somewhat ambiguous messages, stating on the one hand that the problem of the UK joining the monetary union is a matter of *when* rather than *if,* but at the same time emphasising the idea of the special position and role that this country could play in relation to the USA, as a go-between, an intermediary between Europe and the continent with which the UK has always had so many historical links. The two things may be related in so far as they may both express the unusual position of the UK, suspended on the dividing line between the two continents, and with ambivalent relationships with both worlds.

The relationship between the UK and the USA is deeply complicated, and may perhaps be as ambivalent as the UK's relationship with the other European countries. We must remember, as has been said above, that the UK is historically and culturally the country which fathered its American offspring and raised them, only to be rebelled and fought against, betrayed and rejected by them. This is very much a kind of Oedipal history.

As far as the UK is concerned, it cannot stop hanging on to the memory of what the country once was. Whereas American children may still feel attached to the former parent, representing symbolically their original roots, they no longer need a parent UK to help them find their place in the world. They have already come of age a long time ago, since their declaration of independence. It is rather the ageing parent country that is reluctant to let its offspring go and is itself needing help and support in dealing with its own identity crisis.

It could perhaps be argued that the ambivalence the UK is experiencing about fully embarking on this new adventure with its new European partners can be attributed in large part to the fact that it has not yet fully come to terms with the huge transformations it has gone through, and with the changes that have so significantly affected its international role in the second half of the twentieth century. I am referring to the loss of the British Empire, and to the prestige and power that were associated with it.

There is a remarkable discrepancy between the magnitude of this change and the relative silence that has surrounded it. I wonder whether this is because it is such a delicate, sensitive and painful topic that it simply cannot be talked about and tolerated. This taboo might indeed have become a sort of collective defence. I suppose this loss may have come to constitute a sort of narcissistic wound for the British people, and much more of a blow to the British national identity than may have been acknowledged so far.

Moses-Hushovski has described what can happen when people's experience of 'shame' produces, as a reactive consequence, a mental rigidity aimed at correcting those events which they feel are responsible for their suffering. She introduces the term 'deployment' and defines it as a 'rigid self-programming into a system of attitudes, roles, positions and behaviour aimed at protecting the person's self esteem and dignity' (Moses-Hushovski 1996). Her idea seems to refer to a kind of defensive ideological attitude, which has lost contact with the present-day reality and stems from old and past humiliating experiences. To protect themselves from the feelings of shame and defeat, people may end up offending in turn and putting shame on others as a defensive measure.

It is my contention that there is something of this kind of defensiveness in the attitude of some sections of the British people who fight so fiercely against the idea of the EU, the euro or even the new metric measurement system. Volkan (1994, 1996), a psychoanalyst who has applied psychoanalytical concepts and ideas in very creative and interesting ways to relationships within and between nations and large groups, has written a lot on this topic. I think some of his theories can help us to understand better what may have been happening in this country in recent years.

He introduces the term 'chosen trauma' which he defines as 'that historical event that makes a large group feel helpless and victimized by another large group, and share a humiliating injury'. He adds that such an event 'marks their ethnic identity'. He also states that when such an event (or series of events and circumstances, as in this case) is highly emotionally charged, it can become a serious threat to one's own ethnic identity and induce an unbearable anxiety.

Volkan's model refers to historical facts which have been 'chosen' and 'elected' to represent and symbolise a particular situation which has caused a lot of suffering and pain to the people who have lived through it. It seems to me that the UK has not chosen a symbolic event that has been charged with the feelings of and can therefore mark the loss of the Empire. Usually there is the memory of a lost battle, of a particular leader who is chosen as a mythical figure, or a specific event which has been taken to sum up a complex set of circumstances, but in this case there is no such thing. It is as if we were in the presence of a dead body, of a corpse, but with no funeral. This might contribute to making things even more difficult to work through.

The 'chosen' elements in this case may instead be what Volkan calls the 'chosen glories', that is those events whose celebrations become very important as reactions to the traumatic event, as they are trying to deny it, reinforce the people's self-worth, and reassure their shaken identity: events such as the 'Battle of Britain' during the last war, for instance, or those repeated movies that recreate the atmosphere and the splendours of the Victorian era, or the mockery and defeat of the German Nazis. A symbolic ritual celebration which may fit in with Volkan's 'chosen glories' theory is 'Guy Fawkes' night. It is interesting to underline that in this case it deals with the celebration of an event that *did not* take place (the blowing up of Parliament), and which the establishment had managed to avoid, rather than with an event that actually occurred.

It seems more important here to choose and celebrate a *non-event*, in the sense of something that did not happen and therefore did not impinge upon the maintaining and safeguarding of the country's usual regime, than to celebrate an event that *did happen* and that might have been associated with changes and modifications, even though of a positive and constructive nature. The avoided danger and the preservation of the status quo are more important in the collective unconscious than a conquered and mastered new challenge. This could perhaps throw light on the UK's tendency to stick to its traditions, stressing and underlining its need for stability and sameness as its most worthy shared value. Change and novelty, however good and profitable, would probably not create such huge enthusiasm, nor any great occasion for celebration. In this sense, the novelty of joining the EU could not be seen as positive.

The celebration of Remembrance Sunday is another very important ritual in the nation's life that may contain a mixture of 'chosen traumas' as well as 'chosen glories'. It deals with two war victories of the country, which are remembered with pride, but at the same time it contains sorrow for the loss and sacrifice of those who died fighting for their country.

I wonder why only the two world wars, compared with all the other wars that the UK has gone through in the past, have become so emotionally charged and important for the whole nation as to require such a widely shared and deeply felt commemoration. Of course they had some devastating effects which were previously unheard of, but the very large number of soldiers that were killed or wounded in itself may not be enough to explain it. Probably one of the things that makes them different from the previous wars has to do with the fact that World War I was the first war to have been fought by the 'ordinary people' and not only by a professional army, thereby making it much more 'shared' and a group national event.

Another possibility, as far as World War II is concerned, is that with the end of it there might have been the feeling that a real change of era was taking place, and that from then on nothing would ever be the same again, including the Empire and the UK's leading position internationally. One of the things which did change, for instance, as many observers have noticed, was the substantial shift in the attitude of the citizens towards the state that followed World War II. Whereas up to then they had been prepared to sacrifice their own lives for it, after the war the individual's needs seemed to prevail over the state's. These were the years of the welfare state, of the NHS and of more extensive education for all.

In order to describe the turbulent feelings of a large group when confronted with threatening circumstances, Volkan uses the analogy of a big canvas tent, made from a double layer of cloth. The smaller layer fits the individual 'snugly' whereas the larger of these layers protects collectively the individuals contained in the tent, like a mother. When external pressures occur, it is as if the tent is shaken under a storm, needing extra care to make it stronger to endure the adverse elements. It is then that, according to Volkan's metaphor, individuals try to react collectively against the new danger by building up stronger patches on the tent's fabric. In other words, during difficult times of crisis they will need to find in their history, tradition and culture, something strong and self-reassuring enough that can be used to counteract the new threat to their self-esteem. Good parts of themselves need to be found and externalised, in order to make the ethnic tent stronger once more. This is the process of the formation of the 'chosen glories', which are then transformed into myths and rituals. These reassuring symbols become as important to those belonging to the community, as the pole which holds the tent. At the same time, the unacceptable and bad parts of themselves are projected onto the canvas of the 'enemy's tent', and this is also how enemies begin to be established and differentiated from friends. 'What makes the large group identity whole is the intertwining of chosen traumas and chosen glories into the fabric of the tent's canvas...the group draws the mental representation of a traumatic event into its very identity' (Volkan 1994).

These words may be revealing if we try to apply them to the present-day UK. The shaken tent may very well be compared to the shaken identity of a country whose former glory has been rapidly and drastically shrinking, and the projection of the bad parts of oneself onto the enemy group's tent may be compared to all the criticisms that are being thrown at the EU. If we wished to add a bit more to Volkan's image of the large tent, looking at it with some sense of humour, we could perhaps argue that the British people may be thinking of the European Super Tent as a sort of Millennium Dome Tent, that they would have liked to have been very grandiose but that has resulted instead in a big flop.

If we think how in the past centuries the UK had such a central and dominant position in so many parts of the world, extending its Empire or influence to all the five continents, spreading its language and culture to a greater or lesser degree, virtually everywhere, it becomes easier to appreciate how threatening and humiliating it may feel having to give up even a small part of its decisional powers to another political authority.

If it is true that such a colonialist and imperialistic element is still split off and repressed in the collective unconscious phantasy of the British people, we can perhaps understand a bit better the socio-psychopathological phenomenon of hooliganism, which has arisen in the last few decades and has become a very well-known and embarrassing topic of discussion in the popular press. It could be argued that the violence sports fans display overseas represents the acting out of split-off feelings of dominance, powerfulness and superiority over those countries that have been projectively identified in the less cultured strata of the population. There is such a contrast between the blind rage and violence expressed by those few on the one hand, and the values of respectful fair play, reasonableness, understanding and compromise that one can experience in everyday life in Britain on the other, that one can make sense of this contrast by hypothesising a huge projective splitting that produces this extreme bipolarity. Citizens are either very good, perhaps too good to be true, or extremely destructive, arrogant and very aggressive. These may be some of the underlying feelings that impinge on the relationships with the new sibling countries that belong to the same European family, and its parliament.

The basic question that can be raised out of all this is then whether the UK has been able to mourn enough what it has lost, before moving forward to adapt itself to the changed circumstances of new times and new opportunities.

The Italian over-idealisation of the EU

The attitude of Italy towards the EU could not have been more different than the one referred to above, adopted by the British. Italy has always been a very keen supporter of the EU since its very beginning, and joining the euro has been a central point of its recent governments' manifesto.

It is a fact that such a policy and joining the Union coincided, for the first time since the end of World War II, with a total change in the country's public expenditure policy. Whereas previously no Italian government had been able or willing to risk its own good standing in public opinion through unpopular financial reforms and restraints, the need to conform to the Maastricht expectations in order to join the euro provided an acceptable justification for it to impose a hard-line policy on its people. The authority that would not have been easy to use from *inside* the Italian political system could now be applied from *outside* it, that is, from Brussels. The strategy was due to a 'basic lack of trust from some politicians on the government capacities to force unpopular economic measures onto its citizens, as well as on the difficulties in containing administrative corruption' (Connolly 1995).

Another aspect of the different attitude of Italy towards the EU is more deeply rooted in its historical past. First of all, Italy only became a unified kingdom in 1861, very recently in historical terms, through the merging of many parts of its territory which had been separated for a very long time. Some of these areas had also been occupied by foreign powers. Having to find a way of being together with the other European states could perhaps be taken almost as a 'historical compulsion to repeat', if we think how the Italian state came into being in the first place.

The tradition of the city states, which were very different from one another, had been a peculiar feature of the Italian historical scenario for centuries, since the Renaissance. The popular saying in Italy, 'We have made Italy, now we have got to make the Italians', referred to this peculiarity. Each Italian region had developed over time very specific local traditions and cultures. Political and economic differences had overlapped with morphological and geographical ones. Dialects, food, customs and habits of the people, as well as local climates, were all quite different from one another in the various areas of the country. Peer relationships between the citizens of the different regions and cities were difficult, and the national atmosphere is still characterised today by sibling rivalries between different geographical areas, probably due to a large extent to that ongoing tradition. The conflict between the more opulent north and the less developed south is a very well-known example.

In this context, having to rely on a centralised and external authority, like the one offered by Brussels, might have provided a temporary solution to the problem of a national identity not yet consolidated, and a way of defusing conflicts within the national territory.

It is also relevant to add that, unlike the UK, Italy did not have an empire to lose and to mourn, apart from the very limited and rather desperate attempts of fascism to join the colonial powers through the annexing of Ethiopia and Albania and its ruling of Libya. Italy's strivings in fact had always been totally the opposite, that is, to remove foreign dominations from its soil. After all, the Austro-Hungarian Empire was still occupying a large part of its territory until the end of World War I.

The post-war 'latency years' of the nuclear threat era, and its 'relative stability'

Moving away now from the peculiarities of the respective positions of the UK and Italy over the issue of the EU, I would like to make a few remarks on the general atmosphere that we have been living in, in our continent, during the last few decades.

A lot of very complex events have taken place in Europe since the end of World War II that have turned our continent into quite a different place to be and to live in. Radical political changes have occurred, new borders have been established, new governments have been set up, old problems overcome, and new ones faced. To begin with, and above all, we witnessed the end of the era of dictatorships, such as the ones that ruled Germany, Italy and Spain. That period had brought with it an enormous amount of destruction and hatred, and left deeply rooted scars in many people and countries. The ensuing years brought with them, along with the need for reconstruction, a newly found spirit of co-operation that attempted to keep at bay the risk of similar events happening again, and causing pain and destruction once more.

Within this context, since the 1950s and the Treaty of Rome (1957), and during the decades that followed, a new trend seemed to emerge of connections between different European countries, whereby various new forms of agreements, partnerships and associations were drawn up and organisational bodies established at various levels: military (Western European Union), production (European Coal and Steel Community) and political (Committee of Permanent Representatives, European Council, European Parliament).

Meanwhile in the Eastern block the USSR had shown quite clearly to the world its determination to keep its stance in the international political arena, through the suppression of the Hungarian revolution, and the invasion of Czechoslovakia. On the western side of the European Continent there was a relative period of stability. The reality, though, of that stability might not have been as it seemed.

Since we were in fact in the period of the Cold War between the western and eastern superpowers, it may be said that such a stability was somehow being imposed and forced upon western Europe, by both the USA and the overall international situation, which could not allow much internal conflict. Most political tensions had to be projected and focused on international relations between the eastern and western blocs. That had to be the arena where the struggles would mainly be concentrated. We became accustomed to being exposed in those years to the tensions and rivalries between the two superpowers, the USA and the USSR. The ensuing phantasies of total annihilation that were bound to be associated with the risk of a third (atomic) world war were an integral part of the whole picture.

The position and role of the Europeans could then have been compared to that of frail and weakened children, who could only witness in total impotence and paralysing stillness the deadly threats that the parents (USA and USSR) seemed to be casting at each other. Such a disabling deadlock in the world situation had probably produced, as a side issue, a devitalising effect on the forces at work in the political arena. We knew we had to be careful, respecting with underlying terror the precarious balance of the two opposing ideological worlds, capitalism and communism. They must have been thought of as capable of causing unimaginable disasters, had they been carelessly provoked by negligence, and too abruptly. The memory of the last war must have also been very present in most people's minds, and acted as another deterrent against risky and trouble-making movements. The rebelliousness of the younger generations in the late 1960s, the movement against the Vietnam War and that new wave of unrest were probably as much (or as little) opposition and internal struggle as could be tolerated.

It is possible that in those circumstances the level of anxiety was too high to bear, and that a part of it had to become unconscious. If such a hypothesis is correct, this massively defended state of affairs may have then produced an almost paradoxical feeling of stability, if not quite of well-being! In fact, and in spite of the underlying international tensions, in a strange way the status quo of those years may be looked upon by some as a more reassuring and containing time than the one we are going through right now.

The existing political balance and geographical boundaries were very firmly defined and established, and quite untouchable. The USSR had already reminded the world that the Yalta agreement still stood, and that it was not prepared to make any concessions. Such a clearly delineated situation must have had its corresponding mirroring on the mental functioning of the people. A lot was being feared, a lot was being repressed, but as a secondary gain there seemed to be some level of mental containment. In other words there was at least the safety of knowing where we all stood, for better or worse, and on which side of the Iron Curtain we were. To continue the metaphor, the children knew that there was a limit to what they could do, and to their naughtiness.

The emergence of the 'people's adolescence' and political unrest

Let us look at the unrest and instability that has been unleashed in the European Continent in the last 10–15 years, following the fall of the Berlin Wall and communism, the dissolution of the USSR, the end of the Cold War and the dissolution of the former Yugoslavia.

The Eastern bloc quickly split up into several independent countries that had until then been forcibly kept united, and Russia under Yeltsin quickly became a very depleted and impoverished state, which had lost a lot of its previously terrifying military power. It had also lost a large part of its international role and prestige. The wars within its former areas of influence showed how the superpower was not after all so powerful and dangerous anymore, in Afghanistan and later in Chechnya. The omnipotent, dangerous and threatening father had suddenly shown his more fragile side to his developing children. The ensuing rebellions of the satellite children-countries against the father became like a sudden eruption of lava. After a prolonged and silent phase the volcano seemed now to explode with a newly found vigour, and spread around like a plague.

After the fall of the Iron Curtain in 1989, there were radical movements between and within countries, and the balance of power was overturned. A further illustration of this kind of process can be found in what happened to the Italian government. An internal political struggle in the Italian political scene was set in motion, that would have been unthinkable throughout the preceding years, when the country's stability on the international scene was of paramount interest for the western powers. The Christian Democrats had held power tightly for more than four decades, until just a short time after the fall of the Berlin Wall. A totally destabilising period of judicial proceedings against corrupted administrators and politicians, called the 'cleaned hands court case', ensued, and in a relatively short space of time led to the radical disappearance of two of the major parties that had ruled the country for forty years, the Christian Democrats and the Socialists.

The 'children' could now express a little more safely their anger at their parents, and deal with it more openly. Widening the metaphor even more, it could be said that it was as if some of the European citizens had suddenly begun to get out of the so-called latency period, and were getting closer to their own adolescence. After a time characterised by better control over their instinctual urges, mostly due to the fear of the retaliatory responses of their international 'parents', the people seemed to go through a new phase where they became much more aware of their own power than ever before, discovered new possibilities that had been unknown to them till then, and set in motion a process which in due course would bring them to better individuation, independence and autonomy. It can be argued that for the first time in many decades the people of Europe, in both the east and the west, were finding strength and authority to challenge their rulers, and claim more freedom and autonomy than they had ever done before.

Such changes could not have happened, had the international scene not changed so much. The relaxation between the superpowers could now allow for some conflicts within the European continent to take place, that would have been totally unthinkable just a few years before. The conflict that had to be externalised and projected outside till then, could now be retaken inside and dealt with where it actually belonged. Somehow, it could be said that the anxiety had eventually been redistributed more evenly everywhere.

Of course, all this has not been accomplished without a price that at times has been extremely hard to pay. The splitting of Yugoslavia and the ensuing bloodshed, to mention just one development, has been one of the most tragic of the kinds of situations that have developed in this new climate. On the other hand, it is true that such new processes, disturbing as they may have been because so new and radical, hitting people who were not prepared to deal with such unexpected occurrences, also produced an aspect of relief and excitement. They have posed new challenges that can now be dealt with for the first time in half a century and much more openly than had ever been possible in the past.

Political changes in Europe, clinical work and identity

I believe there are a lot of connections between some of the most important political and social changes in Europe since World War II, and the sense of identity of the people. I also believe that these changes have had some impact on the clinical work of the analyst.

To explore that, I would like now to focus my attention on the importance of migrations and related cultural tensions. I will then look at how changes in the nation states' international roles can have some impact on the changing sense of identity of institutions as well as of people. I will also share a few thoughts on the emergence of new regionalisms as contrasted with processes of fusion and globalisation, and the changing concept of nation as connected with the one of social pathology. To conclude, I will make reference to a particular model of cultural integration that could be relevant for the present situation in the EU.

It has been calculated that in three decades between the 1950s and the 1970s about 15 million international migrants have moved between European countries (Liebkind 1989). After 1989 and the fall of communism, these movements of people across international boundaries continued. We can see almost daily the pressures of migration from countries such as Turkey, Yugoslavia, Albania and the former USSR, not only on the eastern and southern coasts of Europe but also on the northern regions of the Continent and the Channel.

Vast masses of people have crossed geographical boundaries which they did not expect to be able to cross in the foreseeable future, and have ended up being confronted with new cultures and ways of life. In fact, one of the most important issues relevant to the problems posed by an organisation of countries such as the EU has to do with the predictable difficulties arising out of the need for a common language and set of values and priorities, taking into account all its peoples' different cultures, traditions and national histories.

These tensions are also bound to be reflected in the clinical work of the analyst. In present-day clinical practice, and even more so when the clinician is working in a very cosmopolitan city, he/she is very likely to encounter people coming from all sorts of different backgrounds and cultures. These discontinu- ities can often be very traumatic and may require from him/her a considerable sensitivity in order to be tackled appropriately. There is a challenge in our clinical work whenever we have to distinguish between what may belong to the individual psychopathology, and what may have to do instead with the patient's (or the analyst's, for that matter) own cultural background, and/or the social psychopathology of either's country of origin, which can be more or less ego-syntonic.

The analyst himself, and his own sense of personal identity, are bound to be affected by the socio-political, national and international changes developing around the place where he carries out his profession. The local circumstances where he operates may have become more or less conducive to an analytical way of working. His conscious and unconscious fantasies will be more or less conditioned, favourably or unfavourably, by the changes that have been occurring in the surrounding society and differing culture, which will have produced in him equally modified expectations, fears and hopes.

These considerations become even more relevant if, as in my own case, the analyst too contains within himself more than one cultural identity, on top of the patient's. In the end we may need to deal with (at least) three different sets of cultural variables: the one operating where the treatment is taking place, the one belonging to the patient's own background and the one belonging to the analyst.

Having worked for many years as a psychoanalyst, with individuals and groups, in both Italy and the UK, and within Italy in various different regions with quite distinct cultural features, I have often thought about how much could be said about the different psychopathologies that prevail in the various socio-cultural contexts. The clinical vignettes and theoretical considerations that could be drawn from these experiences would be endless, and probably may constitute one day the subject of another paper in another book. However, it might perhaps help to describe here at least one of these kinds of situations, so as to give some idea of the kind of things I am referring to.

What comes first to mind, for instance, probably because it has been one of the most striking, is the totally different way in which people in the two cultures seem to react when they are dealing with issues of separation and indi- viduation. Whenever the point of termination of a treatment is reached with an Italian patient, and a mutually agreed date for the ending has been established, the closer one gets to it the more charged the whole issue tends to become, and the more the analyst may need to renegotiate the terms of the separation. With a

British patient, the very same issue tends to be handled in quite a different manner. So much so that at times, in my own countertransference, I have felt a bit puzzled that people I had been working with for several years, and with whom I had shared a lot of very important experiences, could accept with such apparent ease the ending of treatment and separation from the therapeutic relationship. That behaviour has seemed to me to show almost an emotional lack of attachment and responsiveness, that did not appear to be proportionate to the importance of the event. At times, I have even gone so far as to wonder whether I might have done anything wrong, or failed to pick up and notice something which I should have, while trying to come to terms with such a relatively 'cool' way of accepting the inevitability of the situation and the separation.

Only after repeated experiences of this kind and much thought on my part about what was going on, could such a behaviour be understood and made sense of. I had to look at it in the wider social and cultural context, bearing in mind and giving the necessary attention to the peculiarities of the family structure and child training habits of the two countries, taking into account all the due (consistent) differences and traditions. Without wishing to go into too much detail, it is enough to say here that whereas early separation and independence of the child from the parents is supported and encouraged by the British, for instance through the boarding school system, the Italian regime tends to go in the opposite direction. In Italy, the never-ending adolescence that allows children to stay on and live with their own families of origin till marriage is a well-known and relatively widespread phenomenon. The myth of the so called 'Great (Mediterranean, over-protective) Mother' described by some analytical psychologists is very much related to this. The very dependable, but over-controlling and individuation-inhibiting 'Mafia' family could also be taken as another form of the same socio-pathological process.

Bearing all this in mind, it is not surprising that when I was working in Sicily about 70 per cent of my Italian patients, in one way or another, used to display at least some form of agoraphobia and/or separation anxiety.

On a different level, I have very often heard among British patients stories of people who had been involved for many years in a relationship, and then suddenly disappeared from it out of the blue, with no warnings of any kind to their partner of any underlying conflict which must have been there for a long time, mounting up towards that drastic and abrupt conclusion. This also shows how differently people in the two cultures tend to deal with problems of aggression and conflict, besides those of separation.

The situation described above would seldom appear among Italians, among whom the clinician would much more often find himself having to deal with an *excess*, if anything, of open and direct aggression, than an external lack of it.

The same differences would equally apply to a lot of other features, but it would take us too far away from our main theme to discuss them here any further.

I have mentioned above the changes that have taken place in the former USSR and in the Balkans. Under those circumstances I suppose we can understand how and why new identities had to be formed, with much stronger boundaries than ever before between inclusion and exclusion from membership of specific groups (ethnic, national, and religious). Former neighbours with whom people had shared many years of life experiences had suddenly turned into enraged enemies who became able to commit all sorts of atrocities. Old friends and allies have become enemies and old enemies have been turned into new allies. A new process of reorientation and considerable psychological readjustment is now needed by many people whose sense of identity has suffered very serious blows.

These changes extend beyond individual citizens and group of people, to include also international institutions and organisations. For example, we could think about how an organisation such as NATO, which was originally created to counterbalance the hegemonic threat of the former USSR, is struggling nowadays to justify its own existence, and is going through its own identity crisis due to the lack of its primary *raison d'être*. The Atlantic alliance needs now to redefine its own aims and targets, and it will presumably need to look for some other enemy.

The USSR became for several decades a sort of container for many negative externalised projections from a large section of the population in many western countries. Somehow it was for them a highly negatively charged object, thought of as a common enemy. Once again we can notice a shift in the direction of the conflict which, after being targeted initially at the USSR as the 'external enemy', now seems to be turning itself inwards. It is moving from the east towards the west, in the dynamic of tensions within this part of the world, in particular between Europe and the USA.

It has been reported in the media recently how some anxiety has been expressed by the USA administration at the recent plan to create a new European military 'rapid reaction force'. The fact that a Finnish general was put in charge of this new military force seems to encourage those worries, in the light of the fact that Finland has always been outside NATO. Another dispute seems to have arisen lately between the Old Continent and the western super-power on the latter's change of attitude concerning energy policy, and its abandonment of the Kyoto agreement. A new political philosophy of the new American administration seems to be heading straight for a collision course with its own allies.

To a new observer on the international scene of today, it would be difficult to distinguish which country is ally or enemy to which other one, and why.

In other words, once the balance of power and the International status of the major countries in the world change, everything else is bound to be affected, and individual and group identities have to go through a long process of readjustment and redefinition.

Group merging and splitting in Europe: the new regionalisms and globalisation

Other elements that have been contributing to the changing sense of identity of many people throughout the world, and have increased the level of their anxiety, are the so-called 'globalisation' process, and the reactions against it. There seems to be a double tendency of most kinds of groups to aggregate themselves into larger units, and also to break away from already existing entities to form smaller ones. This applies to groups operating in the most diverse sectors of society, ranging from the merely associative, professional and organisational levels, to the financial, industrial-productive, and political ones.

These trends have developed much more quickly than ever before in the last few decades, under the pressures of the development of information technology, transport and communications. The tendency towards merging has been self-evident in the area of commerce, industry and finance where in the process of growing, larger organisations often absorb the smaller ones. The concentration of power and wealth into fewer and larger groups is a very well-known phenomenon of our times. The so-called multi-nationals are the most obvious expression of this and they probably constitute one of the most easily identifiable aspects of capitalism. The difficulty such a trend has produced for the smaller organisation to maintain its peculiar identity and to survive, is very well known.

To quote only one among the many possible examples, drawn from the familiar surroundings of city life, we could think about how hypermarkets often mushroom at such a quick pace that they totally alter the way of life of city centres and their identity. The trend has become so severe in its potential implications that some restrictive legislation has been required.

Moving into the socio-political scenario, these two opposite movements towards merging and splitting have emerged even more dramatically. In the recent developments of the European nation states, these movements have come to constitute a problematic dualism, and they have become more clearly observable in this part of the world than anywhere else. Talking about dichotomy in Europe, Pomian has pointed out how 'we are watching nowadays the simultaneous action of two opposite forces, of which one is pushing towards a deepening and enlargement of the European integration, with the ideal, in due course, of a federal Europe, the united states of Europe, as well as the opposite force aiming at underlining the specificity, the peculiarity and the national identity, and to oppose whatever is perceived by the members of the nation as a threat for its own existence' (Pomian 1997).

Such bipolarity appears quite clearly if we think for example about those eastern European countries who are still wishing to join the EU, as contrasted with those who are striving instead to achieve their independence from the already existing nation states, and individuate as separate and smaller units.

Most European states, in the east as well as in the west, display these tensions. In the east this has happened with the splitting of the former USSR, but also in the west there have been tendencies to split off the large national groups into sub-groups. This is what has been happening to the Basque regions in Spain, to the Northern League in Italy, to Corsica in France, to Flanders in Belgium, to Ireland, Scotland and Wales in the UK, and in the splitting of Czechoslovakia.

In considering these tendencies of groups to split up, it has to be remembered what Nitsun says about the 'anti-group', considered by him to be a universal component that threatens the integrity of the group almost by default, and which is part of a universal dialectical process that could almost be considered physiological (Nitsun 1996). What Nitsun describes is certainly a component of this process, but it is equally useful to be aware of what Pomian says about this, that is, that the differing direction that the history of groups takes, in terms of merging versus splitting, seems to be connected with the specific phases of the political and socio-economic cycle they are going through. According to him, the tendency to split up would seem to prevail at times of crisis or slowing down of growth, and the tendency to merge would seem to prevail in the case of fast and strong development (Pomian 1997).

Which one of these may be more applicable to our present circumstances is open to discussion. What we can say for the time being is that both forces seem to be acting equally strongly.

Regionalism as opposed to globalisation expresses the anxiety of not being able to have one's own say even about things which are directly related to one's own welfare and well-being, because they are instead decided by a centralised authority. Such demands are born out of the need to take a more active participation in the management of the public good, and to overcome the anomy and the sense of alienation that can be induced when institutional life becomes excessively fragmented. That could become one of the likely thresholds beyond which groups tend to reverse their direction from merging to splitting.

The excessive elaboration into a complicated structure of government that can be very difficult to manage effectively has been one subject of the current critical remarks which are often being made about EU organisation. Its apparatus is considered by some almost as a sort of white elephant, which is destined to impinge on the functionality of the democratic process.

The conflict between large groups and smaller sub-groups can be compared, on a different scale, to the tensions that exist between the individual and the group. Referring to such a conflict, and to the reiterated attempts of individuals to get away from what is felt to be too restrictive a demand imposed on him/her by the group, Alford cites Connolly's 'paradox of politics' (Connolly 1991), in which he underlines how 'in order to protect their individuality, individuals destroy the one entity that could, if properly organised, help them realize it' (Alford 1994).

Perhaps we could argue that something similar might also be applicable to the international relations between the European nation states. This may be the case for those countries which are very reluctant to join the EU because they fear that the abandonment of their full autonomy and independence could jeopardise their best interests, and which then may actually create the self-fulfilling prophecy that they had tried so hard to avoid.

Emphasising another aspect of the individual-group relationship, Alford coins the term 'schizoid compromise' pointing at what he feels is an insoluble contradiction, while referring in particular to the prevailing conditions of the American way of life: the irreconcilable attempt of the individual to keep his freedom and independence, while wishing also to merge with and be one with the group. He argues that while there seems to be a tendency and a wish to keep and defend very strongly one's own freedom and lifestyle in that cultural context, there is at the same time an equally great expectation to conform to the group's norms. The final product of these divergent needs could easily become, according to him, an impossible task.

On a larger scale, and in a wider sense than the merely local political one, when we think about globalisation there seems to be anxiety about being exposed to the control of invisible (economic) forces that do not know any geographical boundaries, nor local traditions and cultures, and seem to be prepared to spread around like a plague, taking over, manipulating and swallowing up everyone and everything they find on their path. In light of this, the efforts smaller entities are prepared to take to protect their own identity against the 'invasion' of such forces becomes understandable.

Recently, we have seen forms of protest and rebelliousness directed at the 'global' summits of the world economic organisations, in various places around the world, from Seattle to Quebec and London. However limited the importance that the decision-making authorities attribute to these protesting movements, they nevertheless constitute some new symptoms of a growing need to react against the threats to their identity that people are experiencing, and so deserve some attention.

The nation as transitional object and the concept of social pathology

Within this dilemma between the two extremes of globalisation and localised regionalisms, some have wondered whether any room will still be left for nation states to keep their meaning and play a useful function. Some have argued that the concept of nation as a territorial state with geographical boundaries is only a European invention (Thibaud 1997; Geertz 1995). Others have supported the view that in spite of the crisis the concept has been going through in the last few decades, the nations are still bound to be the privileged territory of politics and culture, if not necessarily of the economy, which cannot but work on a worldwide dimension (Pomian 1997).

In spite of these doubts, several psychoanalytically oriented writers have expressed quite similar views on the usefulness of the concept of the nation as a bridge and as a shared space between the individual and the group, looked at from the Winnicottian perspective of the transitional object (Winnicott 1958).

Solan's concept of 'jointness', for instance, seems to be reminiscent of the above in so far as it refers to the link between the subject and the object, the citizen and society, where separateness is safeguarded, but both partners are sharing a commonly cathected (emotionally charged) space that is meaningful to both. Merging and separateness are the two extremes of a continuum where boundaries can occasionally become more or less blurred. The nation in this sense can constitute this shared space (Solan 1996).

Kristeva seems to follow a similar line of thinking when she describes the nation as transitional object, as an 'intermediate area of experiencing...to which inner reality and external life both contribute...a resting place for the individual engaged in the perpetual human task of keeping inner and outer reality separate yet inter-related' (Kristeva 1993). As with the transitional object which is abandoned when it has fulfilled its function and the child has developed, in a similar way a 'good enough territory' can be one day left behind, when the citizen has grown into a more mature, individuated human being, capable of becoming a potential cosmopolitan.

I have found particularly interesting the contribution of Prager who has also used the idea of the transitional object and space, but has taken it beyond the concept of the nation. He has linked it up with politics in general, as the place where illusion and playfulness can take place. Politics in his vision can be taken as a kind of intermediate area and a common ground between the object (the external reality, the rulers) and the subjects (the citizens), where the 'illusion' would allow the latter to feel that they have contributed to the creation of the former. The citizen's fantasy and creativity would then contribute to the discussion of possible alternatives for the management of society. 'Playing, in this sense, is the art of possible which can be thought and shared between object and subject' (Prager 1993).

If and when the politics degenerate into nationalism, then playfulness is not being used any more; one political system is substituted with another one, and whatever is different from the dominant ideology becomes charged with negative projections and gets attacked and criticised because of that. That is how 'the enemy' is produced. This 'politics of narcissism', as he calls it, is the regime where there is no dialectic any more and no views are allowed other than the ones of the ruling class. Diversity is flattened, playfulness is ruled out and creativity is destined to stagnation. These kind of circumstances, he continues, would be the expression of what he defines as a 'social pathology', a sort of 'failure of the environment to enable, or facilitate, the development of illusion' (Prager 1993). It would be a one-dimensional (narcissistic) way of living, reminiscent of what has been described by Marcuse in the 1960s, in his critique of contemporary society (Marcuse 1967).

In more favourable circumstances, Prager emphasises how society can fulfil the function of a 'facilitating environment' to its child/citizen, allowing the latter to attack it, but at the same time not letting itself be destroyed by it. In this way, through being a 'real external object' society would help the subject to develop and differentiate. In other words, he seems to be saying that society needs to make itself available to be 'used as an object', in the Winnicottian sense, and also be a 'good enough mother' as well as a 'facilitating environment' to its child/citizen.

Towards a model of cultural integration

I have tried to explore some of the problems posed by the EU in a changing world, and the challenges of finding a way for so many differing nation states to stay together as a democratic group of peers and develop a common way of thinking and political behaviour, while at the same time maintaining their own individuality, peculiarity and national identity.

In this context, it might be useful to look at a model of integration between cultures described by Brague, that could provide some useful clues (Brague 1998). Brague has made reference to the Romans, and to their ways of integrating into their own culture the new ones that they were discovering and conquering. He describes how in his view the Romans seem to have had a rather peculiar relationship with their historical origin. He recalls the myth of Rome's foundation by Aeneas, who left Troy with his father and his gods after the town had been sacked by the Greeks, moving to the new Latin land. The legend, according to him, shows how much embedded in the Roman identity is the idea of transplanting an old culture into new soil. The old and new overlap and fuse into a renewed and reproductive beginning.

He believes that this feature of reinterpreting in the present the values and principles of the past constitutes a central element of the Roman attitude to culture and civilisation. He calls that the principle of 'secondariness', which he considers to be fundamental to Roman culture. He underlines how Romans had always shown a great respect and appreciation for the classicism of Greek culture, from which they were not afraid to learn, while at the same time acknowledging the latter's superiority when compared to themselves. He adds to that the belief that the Roman Empire and its thirst for conquest probably had its roots in a sense of inferiority to the objects of their invasions. He suggests that a similar dynamic may also have been active in leading some European people to colonialism. This ability to respect and admire the qualities of the stranger so much that you integrate him/her and make him/her part of your own identity is described by Brague as one of the best assets of the Roman mentality and one that could be very useful to bear in mind.

This could be of particular relevance in present-day Europe, at a time of radical change and fragmentation.

The present circumstances require a huge effort by all the participants to find better ways of integrating our worlds and to turn our differences into something productive and creative, to everybody's advantage rather than to our detriment.

References

Alford, F.C. (1994) *Group Psychology and Political Theory.* Yale: Yale University Press.

Brague, R. (1998) *Il Futuro dell'Occidente. Nel Modello Romano la Salvezza dell' Europa.* Milano: Rusconi Ed.

Connolly, B. (1995) *The Rotten Heart of Europe – The Dirty War for Europe's Money.* London, Boston: Faber & Faber, pp.379–380.

Connolly, W.E. (1991) *Identity/Difference: Democratic Negotiations of Political Paradox.* Ithaca, New York: Cornell University Press.

Encyclopedia Britannica (1978) USA: Encyclopedia Britannica Inc.

Geertz, C. (1995) *Mondo Globale, Mondi Locali.* Bologna: Il Mulino Publ., p.84.

Kristeva, J. (1993) *Nations Without Nationalism.* New York: Columbia University Press.

Liebkind, K. (1985) 'Some problems in the theory and application of cultural pluralism: the social psychology of minority identity.' In UNESCO *Cultural Pluralism and Cultural Identity: The Experience of Canada, Finland and Yugoslavia.* Paris: UNESCO.

Liebkind, K. (ed) (1989) *New Identities in Europe.* Aldershot: Gower Publishing Company Ltd, in association with the European Science Foundation Strasbourg, France.

Marcuse, H. (1967) *L'Uomo A Una Dimensione.* Torino: Einaudi.

Moses, R. (1995) 'Foreword: the pitfalls and promises of group psychotherapists addressing the political process.' In M.F. Ettin, J.W. Fidler and B.D. Cohen (eds) *Group Process and Political Dynamics.* Madison, Connecticut: International Universities Press Inc. Publishers, p.xiii–xvii.

Moses-Hushovski, R. (1996) 'Remaining in the bunker long after the war is over: deployment in the individual, the group, the nation.' In L. Rangell and R. Moses-Hushovski (eds) *Psychoanalysis at the Political Border – Essays in Honor of Rafael Moses.* Madison, USA: International Universities Press, p.96.

Nitsun, M. (1996) *The Anti-Group: Destructive Forces in the Group and their Creative Potential.* London and New York: Routledge.

Pomian, K. (1997) 'The nation in question.' In Boissonnat *et al.* (eds) *Entre Mondialisation et Nations, Quelle Europe?* Semaines Sociales de France, Paris. Isy-les-Moulineaux: Bayard Editions/Centurion.

Prager, J. (1993) 'Politics and illusions: a psychoanalytic exploration of nationalism.' In J. Prager and M. Rustin (eds) *Psychoanalytic Sociology.* Aldershot and Brookfield: Edward Elgar Publisher Ltd., Volume II, pp.303–322.

Rangell, L. (1996) 'Rafael Moses, psychoanalyst of the Middle East.' In L. Rangell and R. Moses-Hushovski (eds) *Psychoanalysis at the Political Border – Essays in Honor of Rafael Moses.* Madison, USA: International Universities Press, pp.3–15.

Solan, R. (1996) 'The leader and the led – their mutual needs.' In L. Rangell and R. Moses-Hushovski (eds) *Psychoanalysis at the Political Border–Essays in Honor of Rafael Moses.* Madison, USA: International Universities Press, pp.237–256.

Thibaud, P. (1997) 'The nation in question.' In Boissonnat *et al.* (eds) *Entre Mondialisation et Nations, Quelle Europe?* Semaines Sociales de France, Paris. Isy-les Moulineaux: Bayard Editions/Centurion, pp.40–69.

Volkan, V.D. (1994) *The Need to Have Enemies and Allies: From Clinical Practice to International Relationships.* New Jersey: J. Aronson Inc.

Volkan, V.D. (1996) 'Intergenerational transmission and "chosen" traumas: a link between the psychology of the individual and that of the ethnic group.' In L. Rangell and R. Moses-Hushovski (eds) *Psychoanalysis at the Political Border – Essays in Honor of Rafael Moses.* Madison, USA: International Universities Press, pp.257–279.

Winnicott, D. (1958) *Transitional Objects and Transitional Phenomena.* New York: Basic Books.

CHAPTER 8

Reconnecting with our World

Chris Johnstone

As I write this chapter, the heaviest rains ever recorded fall on Britain. The little stream I used to paddle in as a child has flooded neighbouring fields, and thousands of people have been evacuated from their homes. Extreme weather events like this are likely to become more common as global warming increases (Houghton *et al.* 1996), leading to concerns about our world and our collective future. As individuals, we can easily feel overwhelmed by the scale of this and other global issues, to such an extent that they become difficult to face. In other areas where problems are difficult to face alone, groupwork has proved useful in helping people find their power to make changes. In my work as a group therapist in the addictions treatment field, I often see people draw strength from the group to face challenges they have found too much when facing by themselves. Can groupwork help us find the courage and inner resources to face and respond to the problems of our world? This chapter aims to introduce and explore an approach to working with groups that sets out to do just that.

I have written this chapter in three parts. Firstly I will give some historical background and introduce the ideas behind this approach. I will then describe methods used in practice. Lastly I will reflect on issues that have come up in my experience of facilitating this type of groupwork over the last ten years. I will also report the results of a follow-up study looking at outcomes for participants at workshops I have run.

The historical background and the ideas behind this approach
How it began

Over twenty years ago, a form of groupwork developed that provided a forum for sharing concerns about global issues. Then, as now, many people felt overwhelmed and powerless when facing problems such as rising pollution levels, the threat of nuclear war or accident, destruction of natural habitats and the increasing gulf between rich and poor. Some had reached the point of despair, feeling that these problems were too huge for any meaningful response to them to be mounted. Yet being able to acknowledge and express such feelings about the world within a supportive setting was found to be liberating, especially when people experienced their concerns as being shared by others. Some of the hopelessness shifted, leaving participants more energised and empowered. In the late 1970s and early 1980s, workshops offering this form of groupwork became known as 'Despair and Empowerment Workshops', and they quickly spread from North America to Europe, Australia and a range of countries in other parts of the world.

In 1983, Joanna Macy, one of the originators of this approach, published a book entitled *Despair and Personal Power in the Nuclear Age*. Macy had recently completed a doctoral thesis exploring the parallels between systems theory and Buddhism. In her book she wove together psychology, groupwork, spirituality and political activism in describing a model for developing our power to respond to world problems. She saw empowerment as a psychological process, involving an inner shift towards the feeling that 'I can do something about this'. She regarded the way we deal with our feelings about world events as one of the keys to finding this kind of power. When we feel strongly about something, our emotions provide a source of energy that can be tapped into. But if we avoid looking at world problems because the feelings they arouse are too painful, we block our ability to respond. One of the first steps to finding personal power was therefore related to the way we dealt with our pain for the world.

In describing how our emotional reactions can play such a central role in finding our power to respond to world problems, Macy (1983, p.22) presented five principles of Despair and Empowerment work. As these provide a rationale for the workshops, I will introduce each in turn.

1. Feelings of pain for our world are natural and healthy

Two thirds of the world's forest cover has already been chopped down, scientists are talking about a mass extinction of species due to human activity, and over a billion people do not have enough food to eat. When faced with such disturbing realities, it is not surprising if we feel disturbed.

> Confronted with widespread suffering and threats of global disaster, responses of anguish – of fear, anger, and grief and even guilt – are normal. (Macy 1983, p.22)

Participants at workshops often tell me that when they have such feelings, they are not sure what to do with them. Fears of being seen as depressing company or of starting a political argument can make this a difficult area to talk about. As a result, people may end up feeling alone with emotions that are seen as 'too heavy' to share with others. Within the workshops, the first principle helps create a climate of acceptance and validation to feelings people may have previously felt they had to shut away or keep quiet about. Along with this is an understanding that people experience and express their pain or concern in different ways, with a range of inner responses that include sadness, anger, grief, despair, numbness, guilt, dread, agitation or feeling empty. In this chapter I will collectively refer to these feelings as 'pain for the world'. The idea that they are not only natural but also healthy responses suggests that they may have a positive function. This leads to the second principle.

2. This pain is morbid only if denied

One of the things that makes it difficult to talk about concerns for the world is the idea that such 'negative feelings' are unproductive and have no value. For example, I have often heard people say things like 'there's no point in getting upset about the world because there's nothing you can do to change it'. The second principle, however, is based on an understanding that pain is useful when it alerts us to threat or injury in a way that prompts us to respond. In workshops, I sometimes illustrate this by putting my finger over a flame. Because it hurts, I quickly move my finger to avoid burning it. I suggest that psychological distress can sometimes serve a similar function, telling us when we are off course or living in a way that may harm us. Looked at this way, feelings can be seen as a source of information that help us navigate through life. If we block them off or deny them, we close down one of our biological warning systems, leaving us at risk of continuing on a path that is damaging to us. I would like to illustrate this with an example from my work in the addiction field.

CASE HISTORY 1: THE MORBID AVOIDANCE OF PAIN

The first time I met Mark he was yellow. He told me he didn't like feeling upset and that he enjoyed drinking because it smoothed over the difficult times in life. He'd had three hospital admissions in the previous six months after small cuts when shaving had continued to bleed for hours. He'd also been arrested several times after becoming abusive when drunk. After telling me about this he said, 'I think the problem's a bit overblown. I don't think my drinking's too bad'.

I explained to him that his liver wasn't working because of alcohol-induced damage, this leading to his blood clotting problems and the jaundice of his yellow skin. This damage was so severe that if he didn't stop drinking and allow his liver to recover, he could die.

Some weeks later he returned and proudly told me that he had stopped drinking cider. He was drinking lager instead. He had found the information about his liver rather depressing, so he continued drinking to cheer himself up. He was still in his twenties when, some months later and vomiting blood, he died.

If uncomfortable feelings are seen as bad things best avoided, one way of doing this (in the short term at least) is to divert attention away from sources of upset. The danger of this, however, is that it leads to the development of blind spots, where it becomes difficult to look at issues that generate distress. In the language of systems theory, this is referred to as 'blocked feedback'. Such resistance to receiving, noticing or passing on disturbing information makes it difficult to mount an effective response, as problems tend to be played down or ignored.

Blocked feedback can occur at the level of individuals, groups, organisations, governments or society as a whole. For example, with the recent BSE crisis in Britain, information was deliberately withheld from the public for fear that it might generate too much alarm.

> The government was pre-occupied with preventing an alarmist over-reaction to BSE... Ministers followed an approach whose object was sedation. In the first half of 1987 there were restraints on the release of information about BSE. (*The BSE Inquiry Report*, HMSO 2000, paras. 1 and 1179)

Pain for the world can be seen as an alarm bell that alerts us to the wounds and threats we experience on a collective basis. If the alarm is suppressed, the danger is that we mount an ineffectual response, rather like Mark's giving up cider but drinking lager instead. How can we, as a society, allow ourselves to be appropriately alarmed? This leads to the next principle.

3. Information alone is not enough

Telling Mark about his liver was not enough to stop him drinking, just as awareness of environmental problems is not enough in itself to make our society give up ecologically destructive activities. As Macy writes:

> It is not sufficient to discuss the present crisis on the informational level alone, or seek to arouse the public to action by delivering ever more terrifying facts and figures. Information by itself can increase resistance, deepening the sense of apathy and powerlessness. We need to help each other process this information on an affective level, if we are to digest it on the cognitive level. (Macy 1983, p.xiii)

Sometimes we can know about something, but the full implications of it may not have sunk in. The following comment from one of my clients illustrates this:

> I knew the damage that drinking was doing to me. But it was on a head level. I didn't really care – until my best friend died. He was alcoholic too, and at that point I knew that if I didn't do something I'd be next. (John, recovering alcoholic)

Part of digesting information is taking on board what it means to us and experiencing any feelings we have about this. But if these feelings are seen as threatening, this creates a barrier to fully absorbing the information. Even though we may be aware of something at a superficial level, the full implications do not sink in. It may take a crisis or extreme event to push a disturbing piece of information into fuller awareness. This is why crisis can become an important turning point.

However, crisis is not always a turning point; one of the things that makes a difference here is the way the feelings are dealt with. If the experience of alarm is blotted out, the crisis may become just another point on a continued downward spiral. But if the shock is felt and taken on board, then awareness of the problem shifts from a head level to a heart level. When we know in our hearts that something is true, we are more likely to want to do something about it. In recovery from addiction, this shift to a deeper level of knowing is referred to as 'hitting bottom'. This is when someone feels the pain of where their addictive behaviour is taking them, experiencing the alarm and the horror in a way that motivates them to change.

What we are looking at here is the importance of emotions to both awareness and motivation. Uncomfortable feelings are threatening, and because of this we often seek, either consciously or unconsciously, to avoid them. This can have the effect of closing down both awareness and motivation, leading to disinterest and apathy. One of the purposes of Despair and Empowerment work is to help us overcome our own resistances, so that we can face the disturbing realities of our times and feel supported in any emotional reactions we have to them. Making room for our feelings is a way of valuing them, for they are seen not only as part of the process of digesting information but also as a source of direction, purpose, energy and determination. I would like to illustrate this with an example from my own life.

CASE HISTORY 2: THE BOY WITH MATCHSTICK ARMS

In 1984, while a medical student on elective in Sri Lanka, I encountered the reality of human starvation for the first time. I visited a centre for abandoned malnourished children, and remember hand-feeding a two-year-old boy who had recently been found. With his matchstick arms and legs, he was a shocking sight. However, the memory got stuck somewhere inside me and I didn't think much about it until four years later when, at a weekend workshop, I was invited to talk about what I mourned for in our world. I remembered him, and as I described holding him, looking into his empty shrunken eyes, I started crying. I continued to cry in a way I'd never done before. I'd always known that people starve, I'd even seen it, but never before had I been given the room to express how I felt about it. It is *so* sad. Every day tens of thousands of children like him die because they don't have enough food to eat. With my sadness I also felt angry that we allow this to continue – and angry at myself too, that I'd found it so easy to forget about. After the workshop I felt a burning determination to do something about the problem of world hunger.

As I write the above paragraph, I feel my eyes get moist and tears form. I think back to holding that child and also to the workshop where I had held him again, only this time in my heart and mind. That weekend was a turning point for me. It touched me so deeply that afterwards I decided to train in groupwork so that I could facilitate these workshops. This area of work seemed to offer something missing in politics – space for tenderness, for the heart. Looking at world problems is generally regarded as difficult and depressing, to the point where for many it is a heart-sink area they would prefer to avoid. But I found that after the workshop I did not feel depressed. Even though I had touched into a deep sadness, having the opportunity to express it left me feeling lighter.

Witnessing others express similar feelings created a depth of community and solidarity that I found nourishing. And giving voice to such deeply felt concerns left me feeling inside 'I want to do something about this'. I felt energised, with a renewed feeling of purpose and direction in my life. This was in part related to the next principle.

4. Unblocking repressed feelings releases energy and clears the mind

Many people will recognise the feeling of release that they experience after a good cry or when getting something off their chest that has been bothering them. Group workers may also know how group energy can sag, as if wading through mud, when significant but difficult things remain unsaid, and then how the energy rises again when unspeakable truths finally surface. Having the opportunity to talk about concerns for the world is often experienced as liberating, as it brings into the open fears that are commonly felt but rarely talked about. When we create a space where we can look at the painful realities of our world without having to hide away how this makes us feel, the effort involved in suppressing emotions can be freed up, releasing energy.

5. Unblocking our pain for the world reconnects us with the larger web of life

If someone close to us dies, feelings of grief are regarded as normal and healthy. The pain of loss, though uncomfortable, is a product of our relationship and reflects how important that person has been to us. Likewise, if someone or something we care about has been attacked, we might feel angry, sad, alarmed or concerned. Feelings can be expressions of relationship and of how much people or things matter to us.

Some indigenous tribal cultures have a relationship of closeness with nature where other species are regarded as close relatives. Although that depth of connection has to a large extent been lost in modern industrialised societies, it has not gone completely. When people are given an opportunity to give voice to their feelings for the world, it allows the expression of that part of their being that still feels connected. This brings the world closer, deepening our relationship with it.

The way we look at things

Our sense of relationship with the world is powerfully influenced by the assumptions and ideas of the culture we live in, particularly those to do with how we look at things. Some writers, such as physicist Fritjof Capra (Capra 1982, p.34), have argued that a profound shift is occurring in the way that western society views the world. In a process comparable to the scientific revolution of the seventeenth century, dominant assumptions are being questioned and new ways of looking at things are emerging. There is a pattern to these changes, which Capra identifies as a shift away from reductionist thinking towards a holistic and ecological worldview. I use the terms 'the Lens of Separation' and 'the Lens of Connection' to refer to these different ways of looking at the world, and here describe the way in which this shift in thinking contributes to the conceptual framework behind the Despair and Empowerment approach.

One way of looking at the world involves splitting it up into parts, so reducing complex phenomena down to their basic building blocks. This allows us to understand our world by focusing in on one part at a time, consciously or unconsciously placing a border around each thing we look at in a way that defines it as different and separate from other things. I use the term 'the Lens of Separation' (see Figure 8.1) to describe this approach, as, like a lens, it frames and focuses what we see in a particular way.

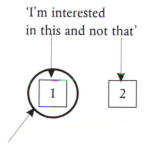

'I'm interested in this and not that'

Narrow frame of attention

- Looks at the world in terms of separate parts

- Narrow focus lens – focuses on one part at a time

- Looks at things in themselves

- Puts a boundary around each thing, with the focus of interest being what is inside the boundary

Figure 8.1 The Lens of Separation

Another way of looking, which I call 'the Lens of Connection' (see Figure 8.2), views everything as connected and interrelated, each thing forming part of larger patterns and wholes.

'I'm interested in how things fit together and in the connections between things'

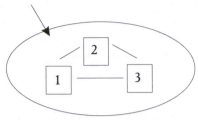

- Sees the world in terms of patterns and relationships
- Wide angle lens – sees the general shape of things
- Looks at things in context
- Looks beyond the boundaries, bringing relationships and larger wholes into view

Figure 8.2 The Lens of Connection

For example, looking at the diagram shown as Figure 8.3, if we focus in on the separate bits, we see squares, but if we stand back and take in the pattern or whole, we see a circle.

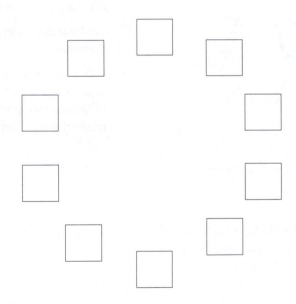

Figure 8.3 A circle of squares

Looking at groups through a Lens of Separation we see separate individuals, while through a Lens of Connection we see the group as a whole. Both views, although different, are valid and useful. When we bring them together, like looking through two eyes, we see with a depth that can focus in on different levels. The Lens of Separation is good for close-up views that reveal the details of small areas, while the Lens of Connection, like a wide angle lens, takes in the larger picture and our relationship to it.

Applying this to how we see ourselves, on one level we are separate individuals, but on another level we are also connected parts of larger wholes. Through a Lens of Separation, we see the distinctness of an individual self, through a Lens of Connection we see a 'connected self' in terms of what we belong to or feel part of. Returning to the analogy of squares and circles, a narrow focus on individual self would see us only as a separate square, while the wider view of a connected self would also see us as part of larger circles. We tend to combine these two views when defining who we are – people usually describe themselves in terms of what makes them unique and also by referring to the groups (e.g. family, ethnic, religious, occupational etc.) they belong to. When we strongly identify with a group, it becomes part of who we are and an important aspect of our identity.

Within western psychology and culture, the balance between these two views of self has been strongly weighted towards the Lens of Separation, leading to a narrow focus on the individual self. From this perspective, the world is seen as something split away and far apart from ourselves (see Figure 8.4).

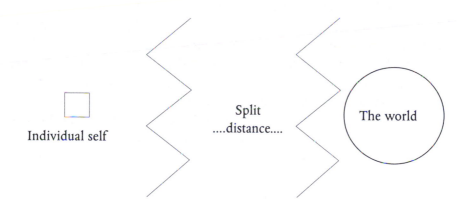

Figure 8.4 A relationship of distance with the world

If we see the world as separate from ourselves, it is easier to believe that there is little we can do to change it. The problems of the world may also seem further away and less relevant to our personal concerns. Looking through a Lens of Separation, it is more difficult to see the links between things. As a result, less attention is given to the social and ecological consequences of decisions and people can unwittingly contribute to ecologically destructive processes. For example, people with savings or pension schemes often have little idea about what their money is actually invested in. Banks or unit trusts, unless ethically screened, will place finance on the basis of short-term profitability, even if this is in ecologically damaging activity that threatens our future.

Within psychotherapy, a conceptual step away from seeing us only as separate individuals comes with the approaches of group analysis and family therapy. Both of these have a wider focus that views the individual as part of larger systems. Foulkes, the originator of the group analytic approach, writes:

> The individual … is part of a social network, a little nodal point, as it were, in this network, and can only artificially be considered in isolation, like a fish out of water. (Foulkes 1948, pp.14–15)

While group analysis and family therapy focus on 'wholes' at the level of group or family, Gaia Theory is a new scientific concept proposing that the earth itself functions as a self-regulating whole. In a striking parallel to the way our bodies control the temperature of our blood, the temperature of the atmosphere appears to have remained relatively stable over the last three and a half billion years, in spite of an estimated 30 per cent increase in the energy coming from the sun over this period (Lovelock 1979, p.18). Atmospheric oxygen levels and the salinity of the oceans also appear to have remained remarkably stable for many millions of years, with evidence growing that these are actively regulated by life itself. Rather than it just being a dead lump of rock, Gaia Theory suggests that the earth is better viewed as a living being that we are part of.

The importance of Gaia Theory psychologically is that it challenges the view that we are just separate individuals. It becomes possible to think of ourselves as being similar to cells within a larger organism, or as part of a group called life. This idea that we are part of the earth, rather than separate from it, has been called 'Deep Ecology'. It involves extending the principle of identification, where our identity is related to the circles or groups we see ourselves as belonging to (Naess 1988, p.28). This approach sees us as part of a larger continuity that connects us not only with other humans but also with other life forms. As this continuity extends both backwards and forwards in time, we are also connected with our ancestors and with future beings. This leads to a wider and deeper sense of self (see Figure 8.5) where, to use the expression of group analyst Farhad Dalal, 'the I is we' (Dalal 1998, p.194).

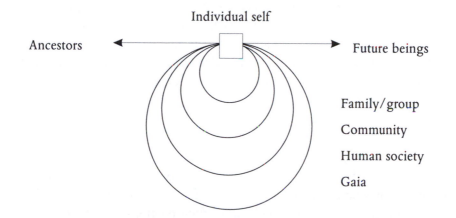

Figure 8.5 A wider and deeper self

This relationship with larger circles can be thought of as an emotional or spiritual connection. We use the term 'spiritual experience' to describe those special moments when we feel a heightened sense of connectedness. As Fritjof Capra writes:

> Ultimately, deep ecological awareness is spiritual or religious awareness. When the concept of the human spirit is understood as the mode of consciousness in which the individual feels a sense of belonging, of connectedness, to the cosmos as a whole, it becomes clear that ecological awareness is spiritual in its deepest essence. (Capra 1996, p.7)

This has an important impact on our motivation to act for our world, as the more we identify with a group the more likely we are to want to act for its well-being. In the past it has been common for people to feel such a connection with their clan, tribe or country. The perspective of Deep Ecology proposes that beneath our differences as human groupings or different species, we are all members of the same large group of life on earth. When we feel part of our world, and also that the world is part of us, a relationship of care, interest and concern follows naturally. Arne Naess, the Norwegian philosopher who coined the term 'Deep Ecology', writes:

> The requisite care flows naturally if the self is widened and deepened so that protection of free nature is felt and conceived of as protection of our very selves. (Naess 1988, p.29)

This approach provides an important conceptual frame for the groupwork, and to reflect this, the title 'Deep Ecology workshop' has often been used in place of 'Despair and Empowerment'. Emotional reactions to threat, loss and injury elsewhere on the planet are seen as expressions of this wider and deeper self. Making room for these feelings becomes a way of experiencing and deepening our connectedness with life.

Two sides of the same coin

So far I have given greater emphasis to the uncomfortable emotions that can come up when we feel for our world. But this is only one side of the coin. One of the most important ways we generate good feelings is through our relationships with others, and the same can be true of our relationship with the world. Arne Naess writes of the link between joy, identification and relationship:

> Early in life, the social self is sufficiently developed so that we do not prefer to eat a big cake alone. We share the cake with our family and friends. We identify with these people sufficiently to see our joy in their joy, and to see our disappointment in theirs. (Naess 1988, p.28)

In good relationships, there is joy in giving. It is only when we split ourselves apart from the world that we create the artificial polarity between caring for the planet and caring for oneself. Serving the world and feeling connected with life become ways of generating good feelings and meeting important personal needs (e.g. feelings of belonging, spiritual needs, purpose in life). Developing a deeper connection and relationship with our world allows us to receive more from it, and this is particularly true when we look at how we develop our sense of personal power.

Developing personal power

Part of our power comes from our belief about what is possible. If we look through a Lens of Separation and see just our tiny self facing the massive problems of our world, then giving up may seem a logical response. But larger systems are capable of achieving things that you could not imagine from examination of their parts alone. A single termite measures a fraction of an inch, but collectively they construct colonies that are nine foot tall. If we look at ourselves or our actions in isolation, it is easy to dismiss them as ineffectual and empty of power. To see ourselves as part of a larger process involves a shift in vision. When we consider a longer time frame that includes the people who came before us and those who continue after, things which seemed impossible before start to become more realistic. As the saying goes – 'I can't, we can' (see Figure 8.6).

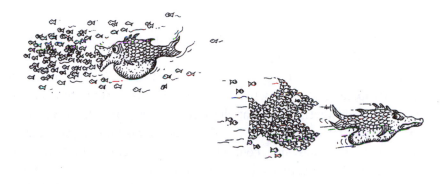

Figure 8.6 'I can't, we can': illustration by Dave Baines, taken from Johnstone (1997, p.41)

When we feel connected with others through membership of the same group or from sharing a common purpose, we are more likely to experience them as allies to draw support from and collaborate with. On one level this can be felt within the group, as the depth of common concern and purpose is expressed. However the scope for finding allies is broadened beyond our immediate human contacts when we see ourselves as part of a wider circle of life. When we identify with and act for our world, it becomes possible to find allies all around us – the trees in the park as well as the ancestors or future beings in our imagination. This is a shift in our experience of reality, where we see ourselves as intimately connected with a larger web of life. These connections, like the roots of a plant, become a source of strength, support and nourishment.

Seeing ourselves as part of something larger also brings the possibility that this larger system may act through us. A brain cell does not come up with a good idea, but participates in one. In a similar way, could we participate in Gaia's self-healing? One of the questions often asked in the workshops is, 'If Gaia were acting through us, what might that lead us to do in our lives?' The power to respond to world problems is seen to come in a large part from this shift in the way we see ourselves. But is it possible to facilitate this shift? Is this something a workshop can help with? The next section introduces methods used in practice during a Deep Ecology workshop.

In practice
Style of facilitation

In this section I introduce some of the methods I use when facilitating workshops based on the model developed by Macy and others (see Macy 1983; Macy and Brown 1998). This model uses an active facilitation approach, guiding participants through a series of experiential exercises within a structured workshop. However, I see the applicability of the approach introduced in the last section as far broader than just this type of workshop. For example, within the contexts of individual counselling, teaching school children, facilitating unstructured groups, or just in living our own lives, the direction of gaze can be out to the world, exploring questions such as 'how do we feel about what's happening?' and 'how can we respond?'

What particularly attracted me to the approach of Deep Ecology was that it brought together areas that were important to me, but which I had previously encountered as separate fields. I call these 'the four directions of Deep Ecology' (see Figure 8.7).

As a result of combining these different areas, this is a hybrid type of groupwork that draws together a mixture of techniques and ways of working. These may include educational input, experiential exercises, story telling, creative expression (e.g. dance, singing), meditation practices, and pragmatic action planning. Each facilitator will interpret the work in their own style and weave together their own unique synthesis of working methods. I have trained and worked closely with Joanna Macy over many years, and so I have been much influenced by her background in Buddhist practice and systems thinking. My own groupwork training was mainly humanistic in orientation, but I also draw on my experience in the addictions recovery field and on my enthusiasm as a musician.

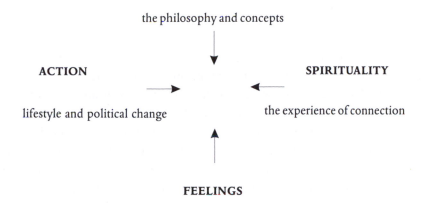

Figure 8.7 The four directions of Deep Ecology

This type of groupwork can be adapted for use in a wide range of settings, and I have been involved in sessions as short as an hour or as long as a month. I find it particularly suitable for residential weekend workshops, as this allows for more depth than that likely to be reached with a single or part-day session. I will therefore base this section on describing the kind of activities found within a weekend workshop.

Five elements

When planning, I think of five main elements which weave in and out of each other and which can also flow as a sequence through a workshop or session. These are:

- clarifying intention
- introducing ideas
- voicing our concerns
- opening to allies
- preparing for action.

I am going to introduce these elements in turn, together with examples of exercises where appropriate. Some of the exercises can be used by themselves in shorter sessions, or adapted for use when working with individuals or if exploring this area by yourself.

1. CLARIFYING INTENTION

The group is going on a journey, the facilitator acting as a guide. What is this journey? Where is it going? Clarifying intention starts with the planning of the workshop, with the decision of what to call it and with the design and distribution of the publicity to advertise it. If the facilitators are clear about their intention and able to effectively communicate this, then the group is more likely to develop the cohesion of a shared purpose. This is particularly important as this is a new area of work and people may have few reference points to give them an idea as to what is likely to happen. For example, some participants came to a Deep Ecology workshop prepared with wellies and spades, because they thought it might involve digging.

I am still unsure about what the best title is to describe this work. 'Despair and Empowerment', while communicating an important aspect, may give the impression that people have to feel despair in order to benefit. I like the title 'Deep Ecology' as this emphasises a relationship of deeper connection with our world, but this may be an unfamiliar or confusing term. In her more recent writings, Joanna Macy uses the term 'the Work that Reconnects' (Macy and Brown 1998, p.5), and for this chapter I have chosen the title 'Reconnecting with our World'. But the potential for ambiguity with any of these titles makes it even more important to be clear to potential participants what the workshops aims to offer. I would identify aims as:

- to provide a safe and supportive space to explore and express our concerns about our world situation
- through sharing these concerns with others, to strengthen the feeling that we are not alone, so that we feel the support of the group
- to positively reframe pain for the world, so that it is valued as a source of information, energy and motivation to act for change
- to deepen our feeling of connection with the larger circle of life, so that we are more able to tap into this as a source of strength and purpose

- to support participants in identifying a goal or project that will help our world, and to explore practical steps they can take to move this forward.

Rainforest activist and workshop facilitator John Seed (Seed *et al.* 1988, p.13) identifies the statement of intention as the single most important element of the workshop. If the intention is to heal our relationship with our world, then everything that follows in the workshop can become an expression of that. Early on in each workshop, I like to check out what people's hopes and fears are, and find out what it was that led them to make the decision to come. Once we have established the direction we are heading in, the journey can proceed.

2. INTRODUCING IDEAS

I have been much influenced by the cognitive-behavioural approach to groupwork, particularly the view that our ability to achieve goals is powerfully affected by the ideas we have. There are always a range of different ways in which we can look at any situation, and some perspectives open up options that others may close down. What I like about this approach is that it gets away from the struggle to prove which idea is right, as ideas are validated by how much they help us make sense of our experience and by whether or not we find them useful. What may be right for one person may not be for another, so this approach makes much more room for differences of opinion within the group. This is particularly important when touching on areas related to politics or spirituality, as these are so often plagued by dogma and party lines. As part of my introduction I tell the group that we aim for a non-dogmatic approach in the way that we facilitate the workshop.

I do find it useful to introduce the ideas behind the Despair and Empowerment and Deep Ecology approaches, because these provide a framework that helps make sense of what we are trying to do together. Some conceptual input therefore forms an integral part of the workshop, and over the course of a weekend there may be one or two sessions of up to an hour where I or my co-facilitator will present ideas and discuss them with the group.

3. VOICING OUR CONCERNS

To open up the area of talking about how we feel about the world, I use a paired listening exercise called 'open ended sentences' (see Macy 1983, p.96). Here is an example of how I might introduce it.

'I would like to introduce a paired listening exercise called "open ended sentences". The aim of this is to provide an opportunity to hear from each other how we think things are going in our world, and how we feel about this. One of you will be the listener, the other the speaker. Decide who wants to listen and who wants to speak first. I am going to offer the first part of a sentence, and the speaker will use this as a starting point to speak for three minutes. The listener's only role is to give your full attention. Try not to say anything, just listen. Speaker, just use this as an opportunity to say anything you want. If you don't know what to say, just come back to the start of the sentence and see what naturally follows it. We will do this with three different starts of sentences, I will call time at the end of each three minutes, and then we will swap over so that the listener first time round becomes the speaker for each of the three topics.'

The sentences I use are:

'When I consider our world situation, I think things are getting…'

'When I think about these things, I feel…'

'I deal with these feelings by…'

Each beginning part of a sentence acts as a springboard, opening up a new area. The first one is looking at thoughts, the second at feelings and the third explores reactions to feelings. In this version of the exercise (there are many others), I am not making assumptions about how people feel. However, if concerns are there, this is a good way of allowing them to surface. When each partner has had their turn at speaking, I pool responses from the group, jotting them down on a board or big piece of paper. Usually there is a mixed picture, with some areas of optimism, but stronger flavours of alarm. Overall most people feel that things are getting worse, and this has also been the finding of MORI and Gallup polls on the subject (Jacobs 1996, p.3). Because this is so rarely talked about, it often comes as a relief to finally get it out into the open.

I see open ended sentences as an opening and deepening exercise, and in a short workshop, it would need to be followed by space or processes to integrate, such as the action planning discussed later. In a longer workshop, this opens the descent into the despair work. To give a fuller expression to the feelings, we would then move into a form such as 'the Truth Mandala'.

The Truth Mandala

To break beyond the taboos that usually block expression of 'negative emotions', we need to create a context of permission where the normal operating codes do not apply. I introduce the idea of a group ritual or ceremony as a way of creating a non-ordinary space that invites us to speak from a wider and deeper sense of self. The Truth Mandala is one such form, and was developed by Joanna Macy in 1992 (see Macy and Brown 1998, p.101). Here is an example of how I might introduce it.

> 'This exercise is an explicit inviting forth of feelings that normally are considered out of bounds. We are creating a circle where we can support each other to share and express some of the feelings we may have for our world, but which we don't normally have opportunity to express. This is a circle of reporting in. We are reporting in about our world situation.'

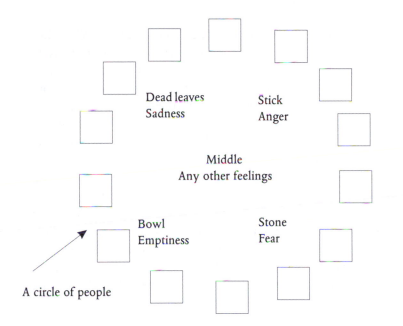

Figure 8.8 The Truth Mandala

I place an object in each of the four quadrants of a circle formed by the group, each one representing a feeling or group of feelings (see Figure 8.8). A pile of dead leaves symbolises the place of sadness, a stick symbolises anger, a stone symbolises fear and an empty bowl symbolises the feeling of emptiness. The centre of the circle may represent any other feelings.

I move into the circle to model the kind of sharing we are inviting. Picking up the stick, I might say:

> 'I feel really angry that the trains have been privatised, and now the services are so appalling that people are even more likely to drive, just at the time when we need to move away from such an over-reliance on cars.'

Continuing with this example, I then stand in the centre and say, 'I also feel guilty that I am a polluter, I am also part of the problem'. And I might then go to the bowl of emptiness and say, 'Sometimes it all feels too much and I don't know how to respond. I feel empty, hopeless, incapable'. I continue to the group:

> 'We have one person in the centre speaking at any one time. When they have finished they go back to join the circle. We don't have to reply to anything that has been said. This is not a debate, it is not about winning people over or being right. It is about having an opportunity to share our concerns and any feelings we may have with them. When someone has finished speaking those in the circle might like to say something like "I hear you", or "me too" if what they've said is something you identify with. But our role in the circle is – like the listener in the open ended sentences – mainly just to give our attention, to witness, to hear each other. I suggest that you listen inside for signals as to when to come and speak. Speak when you feel moved to speak, but don't feel you need say anything if you don't want to. Clues that you may have something to say often include things like feeling your heart pounding, or noticing your lip quivering. If there is someone in the centre, wait for them to finish, then have your turn. There may be silences or gaps after a person has shared. If you feel moved to speak then, then come on in.'

It is worth allowing at least an hour and a half for this process. Larger groups may need more time. People can come into the circle more than once, but should be sensitive to the needs of people who have not yet spoken before coming in several times. There is no strict time limit to the process, but at some point the group may have to balance the desire of people to continue speaking with the desire to get to lunch or to whatever is next in the programme. The role of the facilitator is to introduce and start the process, and then to bring it to a close at the end. They would be unlikely to make any other intervention, other than participating in the process as an active member of the group.

Every time I have participated in this process I have been deeply touched. Even when I have not had much to say myself I have been moved to tears by the sharings of others. Parents have talked of their terror for their children's future, teachers of their frustrations at working in under-resourced schools, city dwellers of their grief that the little stream they used to sit by has been built on. The invitation is to speak our truths, share our concerns, whatever it is that troubles us.

The turning

There is a dynamic to the Despair and Empowerment model that involves three stages – descent, turning and then empowerment (see Figure 8.9). When people allow themselves to descend into their pain for the world, the journey moves towards a bottoming out point where a turning can occur. This process has parallels with the dark night of the soul described in many spiritual traditions, the hitting bottom of addictions recovery and with the alchemical process described by Amélie Noack in Chapter 1.

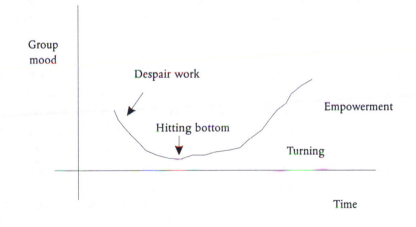

Figure 8.9 The dynamics of Despair and Empowerment work

The turning can be felt as a shift in group mood, sometimes like the sun coming out after a storm. This can occur during a process such as the Truth Mandala, but individual group members experience their own turnings at different points in time. The turning involves a shift or resolution in the distress. It is not that the pain necessarily goes, but that the relationship to it changes. This may follow emotional release, or it may be through no longer feeling alone with it, or through the dawning of a new insight. It may also come with the finding of new allies. Like a plant that grows longer roots during a drought, it is when we are in anguish or perplexed that we can sometimes open to new sources of help. This is one of the reasons why we do the Council of All Beings.

4. OPENING TO ALLIES

The Council of All Beings

I introduce the Council of All Beings as an opportunity to seek out new perspectives and find new allies. It can also be seen as a process for healing our relationship with the rest of life (Seed *et al.* 1988, p.7). With species becoming extinct every day as a result of human activity, our species as a whole has an aggressive relationship to other life forms. To begin to make peace with the rest of life, we use that well-tested tool of conflict resolution work – looking through the eyes of the other party. We do this by imagining that, just for an afternoon, we have taken on the form of a non-human life form, for example imagining ourselves as an ant, an eagle or an oak tree.

We imagine ourselves as attending the ecosystem's equivalent of a special session of the United Nations. We meet to report in on the condition of our world, from the perspective of non-human life forms. We can approach this on a number of levels. We could see it as an improvised group drama, where each of us represents a being and acts as if we were speaking on their behalf – perhaps in a way similar to playback theatre (see Chapter 2). Or we could see it in more mystical terms, as a ceremony or ritual where we allow the spirit of another being to speak through us.

As preparation, participants spend a period of time alone in nature, on a kind of mini vision quest. We go out looking for the being to represent in the council. It may be something we encounter on our journey, or that comes up in our mind while we are wandering. Perhaps the being will choose us. We then gather to make a mask to represent the being. At a prearranged time, we gather to report in from the perspective of assembled beings. This can be completely unstructured, with the facilitator opening the session and then only making minimal interventions. An alternative is to structure it in the form of two rounds. The first of these is a reporting in where each being introduces itself and shares any concerns about the conditions it faces. In the second round, each being is asked to contribute a strength, insight or quality towards the common purpose of protecting life on earth. For example:

> 'I am badger – I come to this council to report the destruction of the forests and attacks on our homes. Gassed and dug up, we are under threat.
>
> To any of those humans who act to protect us, I offer my ability to dart through hedges and wriggle my way through obstacles in my path.'

After the sharing, the facilitator brings the council to a close. Sometimes we have a fire outside where we burn the masks in ceremonial fashion. As we place each mask in the fire, we may thank the being for the insights and strengths they offer.

Some years ago, when I was going through an unhappy period in my life, I sat down by a tree. I looked up and recognised the dark buds – it was Ash. I had been Ash, and I felt a sense of reunion with an old friend. Looking down at my feet, I saw Ivy. I had been Ivy too, at a different Council of All Beings. I felt supported by these two plants; I had a relationship with them that I felt comforted by. My experiences of these councils have had a profound impact on my relationship with the life forms I have represented. They have become significant as allies in my life. I wish to be an ally to them too.

5. PREPARING FOR ACTION

One part of the workshop that I have found particularly useful is when, towards the end, we look at how we apply this approach in our lives. This has allowed me to integrate strong feelings brought up in exercises like the Truth Mandala by helping me focus the energy of my emotions into a specific project. Identifying small practical steps we can take is an important part of the empowerment process. To do this, each participant works through a series of six questions. This is usually done in pairs or groups of three, each person having about 15 minutes. The questions I use, which are adapted from Joanna Macy's book (Macy 1983, p.143), are:

1.   If you imagined that Gaia could act through you, and that you could play a role in the healing of our world, what sort of goal, project or area would you most want to put your energies into?

2.   What specific goal could you realistically aim to achieve in the next 12 months that would contribute towards this?

3.   What strengths or resources do you now have that can help you do this?

4.   What will you need to learn or acquire?

5.   What obstacles are you likely to put in the way of fulfilling this goal?

6.   What can you do in the next three days, no matter how small a step, that will help you reach your goal?

Every time I have done this process it has usefully nudged me forward, encouraging me to clarify what my focus was at the time. Hearing the steps people plan to take over the next three days can be an inspiring way to end the workshop, and also gives participants an opportunity to ask the group for the kind of support they would find helpful in reaching their goals.

Reflections

When I talk with friends and colleagues about this type of workshop, I encounter a mixed response. Some are interested, especially if they are already involved in social or environmental issues. But sometimes people appear puzzled, as though the whole idea of the workshop does not quite make sense to them. Occasionally I encounter the anxiety that to look too deeply at the problems of the world might be dangerous, in that it might trigger a depressive episode or mental breakdown. In this section I would like to look at these concerns and to reflect on my experience of working with groups in this area. I would like to do this by addressing the following questions:

• What is the point of these workshops?

• Do they make any difference?

- Are they safe?
- What is personal and what is planetary?

What is the point of these workshops?

Some years ago I showed a friend a leaflet for a workshop I was running. She pointed out that I had mentioned the word 'pain' four times, but had not mentioned joy once. One of the criticisms of the Despair and Empowerment approach is that it appears to focus on negative emotions in a way that may be unappealing or difficult to make sense of. I encountered a similar reaction when running a session for trainee clinical psychologists. 'Excuse me, why are we doing this?' someone asked, after the open ended sentences exercise. Because the workshops are based upon a perspective that may be new or unfamiliar, the rationale for them may not be clear. This is why I wanted to introduce the ideas at such length in the first section.

The workshops may also make little sense to someone who is not particularly concerned about the condition of our world. The starting point is a perception that things are seriously amiss, which motivates someone to come to a workshop that offers to strengthen their ability to respond.

Do they make any difference?

While I was writing this chapter, a friend called Jade phoned me. She had been to a workshop I had run seven years ago, and so I asked her whether it had made any difference. Here is what she said:

> I can honestly say that I think my life would be different now if I hadn't gone to that workshop. It really changed things for me. Previously I'd been terrified of the prospect of global and ecological collapse. It was so horrifying a thought that I couldn't face it. It was too much to look at world problems, so I tried to shut them out.

> At that workshop, things changed. I faced my horrors and remember thinking 'this is my terror and it is really bad'. Previously I'd been really afraid, but afterwards my nightmares stopped. I felt more accepting, putting things in perspective better, thinking that we just do our best, so I got on with it.

Jade now works for an environmental organisation and I am often inspired by the positive steps she takes to make the world a better place. I think back to the workshop that she came to, and I remember thinking at the time that it had not been that successful. After the workshop I had asked myself, 'How do I know these do any good?' I decided to send a questionnaire to participants of workshops I had facilitated over the previous 12 months to find out whether they had found that it made any difference.

I sent questionnaires to all participants of residential Deep Ecology workshops I had run between December 1992 and November 1993. I sent them a year after each event, so that I could get an idea of longer-term outcomes. I asked people to rate their responses to a series of questions on a five-point scale that included the following options: not at all, slightly, moderately, quite a lot, very deeply. I also asked for additional comments. The questions I asked included:

- Did the workshop give you an opportunity to express your feelings about the state of the earth?

- Did the workshop help you strengthen or deepen your sense of connection with the earth/life on earth?

- Was your experience of the workshop in any way personally healing or beneficial to you?

- Was your experience of the workshop in any way harmful or damaging to you?

- Did your experience of the workshop help strengthen the feeling that you can make a difference to the state of the world?

- Overall, has your experience of the workshop in any way changed your life?

Of 40 questionnaires sent, I received 31 replies. Everyone replied that the workshop had provided the opportunity to express their feelings about the world, and over 70 per cent said that this had been 'quite a lot' or 'very deeply'. Over 90 per cent replied that the workshop had helped strengthen both their sense of connection with the world and their feeling that they could make a difference within it. For over half the respondents to both these questions, this had been either 'quite a lot' or 'very deeply'. Over 80 per cent replied that the experience of the workshop had changed their life, and for this, over a quarter of those who replied had marked the response 'very deeply'.

This is a small-scale study, and was carried out to satisfy personal curiosity rather than academic rigour. To get a more comprehensive view of outcomes, a much larger sample size would be needed. However it does support the view that many people find these workshops an empowering experience and one that deepens their feeling of connection with the world. A smaller proportion – in this case about a quarter – found, like Jade and myself, the workshop to be an important turning point that very deeply changed their lives.

PERSONALLY HEALING

One striking finding of the questionnaire was the high proportion of people who found the workshop to be personally healing. Over 90 per cent of replies rated this area as 'moderately' or more, and over 75 per cent marked the responses of either 'quite a lot' or 'very deeply'. This made it the most highly rated positive outcome of the workshop. A number of participants wrote in their comments that the workshop had been healing in helping promote a sense of integration with a wider picture, one person writing: 'I remember an uncommon and wonderful sense that I *did* (do) have a place in the world'.

This finding supports the idea that an important area of personal need and personal growth is in our relationship with the world. Other factors described as healing were the experience of not being alone in feeling distress for the world and having this distress validated as an appropriate emotional response to world problems. One participant, listing what she had found beneficial, wrote: 'Permission to feel, to grieve, to hate, to rage, to cry – validation that I am not "odd" but responding to an unhealthy situation in a healthy way'.

Are they safe?

I added the question asking about harmful effects because I had encountered the fear that opening up feelings about world problems might be a harmful thing to do. I wanted to check whether there was any evidence of this. Over 80 per cent replied 'not at all', nearly 10 per cent put 'slightly', 3 per cent (one person) marked 'moderately', 3 per cent 'quite a lot' and 3 per cent marked the response 'very deeply'. It is important to add that every one of these people had also marked that they had found the workshop as much or more personally healing, so on balance no one felt harmed by the workshop. Looking at the written comments people had made, no one mentioned feeling depressed or traumatised by their feelings about the world. The negative effects of the workshop that people identified fell into two categories.

PERSONAL ISSUES BROUGHT UP BY THE WORKSHOP

The one person who had marked 'very deeply' for this question also replied that she had found it 'very deeply' personally healing. In her additional comments she stated that she had not found the workshop harmful, but that it had brought up a lot of previously unexpressed personal grief, and that following the workshop she had gone into therapy and been able to move forward with this. She had also left the workshop early, and so missed the integrating potential of exercises used towards the end of the workshop. Other people had also commented on personal grief issues being brought to the surface, and they had identified this as a factor in the workshops that was personally healing.

FACTORS TO DO WITH BEING IN A GROUP

One person commented that they had felt rejected in the group. They also replied that they had found the workshop a moving experience that was personally healing. Other studies (such as Lieberman, Yalom and Miles 1973) have also identified that people feeling rejected or attacked by others is a potential adverse effect of intensive groups. Groups can sometimes painfully recreate earlier difficult life experiences, and as this type of workshop is not a personal therapy group, some of these issues may get missed. However, the solidarity of facing a common threat together can help lift people above their personal issues, and break down some of the barriers that lead to exclusion. One participant listed the positive effects of the workshop as including:

> Increased affection for, understanding and tolerance to other humans, replacing the rejection and hatred and blame I had formerly felt. This allowed more openness and truth between myself and others.

This very feeling of closeness and community was, ironically, what led to a negative effect identified by another participant, who commented: 'It set up connections which never came to anything – disillusion'.

Participants can be left feeling disappointed and abandoned if the warm connections developed during the workshop do not last long afterwards. The only other outcome study of Deep Ecology workshops that I know of, carried out by the eco-psychologist Eshana Bragg in Australia (Bragg 1995), also found that the experience of community felt during the workshop was short-lived afterwards. She recommended that support networks be set up to maintain the supportive connections experienced in the group.

Returning to the question of safety, these findings suggest that rather than it being harmful to open up our feelings about world problems, when this is done in a supportive setting it can be a deeply healing thing to do. However, as with other intensive group experiences, there is a potential for personal issues to come up that do not get resolved, for people to feel rejected within a group and disappointment to follow closeness if it is not sustained.

An assessment of safety also needs to include the question, 'Is it safe not to do this?' While these workshops are only one of many possible ways of responding to the feelings brought up by global issues, the story of Mark described earlier in this chapter suggests that ignoring these feelings may have its own risks.

What is personal and what is planetary?

I think back to the Deep Ecology workshop I went to in 1988, and my tears for the starving children of our world. At the time, I was working as a junior doctor in a children's cancer unit, and a young girl I was looking after was dying of bone cancer. I wondered afterwards whether my tears were not just for the starving but also for her, and for the tragedy of childhood malignancy that I was witnessing. Later still, when working with more personal pain in individual therapy, I wondered whether my tears were also for my own inner wounded child. The tendency when looking through a Lens of Separation is to ask, 'What was I *really* crying for?' and to assume that there is one right answer that makes others wrong. I increasingly value the idea that many things happen at the same time, and that 'both…and…' views are often more accurate than 'either…or…' dichotomies.

Farhad Dalal's book, *Taking the Group Seriously*, has been an important influence in many of the chapters in this book. He wrestles with the interplay of individual and group, and concludes:

> Perhaps the most profound realisation to emerge from these explorations is that mind and thought are not private properties of the individual, but properties of the group. (Dalal 1998, p.225)

He is looking through a Lens of Connection and seeing the group as an entity, where, as he puts it 'the individual is a level of group'. He also quotes Foulkes who wrote: 'In order to see something whole, we have to…step outside of that which we want to see' (Foulkes 1973, p.230).

Perhaps this chapter could have been called 'Taking the World Seriously'. With the photos from astronauts, we are among the first generations of humans ever to have seen images of the earth from the outside – in a way that makes it easier for us to think of it as a whole. The Deep Ecology approach and the branch of psychology becoming known as 'eco-psychology' invite us to see the individual as a level of our world, of Gaia. The workshops introduced in this chapter apply this new psychology to one of the major challenges of the twenty-first century – how we can support each other to face and constructively respond to the problems of our world. The results of the outcome study suggest that facing this challenge is not only good for the planet, but that it is also good for personal healing, well-being and growth.

References

Bragg, E. (1995) *Towards Ecological Self.* Unpublished PhD dissertation, James Cook University, Townsville, North Queensland, Australia.

Capra, F. (1982) *The Turning Point.* London: Flamingo.

Capra, F. (1996) *The Web of Life.* London: HarperCollins.

Dalal, F. (1998) *Taking the Group Seriously.* London: Jessica Kingsley Publishers.

Foulkes, S.H. (1948) *Introduction to Group Analytic Psychotherapy.* William Heinemann Medical Books. Reprinted 1983. London: Karnac.

Foulkes, S.H. (1973) 'The group as matrix of the individual's mental life.' In (1990) *Selected Papers 223–233.* London: Karnac.

HMSO (2000) *The BSE Inquiry Report.* Available via the internet at www.bse.org.uk

Houghton, J.T. *et al.* (eds) (1996) *Climate Change 1995: The Science of Climate Change, Contribution of Working Group 1 to the Second Assessment Report of the Intergovernmental Panel on Climate Change.* New York: Cambridge University Press.

Jacobs, M. (1996) *The Politics of the Real World.* London: Earthscan.

Johnstone, C. (1997) *The Lens of Deep Ecology.* Third Edition. London: The Institute for Deep Ecology (UK). (Price £4, available from the author at 24a, Balmoral Road, Bristol, BS7 9AZ, UK.)

Lieberman. M., Yalom, I. and Miles, M. (1973) *Encounter Groups: First Facts.* New York: Basic Books.

Lovelock, J. (1979) *Gaia – A New Look at Life on Earth.* Oxford: Oxford University Press. Reprinted 1995.

Macy, J. (1983) *Despair and Personal Power in the Nuclear Age.* Philadelphia: New Society Publishers.

Macy, J. and Brown, M. (1998) *Coming Back to Life.* Philadelphia: New Society Publishers.

Naess, A. (1988) 'Self realisation: an ecological approach to being in the world.' In J. Seed *et al.* (eds) *Thinking Like a Mountain.* London: Heretic Books.

Seed, J. (1988) 'To hear within ourselves the sound of the earth crying.' In J. Seed *et al.* (eds) *Thinking Like a Mountain.* London: Heretic Books.

Seed, J. *et al.* (eds) (1988) *Thinking Like a Mountain.* London: Heretic Books.

List of Contributors

Anna Chesner is a registered psychotherapist, psychodrama practitioner and trainer, group analyst and dramatherapist. She is also a playback theatre practitioner. She has published and contributed to a number of books including *Dramatherapy and Supervision* and *Dramatherapy for People with Learning Disabilities*.

Angela Eden has worked in education, community and economic development. Her training in social policy and organisational consultancy led to roles in both public and commercial organisations. She is currently working as a Leadership Development consultant at the Tavistock Institute, an associate trainer with the Industrial Society, and runs a small Consultancy practice specialising in diversity issues for individual, group and team development.

Antonio L.S. Fazio is a sociologist, psychoanalyst and group psychotherapist. He is on the clinical staff of University College London and is involved in training psychoanalysts and group psychotherapists. He is a member of the British and Italian psychoanalytical societies. His main interest has been the application of psychoanalytic principles and concepts to groups, institutions and therapeutic communities, and he has published various papers and a book chapter.

Herb Hahn is a chartered occupational and clinical psychologist, registered supervisor, and psychoanalytic psychotherapist. He has experience of Tavistock Group Relations and Foulkesian Group Analytic approaches and, in addition to his clinical and supervisory practice, he consults internationally to managers, senior executives, groups and organisations. He has contributed chapters on assessment, supervision and social dreaming to edited books on these themes, plus a variety of publications in various professional journals.

Chris Johnstone is a doctor and group therapist working in the addictions treatment field. Over the last ten years he has also been running groups exploring psychological responses to planetary problems. His booklet *The Lens of Deep Ecology*, published by the Institute for Deep Ecology (UK), is required reading for a number of university courses.

Amélie Noack initially trained as an architect, and is now an experienced Jungian analyst currently training as a group analyst. She has for may years been involved in training psychotherapists using experiential methods, and has also had a central role in the work of the Squiggle Foundation.

Peter Tatham is medically qualified and specialises as a Zurich-trained Jungian analyst. He works in full-time analytic practice and has taught and lectured widely, both nationally and internationally. His publications include *The Making of Maleness* (Karnac Books).

Ron Wiener is a sociodramatist, trainer and organisational consultant working for local government, the health service, the private and voluntary sectors and the police force.

Author Index

Subject Index

acting out 27
active imagination 83
aggression
    cultural differences
        176–77
    dealing with 27
alchemy
    albedo stage 30
    circulatio 82
    individuation 36
    model of reality 37–38
    nigredo stage 29, 34,
        207
    putrefactio stage 34–35
    rubedo stage 33
    transformative processes
        15–16
analyst, identity and cultural
    variables 174–75
anger, dealing with 27
anti-group factor 34, 179
anxiety
    in group matrix 25
    repression of 172
    separation 92, 175–77
archetypes
    mother 76–77
    Self 77–80, 82, 83
assessor role, of conductor
    19, 22
attendance, regularity of 22
authority figure
    co-authored books
        10–11
    conductor as 18–19, 22
    need for 33

barriers, in groups 119–20
basic assumptions theory
    (Bion) 119
breaks, dealing with 26–27
British Psychodrama
    Association (BPA) 137,
    147–49, 155

chaos
    meanings of 75
    theory 35

co-leading, and role
    clarification 141–44
co-unconscious (Moreno)
    48
cognitive-behavioural
    approach 203
Cold War
    devitalising effect of
        171–72
    instability following
        173
    stability as gain 172
collective unconscious
    archetypes 76–78
    as matrix 68
colonialism 183
    and loss of empire 165,
        168–69, 179
communication, impact of
    technological change on
        111–12
    see also organisational
        change, and language
community
    education 133
    stories as belonging in
        65
    theatre 64, 152–53
condenser phenomena 24,
    25
conductor
    as bad object 34
    group ending 32
    projection carrier 22
    role of 19–20
        containing 23, 24
        covering 23, 24, 32
        monitoring 24
confidentiality
    experiential groups
        19–20
    playback theatre 54
containment
    conductor role 23, 24
    group 15–16, 25
        alchemy metaphor
        29–30
    playback theatre 49–50,
        54, 55
contributors 8, 9, 217–18
    authority issues 10–11
    dreams of 10–12
control

being in versus being in
    charge 75–76
    issues of 136, 141–42
countertransference
    consultant 129
    erotic relationships
        103–4
    experiential groups 17
    social 161
covering function, of
    conductor 23, 24, 32
creative task, as
    breakthrough 11
crisis, using as turning point
    190
cultural unconscious
    (Henderson) 48

death, dealing with 26
Despair and Empowerment
    workshops see global
    issues, and groupwork
Despair and Personal Power
    in the Nuclear Age 187
dramatherapy 12, 41
    and ritual 51
    see also playback theatre;
        psychodrama
dreams see social dreaming

eco-psychology 215–16
emotions, resistance to
    painful 187–89,
        190–91
empathy 30
employment, and
    technological change
        112
empowerment
    global issues 187
    of group members 134
ending
    cultural factors in
        response to 175–77
    resistance to 31–33
environment-individual
    interaction 36–37
European Union (EU) 160
    co-operation, developing
        spirit of 170–71
    complexity 180
    cultural integration
        183–84
    cultural variance 174